# If These WALLS Could TALK:

## BUFFALO BILLS

# If These **WALLS** Could **TALK:**

## BUFFALO BILLS

*Stories from the Buffalo Bills Sideline, Locker Room, and Press Box*

John Murphy
with Scott Pitoniak

TRIUMPH
B O O K S

Library of Congress Cataloging-in-Publication Data

Names: Murphy, John (Sports broadcaster) author. | Pitoniak, Scott, author.
Title: If these walls could talk: Buffalo Bills: stories from the Buffalo
    Bills sideline, locker room, and press box / John Murphy with Scott
    Pitoniak.
Description: Chicago, Illinois: Triumph Books, [2023]
Identifiers: LCCN 2023019132 | ISBN 9781637271896 (trade paperback)
Subjects: LCSH: Buffalo Bills (Football team)—History. | Football
    players—United States—History. | BISAC: SPORTS & RECREATION
    / Football | TRAVEL / United States / Northeast / Middle Atlantic (NJ,
    NY, PA)
Classification: LCC GV956.B83 .P58 2023 | DDC
    796.332/640974797—dc23/eng/20230421
LC record available at https://lccn.loc.gov/2023019132

This book is available in quantity at special discounts for your group or organization. For further information, contact:
    **Triumph Books LLC**
    814 North Franklin Street
    Chicago, Illinois 60610
    (312) 337-0747
    www.triumphbooks.com

Printed in U.S.A.
ISBN: 978-1-63727-189-6
Design by Amy Carter
Production by Patricia Frey
Photos by AP Images unless otherwise indicated

# CONTENTS

# FOREWORD

I met John Murphy not long after I was drafted in the first round by the Buffalo Bills back in 2009, and we hit it off from the get-go. Whenever he interviewed me or I ran into him at various team or charitable functions he was emceeing around town, Murph treated me incredibly well. I began feeling a connection between us—a connection that's grown into a good friendship over time.

Murph's fun-loving personality, enthusiasm, and dedication to his family and his community hooked me early on. He seemed like a guy you could trust, a guy you could enjoying sitting down with and having a few beers. He was different from many media people I had encountered. My nine seasons with the Bills coincided with the dreaded playoff drought. So, there was considerable negativity surrounding the team during that era, especially in the media, which at times seemed to revel in mocking us and taking cheap shots. I saw right away, though, that Murph wasn't that way at all. Yes, he was honest and called 'em as he saw 'em as a broadcaster, but his critiques were never personal attacks. He was an upbeat guy, and I think he appreciated how hard we players were working to get this thing turned around.

He believed, like we did, that at some point, the Bills would get it right and move in a positive direction, and we finally did in 2017 when we made the playoffs in my final year as a player. That was a great year for me professionally because we had tossed that King Kong off our backs and the backs of Buffalo's wild and wonderful fans.

Sadly, following that memorable season, a neck condition forced me to retire sooner than anticipated. It was a difficult transition, but, fortunately, when the door to the locker room at Highmark Stadium slammed shut, the door to the radio announcer's booth flung open. Not only would I be able to stay connected to the team and game I loved, but I also would be able to work with and be mentored by one of the best play-by-play guys in all of football. I could not have asked for a better guy to break in with.

Before my first Bills radio season in 2019, Murph and I gathered at the team's training facility and did a mock broadcast using video from a game from the previous year. The only advice he gave me was to be myself and have fun. He made me feel at ease from the start. And although I had enjoyed listening to his highlight calls when I was a player, it wasn't until I began working with him that I realized just how good he is.

I'd been listening to games since my days growing up in Cincinnati, when the radio voices of Reds broadcasters Marty Brennaman and Joe Nuxhall filled our house on a daily basis.

And Murph reminded me of those broadcasters, the way he sets the scene so perfectly and paints pictures with his words just like Brennaman and Nuxhall used to do. They made you feel like you were at the ballpark. Murph makes you feel you are there with us at Highmark Stadium: "The Bills are moving left to right toward the tunnel end of the stadium. They're dressed from top to bottom in their blue uniforms with their white helmets. The Steelers are in their gold pants with their white jerseys and trademark black helmets. It's an absolutely beautiful day for a football game, isn't it, Eric? The sun is shining in Orchard Park, but the flags above the uprights are swirling, so we'll keep an eye on what impact that might have on the passing and kicking games. Here…we…go!"

It sounds so easy, so simple, but it isn't. There's an artistry to it, and Murph is so good at it. The other thing I love about working with him is that he's perfect not only at setting the scene, but also at setting me up for success. He has a feel for the flow of the game. He picks up on points that need to be made as the broadcast unfolds, but instead of making them himself, he'll ask me to elaborate on Josh Allen's decision to throw the ball to Stefon Diggs in a certain situation or why Von Miller was able to beat a left tackle with a swim move to get to the quarterback. Again, Murph could make the points himself and take credit, but instead he dishes off to me so I can shine and give a player's perspective. Not all play-by-play guys are like that. But Murph is always unselfish in that way.

I think the great play-by-play guys are like great point guards. They're great at assisting their color men, putting them in position to succeed. Color guys are always at the mercy of their play-by-play guys. Murph always puts me in position to succeed.

I think we've developed a good chemistry over time. He knows how to keep things loose. Yes, there are occasions when he wants me to become analytical, to get to the core of why a play succeeded or failed. But he's also taught me that I need to put Football 401 knowledge into Football 101 terms, so it's understandable and digestible to the casual fan. He's shown me how to make the broadcast informative and also make it feel like we are talking to our buddies over beers at a tailgate.

The other thing Murph has going for him is he's a lifelong Buffalonian and has been around for a huge chunk of Bills history, going back to his boyhood days attending games at old War Memorial Stadium during Buffalo's AFL era. That wealth of knowledge enables him to put things into historical context and adds great depth to the broadcast. He's pretty much seen it all.

As you turn these pages, Murph and his friend, longtime Bills chronicler and author Scott Pitoniak, will take you on a journey through the team's rich history—from Jack Kemp to Jim Kelly to Josh Allen.

You'll also get a feel for Murph's deep, passionate Buffalo roots, his friendship with the original "Voice of the Bills"—Van Miller—and how he unwittingly wound up landing this dream job. There are tons of behind-the-scenes stories, many of which have never been told before. The players, coaches, and administrators come to life.

The book is written in Murph's distinctive voice. So, you'll feel as if you're sitting there right next to him. That's something I'm privileged to do every time the Bills play. I've been fortunate to kick off my broadcast career with him and even more fortunate to be able to call him my friend. Enjoy the read and go Bills!

—*Eric Wood, former Bills Pro Bowl center and current Bills color commentator*

# INTRODUCTION

Though it happened six decades ago, there are times when it feels like six minutes ago. In fact, when I think about it, it's like I'm a wide-eyed, nine-year-old all over again. New Year's Day 1967 remains indelible in my mind—and will for as long as I live—because that's the day I attended my first Buffalo Bills home game at War Memorial Stadium, the big concrete bowl on the corner of Jefferson and Best on the east side of the city.

And what makes that day even more memorable is that this wasn't just any old Bills home game. It just so happened to be the American Football League Championship Game against the Kansas City Chiefs. The winner would advance to play Vince Lombardi's National Football League champion Green Bay Packers in the showdown that became known three years later as the Super Bowl. I don't know how my dad managed it, but he somehow finagled four tickets and took me and my brothers, Mark and Matt, that day. I was beyond excited. This was like Christmas morning, Easter Sunday, the Fourth of July, and several other holidays all rolled into one. I grew up in Lockport, a small, working-class suburb about 45 minutes north of the city, and any trip to Buffalo was a big deal to me. Buffalo just seemed like a huge metropolis, and I guess it was compared to Lockport, which in those days had a population of about 26,000.

Listening to Van Miller's radio descriptions of Bills games at War Memorial Stadium definitely had whet my appetite for this moment. So, too, had watching Sunday telecasts of games on our grainy black-and-white television and reading stories and looking at newspaper photos in the *Courier-Express* and *Buffalo Evening News*. But nothing can fully prepare you for the experience of being there and absorbing the sights, sounds, and smells—and sharing all of it with others bonded by a love of their hometown team.

I vividly remember herding like cattle up the steps to the stadium and the sense of excitement and anticipation I felt. I finally was going to be able to see my heroes in the flesh, in living color. I can still smell the aroma of the hot dogs grilling in the concourses. I can still recall sitting on the concrete high above the 15-yard line, watching quarterback Jack Kemp warming up with wide receiver Elbert "Golden Wheels" Dubenion. (Man, I love that nickname.)

And I can remember how quickly the air of excitement rushed out of me and my 42,080 fellow fanatics that day as the Bills fell behind early and wound up being shellacked 31–7. What a downer.

As we walked out, I was crestfallen like everyone else. But I also couldn't wait to experience another Bills football game at War Memorial. Despite the disappointing, lopsided outcome, that day had cemented my love for the team and my desire to keep coming back for more. I was hooked. For life.

In retrospect, that experience also prepared me for the sports misery that would follow. Because to be a Bills fan, or a Buffalo sports fan for that matter, is to know heartbreak. And, believe me, we've endured more than our fair share through the decades. But it's also about knowing how to keep the faith and keep on loving despite the gut punches, despite sometimes not being loved back in return. And I think that's a huge part of being not only a Bills fan, but also a Buffalonian. We're an abused but resilient lot. We know a thing or two about getting up after being knocked down.

Never, in a million years, could I have envisioned the personal journey I would travel since that unforgettable day at War Memorial 57 years ago. Believe me when I say this wasn't planned. It just sort of happened, and I couldn't be more thrilled or grateful that it did. I would go from being a fan of my hometown team to being the broadcast voice of my hometown team. And along the way, I would have the opportunity to work alongside and then succeed my hero and the man who will always be in my mind the "Voice of the Bills"—Van "The Man" Miller.

It blows my mind that I've been at this now since 1984, including the last 19 years as the play-by-play guy. Toss in the preseason and the postseason, and I've been behind the microphone for more than 600 Bills games. So, I've had an opportunity to chronicle a huge chunk of this team's history—from Joe Ferguson to Jim Kelly to Josh Allen (with a litany of forgettable quarterbacks interspersed between those guys); from Chuck Knox to Marv Levy to Sean McDermott; from Stew Barber to Bill Polian to Brandon Beane; from Rich to Ralph to Highmark Stadium; from Talkin' Proud to basement finishes to Super Bowl participants to a long, long drought to Super Bowl contenders again.

It's been one hell of a journey since that first trip with my dad and brothers. And, hopefully, it's far from being over. I hope you will join me and my coauthor and friend Scott Pitoniak on this roller-coaster trek through Bills history on the following pages. As Van "The Man" would say, "Fasten your seatbelts." I hope you enjoy the ride as much as I have.

# CHAPTER 1
## JOSH ALLEN

There are numerous reasons why happy days are here again for the Buffalo Bills, why after such a long stretch of gory days that we're experiencing glory days once more. Clearly, the fact the Bills are run by their best coaching/general manager combination since the Marv Levy/ Bill Polian leadership team of the Super Bowl era is of paramount importance. Whether it's business, politics, or sports, having strong, intelligent, caring leaders matter. And in Sean McDermott and Brandon Beane, the current Bills have two guys who not only have a vision, but also the wisdom and courage of their convictions to make that vision come true. They've done a masterful job completely overhauling this roster. They've turned a team of pretenders into a team of contenders. And they've done so in a remarkably short period of time.

But if pressed to cite the No. 1 reason the Bills are again in legitimate contention for a Lombardi Trophy, I would answer simply with two words: Josh Allen. The National Football League has long been a quarterback-centric league—probably more so now than ever given the numerous rule and strategic changes that enable quarterbacks and receivers to put up Madden-like video game numbers. And in Allen, Buffalo has finally found its next Jack Kemp, its next Jim Kelly—a quarterback with the ability and moxie to take a team to the promised land, a quarterback who's a perfect fit for these times and these Bills.

With Allen, history seems to be repeating itself, and it's been a blast to describe it as it unfolds—especially after enduring so many mediocre seasons in a row. As I witnessed in my youth, Kemp became the missing piece in Buffalo's run to consecutive AFL titles in 1964 and 1965. Kelly, of course, took over a team that went 2–14 and finished at the bottom of the NFL standings in 1984 and 1985 and then willed it to an unprecedented four consecutive Super Bowls. And now all these decades later, the ball and the torch have been handed to Allen.

It's interesting when I think back to the parallels between these three glory eras of Bills football. Neither Kemp, who hailed from Southern

California, nor Kelly, who grew up in a dot-on-the-map-coal-mining town north of Pittsburgh, wanted to come here. In fact, they fought tooth and nail not to come. But after they arrived and lived here for awhile, they saw what a truly great place this is. They became one of us and opted not to leave—even after their playing days were done.

Allen differed from Kemp and Kelly in one big respect. When the Bills shocked many by moving up in the 2018 NFL Draft to select him with the seventh overall pick, he couldn't wait to get to Buffalo. Though he grew up in a rural, Northern California town, Allen, I think, related to us right away. He understood us and became one of us immediately. He really is built for Buffalo. It's been a perfect fit between quarterback and town—the football version of beef on weck.

I suspect part of that has to do with the fact Allen, like we Buffalonians, carries a chip on his shoulder. He knows what it's like to be overlooked and ridiculed. We do, too. For as long as I can remember, it seems like people have taken shots at us. I have vivid memories of Johnny Carson making fun of us on his late-night monologues, citing our Siberian-like winters and lagging economy. I remember being unnerved by a *Sports Illustrated* article in the late 1960s that ragged on us about our many warts and said Buffalo didn't deserve to have an NFL team.

Admittedly, some of the criticism may have been justified. I mean, there's no denying we have harsh winters. Heck, we had six feet of snow dumped on us in November of 2022, forcing a game against the Cleveland Browns to be moved to Detroit. And the economy did indeed tank after Lackawanna Steel shuttered its plants in the early 1980s. And our football team—the thing we hang our hats and collective self-esteem on—did go through that 17-year stretch when it didn't make the play-offs, which is really tough to do, considering the NFL draft is set up to help bad teams become good if you pick the right players.

But we've always been a hardy, resilient lot. You may knock us down, but you can't keep us down. To invoke a line from those defunct Buffalo factories, "from the hottest furnaces is forged the strongest steel." We do have steely resolve.

We're known as the City of No Illusions and the City of Good Neighbors and we epitomize and embrace both of those phrases. The people here are genuine. There's few airs about us. And, man, do we ever love our football. It's a huge, huge part of who we are. It's a big part of our identity. There are occasions when maybe we invest too much emotion, self-worth, and dollars into the Bills, but even in bad times, they've been a source of community pride. Unlike big cities, we don't have as many sports teams or other diversions to occupy our time. When you think about it, the fact Buffalo has an NFL franchise really doesn't make sense given our small size compared to all other markets but Green Bay. But we do have an NFL franchise, and it gives us a certain gravitas, makes us big time. When the Bills beat teams from New York or Chicago or L.A., Buffalonians feel a sense of David vs. Goliath conquest. They puff their chests out.

There's been a lot of chest puffing over Buffalo's pride and joy in recent years, thanks to Allen. Like the mid-1960s, early 1980s, and early 1990s, this truly is a time for Talkin' Proud. A time to shout. A new glory era.

As a quarterback Allen has done things no one—not even Patrick Mahomes nor Tom Brady—has ever done. And what's made him even more special is the way he's won fans over off the field. It's really cool how he's connected with Kelly. The two have formed a special bond. Kelly advised him early on to embrace the city, and Allen has followed through on that advice big time.

You won't find too many athletes better with fans than Allen, especially the way he treats young fans. I love the way he prioritizes the kids whenever he signs autographs or gives away his jerseys or equipment. And I love the way he interacts with them. Before an open practice in August 2022 at Highmark Stadium, I'll never forget how he went up and

Quarterback Josh Allen runs during the Buffalo Bills' win in the 2022 regular-season finale. That victory represented the Bills' third straight win against the New England Patriots.

down the sidelines tossing passes to kids in the stands. He must have spent about 45 minutes doing that. Imagine what a thrill that was for each of those kids. They will remember that moment for as long as they live. And they'll be Allen fans and Bills fans forever because he took that time to make those connections. He's such a great ambassador for his team and his adopted city. He's so genuine, so real. There's no pretense about him. Just like Buffalonians.

In fact, if you didn't know any better, you'd say Allen was from Western New York, not Northern California. I think he can relate to the BS we often have to endure because he's gone through similar malarkey much of his life. At his core, Allen is a small-town guy who had been overlooked pretty much every step of his journey. Try as he may, he couldn't get any Division I college football program to take a serious look at him in high school. So he had to start out at a junior college. While there he grew several inches, put up some big numbers, and showed off his powerful arm, but only two schools—Wyoming and Eastern Michigan—offered scholarships. And the Wyoming scholarship only materialized after the school's first choice, Eric Dungey, opted to go to Syracuse.

Allen played well at Wyoming—an off-the-radar school—but didn't dominate the way many experts wanted him to. So when it came time for the NFL draft, critics staged an all-out blitz. Among the negative reviews:

*Strong arm but too erratic, too inconsistent.*

*Doesn't do a great job reading defenses or going through his progressions.*

*Relies too much on his arm, forcing passes into coverage.*

*Relies too much on his legs, taking off and running when he should be staying in the pocket.*

*Didn't play in a Power Five Conference. Went against inferior competition and didn't dominate.*

*Risky pick. Good chance he'll wind up being a bust.*

Fortunately, Josh didn't listen to the noise emanating from the peanut gallery. He'd been down this road many times before, and like, Buffalonians, who endured their share of being trashed upon, he basically said, "Screw you."

Fortunately, the McBeane team of McDermott and Beane didn't listen to the so-called experts either. They saw enormous potential in Allen. So they gambled their reputations on him—and won big time. It's interesting, thinking back to the negative reaction of many Bills fans and media after Allen was selected. By no means am I going to tell you that I was some clairvoyant who knew Allen was going to be this good. No one did. Not even McDermott or Beane, who, if truth be told, might have chosen Sam Darnold out of the University of Southern California had he not been selected third overall by the New York Jets and somehow was still available at Buffalo's No. 7 slot.

But unlike many members of the media and many Bills fans, I was more than willing to give Allen the benefit of the doubt. I told listeners on the *One Bills Live* television/radio show I cohosted: "Sheesh! Give the kid a chance. Don't rush to judgment."

I guess some of the media and fans' skepticism was understandable because of the Bills checkered history picking and developing quarterbacks. The memory of how Buffalo had traded back to select EJ Manuel with the 16th overall selection in the 2013 draft was still painfully vivid in the minds of many. That pick instantaneously was labeled a reach by the Bills. Some NFL scouts and personnel people said the Florida State quarterback likely would have been available in the second round, maybe even in the third.

Buddy Nix, the general manager at the time, was about to retire and turn over the reins to Doug Whaley and said he was going to find Buffalo its quarterback of the future before heading off into the sunset. In hindsight it was a desperation pick. Manuel was a good person, but as a pro quarterback, he wound up being a dud rather than a stud, throwing

19 touchdown passes and 15 interceptions in 17 starts over four seasons before being released.

Longer history was at play here, too, as Bills followers reeled off the busload of quarterbacks who had passed through Buffalo since Kelly's retirement following the 1996 season. Between Kelly and Allen, 17 different players had lined up behind center for the Bills.

That kind of instability at the most important position on the field explains why the franchise went 17 seasons without a playoff berth. It also helps explain why some critics were dismissing Allen before he had even taken his first NFL snap. I thought that was patently unfair.

Yes, the Bills history with quarterbacks had been bad for a long time, but what did that have to do with Allen? Nothing really. He deserved to be judged on his own merits, not the performances of Manuel, J.P. Losman, Trent Edwards, Rob Johnson, or any other Buffalo predecessor.

Despite all the quarterback misses, the Bills had no choice but to keep swinging in hopes they finally would get ahold of one. And, boy, did they ever get ahold of one with Allen. So far, this has been a tape-measure home run, a grand slam of a pick, the kind that makes a general manager and a coach look like geniuses and cements their legacies.

Success, though, didn't come immediately for Allen. It rarely does with any rookie quarterback—even ones who wind up in the Pro Football Hall of Fame. He was raw and definitely tried to do too much early on, which led to turnovers and losses. It reminded me a bit of the struggles Kelly experienced in his first few years, though in retrospect, Allen wound up progressing more rapidly.

The Bills coaches, especially first-time NFL offensive coordinator Brian Daboll, marveled at Allen's size (6'5", 245 pounds), arm, and athleticism, but they also knew he was a lump of clay that needed to be molded. He needed a lot of fine-tuning, and the original gameplan was to go slowly with him. They were hoping they would be able to do what Kansas City Chiefs coach Andy Reid had done with Mahomes during the quarterback's rookie year: have him stand on the sidelines, watch, and learn while a veteran served as a bridge quarterback.

But there was a world of difference between Mahomes' and Allen's situations. The Chiefs were a perennial playoff team and had Alex Smith, a quarterback who was still at the top of his game in his 13th season. He'd already been to a Super Bowl and three Pro Bowls. He was the ideal guy to tide the Chiefs over while mentoring Mahomes. Plus, in Reid, Mahomes had an established, long-in-the-tooth coach with a reputation for developing outstanding quarterbacks and creating offenses that catered to their strengths.

The Bills had hoped to do the same with Allen. But they were coming off a fluke-ish playoff appearance and had just parted ways with inconsistent quarterback Tyrod Taylor. Unfortunately, they didn't have an established veteran to allow Allen time to be mentored and ease into the job. Instead, they had Nathan Peterman, who turned out to be a disaster.

The year before drafting Allen, Buffalo had taken a flyer on Peterman, selecting him in the fifth round in hopes of perhaps finding a diamond in the rough. He had been a very good quarterback at the University of Pittsburgh, shattering the school passing records of Pro Football Hall of Famer Dan Marino and Alex Van Pelt, who quarterbacked the Bills for several seasons before joining me in the booth as my color analyst when I took over the play-by-play duties from Van Miller.

McDermott clearly saw something in Peterman that others didn't see. Peterman wound up beating out Allen and third-year veteran AJ McCarron in training camp for the right to start the 2018 season opener on the road against the Baltimore Ravens. With Taylor and the offense floundering a year earlier, McDermott opted to shake the Bills from their lethargy by starting Peterman in a late-season game against the Chargers in Los Angeles. What transpired was probably the worst half of quarterbacking I or anyone else has ever witnessed. Poor Peterman wound up throwing five interceptions, and the Bills had their asses handed to them in a 54–23 loss.

Many thought that ignominious debut would be the last we'd ever hear of Peterman, but McDermott hadn't completely lost faith in him, though he did insert Taylor back into the starting lineup following Peterman's debacle. Peterman was back on the roster in 2018 and shockingly was given that Opening Day start. Once again, things did not go well for him, as he completed just five-of-18 passes for 24 yards and was picked off twice before being benched in the second quarter of a 47–3 beatdown by the Ravens. Allen entered a game whose outcome already had been decided. Baltimore's pass rushers were pinning their ears back at that point, and, though Allen understandably struggled while running for his life, he did manage to show some flashes.

McDermott had finally seen the error of his ways regarding Peterman, and the plans to go slowly with Allen were scrapped. The Bills had no choice really but to start the rookie at quarterback in Week Two against the Los Angeles Chargers in Orchard Park. Although the Bills lost 31–20 that day, Allen enjoyed a few good moments while learning the NFL game on the fly. Yes, he was picked off twice, but he also managed to throw for 245 yards and connect on his first pro touchdown pass. (In case you're wondering, it was a two-yard toss to Kelvin Benjamin in the back of the end zone.) Allen also picked up 32 yards on eight carries.

The next week, the Bills traveled to Minnesota to play the Vikings, a loaded team that some pundits predicted would win the Super Bowl. No one was giving Buffalo much of a chance. The oddsmakers in Las Vegas clearly hadn't been impressed with Allen's starting debut nor his supporting cast, establishing Buffalo as 17-point underdogs. One bettor was so certain the Vikings would cover the point-spread that he plopped down $9,000. Thanks to Allen, that guy and many others wound up losing a ton of money.

In the biggest upset the NFL had seen in 23 years, the Bills clobbered the Vikings 27–6 in a game that wasn't even that close. Allen wound up scrambling for a 10-yard score on Buffalo's first possession. After a Stephen Hauschka field goal made it 10–0, Allen rifled a 26-yard touchdown pass to Jason Croom and added a one-yard touchdown run a little later as the Bills zoomed to a 27–0 halftime lead and never looked back. Though Allen's stats weren't eye-popping—196 passing yards, 39 rushing yards—they would have been more robust and the score even more lopsided had his receivers done a better job holding onto the ball.

Not that it mattered. What Allen did that day clearly gave us a glimpse of the greatness to come. Of all the plays he made, none was more spectacular than his impersonation of Olympic gold medal hurdler Edwin Moses in the second quarter. While scrambling to convert a third and 10, Allen went airborne and leapt over Vikings linebacker Anthony Barr. It was a reckless play, but it also was an unforgettable play that spoke to Allen's athleticism and his willingness to do whatever it takes on the football field to win. I obviously went wild in the booth, trying to describe what had just happened. Barr wasn't the only guy Allen caught by surprise on that play. It was amazing.

Of all the plays by NFL players that week and that season for that matter, that one truly stuck out. Not surprisingly, the video of Air Josh went viral and spawned thousands of humorous, clever memes. I remember getting a chuckle of a few in particular that showed Allen leaping over the Empire State Building and Mount Everest. People still talk about it, rave about it, and check it out on YouTube. At Bills training camp at St. John Fisher University in Rochester, New York, some of the team's clever marketing people put a life-sized, cutout photo of the leap on a pole, so that fans could have their pictures taken with the cutout of Allen hurdling them.

Clearly, it's not the kind of thing you want to see Allen doing very often because it's an incredibly risky play that could lead to serious injury.

But it endeared him to fans and teammates because it spoke volumes about him putting his body on the line to win. It also spoke volumes about his athleticism and his toughness, and Buffalo football fans love toughness. It's part of what made Kelly great, too.

After a loss to the Green Bay Packers the next week and a win against the Tennessee Titans, Allen suffered an injury against the Houston Texans when he took a helmet to his right elbow while completing a 39-yard pass to Benjamin. Allen kept shaking his right hand to try to get feeling back in his arm as he jogged down field and actually took another snap before dropping to his knees in pain. He came out of the game and would miss the next four games to allow his elbow to heal.

Interestingly, his return to action was against the Jacksonville Jaguars. And that was noteworthy because before the season loud-mouth Jags cornerback Jalen Ramsey took some shots at Allen, calling him "over-rated" and "trash." Allen didn't have a great day passing, completing just eight-of-19 passes for 160 yards and a touchdown. But he would lead the Bills to a 24–21 victory on the strength of his legs, rushing for 99 yards and another score. That yardage total was a new record for Bills quarterbacks, breaking the mark set by Taylor.

The next week in a four-point loss to the Miami Dolphins, Allen continued his development as a dual-threat quarterback, throwing for 231 yards and two touchdowns and breaking the rushing record he had established the week before by running for 135 yards. That set up a much-hyped matchup between him and his friend, Sam Darnold, whom the Jets had taken that April with the third pick overall. Darnold's team had gotten the better of the duel between rookie quarterbacks that day, but Allen had his moments during the four-point loss. His passing was still sketchy, as he threw for 206 yards and was picked off twice, but his legs remained a potent part of his repertoire as he rushed for 101 yards and one touchdown. That performance enabled him to become the first quarterback in NFL history to run for 95 or more yards in three consecutive games.

After a decisive loss to the New England Patriots, Allen rebounded in his rematch with Miami, continuing a trend of putting up big numbers against the Dolphins that continues to this day. Although he threw his first pick-six, Josh accounted for five touchdowns—three passing, two rushing—and 319 yards in total offense (including 95 rushing) as Buffalo ended a disappointing season on a high note with a 42–17 squishing of the Fish. The sterling performance earned him his first of what would become many AFC Offensive Player of the Week honors.

Allen's rookie season stats were nothing to write home about. He threw more interceptions (12) than touchdown passes (10) and he completed only 53 percent of his throws. It was the lowest completion percentage among NFL starters, and that only fanned the flames of critics fixated on his accuracy issues. He did, though, run for 631 yards and eight touchdowns, and many of the runs were spectacular in nature. He quickly emerged as the Bills best short-yardage runner and goal-line rushing threat. That he had the potential to beat you with his arms or legs was underscored by the fact he was the first Bills quarterback to lead the team in passing and rushing in the same season.

And there were plenty of positive things he did that didn't show up in the stat sheets—intangibles like grit and moxie. He still needed to improve in a lot of areas, and McDermott and Beane believed they could expedite his development by surrounding him with better talent. They needed to shore up the offensive line and get Allen some playmakers, which they did.

I definitely liked what I had seen. Even though Allen hadn't been a world-beater, he hadn't wilted while being surrounded by an average to below-average supporting cast. And he didn't point any fingers at anybody but himself. That's another positive trend that's continued. Even though there have been times when he would have been justified in criticizing teammates or coaches, Allen has never done that publicly. I think that just makes him an even stronger leader in the eyes of his coaches and fellow players. Guys know he has their backs, will fall on the sword for them, and criticizes himself, and that makes his teammates want to work harder and do better to support him.

Despite that 6–10 finish during his rookie season, I was encouraged about the quarterback position and the team's future. As evidenced by their 5–6 record in Josh's starts, the Bills were markedly better with him under center. I believed the interminable search for a worthy successor to Kelly might finally be over. The upside for Allen seemed huge. He clearly had all the physical tools and during his rookie season had precociously established himself as a team leader through example and deed. That's not easy for a first-year quarterback to do, but he had won over everyone, including the veterans with his toughness and determination. His temperament seemed perfectly aligned with Buffalo's. He got us, we got him, and in short order, he would become one of us.

# CHAPTER 2
## ROOTED IN BUFFALO AND ROOTING FOR BUFFALO

Ithink the fact I'm Buffalo born and bred has helped me immensely as a Bills broadcaster because I learned at an early age what makes us tick, what we're all about. So when I'm announcing games, I definitely know who I'm speaking to because I'm one of them and have been my entire life.

I was born in Lockport, a working-class suburb north of Buffalo. In retrospect, I was blessed to grow up there and be a part of a community where people cared for one another. I hail from a large Irish Catholic family. I like to kid that my parents, Matt and Lucille, were pros at pro-creation. They had nine kids in all. I was in the middle of the litter. I joke to my wife, Mary, that studies show that middle children are the most well-adjusted. She usually snickers and shakes her head when I tell her that and reminds me there are exceptions to every rule.

I will say this: being in the middle was great because it allowed me to be in both the big kid group and the little kid group of my family. I had the best of both worlds. We were a tight-knit, working-class family in a tight-knit, working-class town. General Motors had a big plant in Lockport, and it seemed like three-quarters of the town worked there. My dad ran a tire store not far from the factory, and I wound up working there when I got older. So in addition to describing press coverages and wheel routes, I can tell you how much tread you have left on your tires and if you need new ones.

In addition to running Lockport Tire, my dad worked as a politician, serving in the New York State Legislature from 1975 to 1992. Politics runs in our family. My grandfather, whom I never met, was the long-time Democratic party chair of Niagara County. My late brother Matt was a judge for years. And in 2005 my wife was elected as Orchard Park Town Supervisor, following her successful career as a television news reporter. No one ever approached me about running for office, nor did I ever entertain any thoughts of seeking office. But I did enjoy campaign-ing, which I did on behalf of my father, brother, and wife.

The Murphys were a sports-loving family for as long as I can remember. My mom, who was from New York City, was actually a more passionate and knowledgeable fan than my dad. My brother, Mark, who was four years older than I, was the one who really got me interested in sports. I have fond memories of watching *Hockey Night in Canada* telecasts with him in the years before the Buffalo Sabres came to town.

I learned to read at a very early age and wound up being so advanced that my teachers at St. Patrick's Elementary School had me skip a grade level so I wouldn't become disinterested and bored. One of the things I loved reading at an early age were the sports pages of the *Courier-Express* and the *Buffalo Evening News*. Perhaps the person I enjoyed reading most was *Courier-Express* sports columnist Phil Ranallo. He had a talent for making you feel like you were there. He wrote about all Buffalo sports and had a particular fondness for the horses. His descriptions of the horses and the characters at Fort Erie Race Track were so vivid, so real, that I couldn't wait until I was old enough to go there. And Ranallo's stuff was so good that it stood the test of time. I still have a book with a collection of his best columns.

I also became a big fan of Larry Felser, who covered the Bills from the start and later would become the sports columnist of the *Evening News* and a good friend. One of the thrills of my career was being able to do a radio show with him. He was a font of Buffalo sports history knowledge, a walking encyclopedia, and the thing I liked about him was his ability to cut through the BS and get to the truth.

My love of Buffalo sports also was nurtured by radio and television broadcasters, including Stan Barron, Rick Azar, and Ted Darling, the original voice of the Sabres. And perhaps no one nurtured my interest more than Van Miller, who was a ubiquitous presence, doing everything from Bills football to Buffalo Braves NBA games to Niagara basketball to bowling for dollars. Heck, Miller even did non-sports stuff like *It's Academic*, a weekly, *Jeopardy!*-like show in which students from area high schools would match wits. Years later, I would come to realize that my education as a broadcaster was cultivated by listening to Miller and company in my youth. They wound up being some of my greatest teachers.

The Bills were my first sports love, and in hindsight I picked a pretty good time to start following them. In those days CBS carried the NFL games, which usually meant we'd get an abundance of Cleveland Browns and New York Giants telecasts, while NBC carried the upstart AFL. I remember watching Bills games on our black-and-white television with Curt Gowdy and Al DeRogatis providing the play-by-play and color commentary, respectively. Gowdy would go on to do more major sports telecasts than probably any announcer in sports history, and the fact that he was doing AFL games definitely gave us a certain gravitas.

Though my first in-person viewing of professional football didn't go well in the Kansas City Chiefs' annihilation of Buffalo in the 1967 AFL Championship Game at War Memorial Stadium, I was hooked. I couldn't wait to go back again and again and again. War Memorial was built back in 1937 as part of Franklin Roosevelt's alphabet soup program to create jobs during the Great Depression. This massive concrete bowl became known colloquially as The Rockpile, but I refuse to refer to it as that. Some might feel that I'm being overly sensitive here, but I think calling it that was being disrespectful to a place that was named to honor soldiers who had lost their lives fighting for our country.

The old stadium will always be hallowed sports grounds to me because it's where I saw my first Bills game and many more games before the team headed to their new suburban digs in Orchard Park in 1973. War Memorial had character. It was stout and solid—just like us. I was fascinated by the whole place: the looks, the smells, the sounds. I swear I can still smell the aroma of those hot dogs grilling in the concourse. I remember my uncle telling me stories about him and his buddies buying an extra ticket so they could plop their quarter keg of beer in a vacant seat between them. Can you imagine that: *carrying a quarter keg of beer into a stadium?* I doubt you'd be able to sneak that through a stadium metal detector today.

In addition to attending games at War Memorial, I also had an opportunity to go to training camp at Niagara University, which was only about 20 minutes from our home. Training camp wasn't the big production we've come to know since the team moved to St. John Fisher College (now University) two decades ago. It was pretty informal and more intimate back then. There weren't any merchandise or corporate tents or souvenir stands, and crowds were fairly small. This made it much easier to converse with and get autographs from players and coaches.

I'll never forget how I once went there with the intent of meeting Jack Kemp, my favorite Bills player, and getting his autograph. My heart pounded when I saw him walking off the field toward me in full uniform with helmet in hand. But just before he reached the area where we were standing, Kemp was intercepted by a couple of men in suits. They were close enough for us to hear their conversation. The guys were from California, Kemp's home state, and were talking to him about his post-football career political aspirations and his support of then-governor Ronald Reagan's economic agenda. As it turned out, that conversation went on and on and on, and we never did get Kemp's autograph because he had to hurry off to team meetings. I was crestfallen not only because I didn't get to meet him, but also because of what I overheard. I come from a family of Democrats, and it was disappointing for me to discover that Kemp was a Republican.

Years later, I would get a chance to speak with Kemp on several occasions for pregame and halftime interviews on Bills broadcasts. By that time, he was a well-established and well-respected congressman from Western New York. He later would try and fail to secure the Republican presidential nomination and also lose out as the vice presidential candidate during running mate Bob Dole's unsuccessful bid for the Oval

Office in 1996. Although I disagreed with Kemp's politics, I always found him to be a gracious and accommodating interview. He obviously had some great stories from those old AFL days, when he locked horns with coach Lou Saban and fended off Daryle Lamonica, the quarterback who tried to wrest the starting job from him.

Kemp took a lot of grief during his Bills career as fans constantly—and sometimes heatedly—debated whether he or Lamonica should be *the* guy. It led to a funny quote Kemp liked to mention about how the vitriol he had received from Bills fans had prepared him for what he would encounter in the political arena. "I'd already been spat upon, sworn at, and hung in effigy," he liked to say. "So, I had developed the thick skin I would need in Washington."

In addition to the Bills, I was a huge college basketball fan, and my timing was great for that, too. Around 1970, when I was in the seventh or eighth grade, it was a golden era for Buffalo-area college basketball, which featured future Hall of Famers Bob Lanier (St. Bonaventure) and Calvin Murphy (Niagara). And because of Murphy's surname and sublime game and because Niagara's campus was only about 20 minutes from Lockport, I became a huge, huge Niagara fan. And all these years later, I still am.

Miller happened to be doing Niagara games back then, so that helped pique my interest. But little Calvin was the biggest reason I rooted fiercely for the Purple Eagles. Although he stood just 5'9", he could jump out of the gym. He could dunk a basketball from a standing position with either hand. That's how springy his legs were. And he could shoot the lights out, too. Calvin wound up averaging more than 30 points per game during his college career, and if they had the three-point line back then, there's no telling how high his average might have been.

Calvin also somehow became a world-class baton twirler. He'd toss that sucker 20 to 25 feet into the air and catch it without missing a beat. He was so good at it that the Bills actually had him twirl before and during halftime of games at War Memorial Stadium. We caught wind that he was going to march and twirl in the Memorial Day Parade in Lockport. My father knew of my love for Calvin, so when he found out, he contacted a friend of his—Lloyd Patterson—who had been a former Niagara basketball player. My father actually drove to pick up Calvin and brought him to our house. I sat in my backyard, talking to my boyhood sports hero. It was surreal. Years later, I told Mary that I wanted to name our second son Calvin but she put the kibosh on that in a hurry.

In addition to following sports passionately while growing up, I also played them, though not very well. It seemed like the neighborhood kids and I were playing some form of baseball, Wiffle Ball, or kickball every summer day. I was a decent-sized kid and loved playing basketball, too. And I would have loved to have played in high school, but the bottom line was that I wasn't quick enough. I did run some cross country at DeSales Catholic High School, but that probably was the extent of my athletic career—other than golf and the pickup basketball games I played in my 20s and 30s. I guess you could say that I talk a much better game than I play.

The first time I sat before a microphone was in high school. There was a little, bitty radio station in Lockport—WLVL—that broadcast varsity football and basketball games in Niagara County, and I did stats and stuff for them. At the end of the game, I would get to go on the air and read the final stats. That kind of planted the seed for me, but if I said that's when I knew I wanted to make a career of this, I'd be lying. Sometimes you just kind of work hard and luck into things. And that's what happened to me. But I never had this grand scheme of becoming a broadcaster for life. The stars just wound up aligning perfectly for me. And in retrospect I consider myself truly blessed that they did.

At the advice of my high school counselor, I decided to apply to Ithaca College and Syracuse University, two schools that offered broadcasting majors. SU's Newhouse School of Public Communications has

21

since developed a reputation as "Sportscaster U," churning out well-known broadcasters like Bob Costas, Mike Tirico, Marv Albert, Dick Stockton, Len Berman, and Sean McDonough. But back then in the mid-1970s when I was there, the reputation wasn't nearly as big as it has become. I ultimately may have decided on SU because I was a New York Knickerbockers' fan—in addition to being a Buffalo Braves fan—and I read a book by Albert, the longtime play-by-play voice of the Knicks and the National Basketball Association. I read in the book that Albert had attended Syracuse as did previous Knicks announcer, Marty Glickman. So, I said to myself, *All right, I'll go there.*

I did wind up working for a radio station there, but it wasn't WAER, the station where Albert, Costas, Tirico, and so many others had cut their journalistic teeth. Instead, I worked at another student station, WJPZ, where I hosted a music show and became the news director. WJPZ was more of a jazz station. We didn't do any sports there, and the news was kind of just slapped together, but it was broadcasting experience. WAER was where you went if you were truly serious about becoming a sports-caster, but I found the station to be too clubby and clique-ish and I still hadn't figured out what I was going to do with the rest of my life.

My Newhouse professors were good and demanding. One of the prominent ones, a guy by the name of Ernie Andrews, was especially hard on me. My classmates and I would take turns anchoring the campus news, and Andrews essentially told me he didn't like my voice or my delivery. He kind of indicated that I didn't have a future in the business. I didn't take it personally. I just tried to get better, but I did take some satisfaction in eventually proving him wrong. I wonder what he would think of me now.

Interestingly, my favorite college courses had nothing to do with broadcasting. I had always been interested in history and loved literature, so I wound up loving my liberal arts courses. We had a fabulous profes-sor by the name of David Bennett, who taught 20th century American history. His lectures weren't lectures at all but rather performances. He really knew how to bring history to life. I also absolutely loved the constitutional law course I took with Michael Sawyer, who was a nationally renowned expert on the subject, and communications law with Jay Wright, who was a driving force behind the Freedom of Information Act.

I remember talking with my older brother, Matt, about how much I had enjoyed my law courses. He had just become an attorney after finishing law school at the University of Albany and told me I should consider taking the LSATs. So, I did and wound up doing pretty well. After graduating with a degree in broadcasting from Syracuse, I applied and was accepted to the School of Law at the University at Buffalo. Although I believed I could have become a good lawyer and could have had a long career doing it, I quickly realized I didn't have some deep-seeded passion for the law. Looking back on those times and that decision, I realized I still hadn't found what I was looking for or what I wanted to do with the rest of my life.

My pursuit of my law degree didn't even last a semester. I really wasn't into it. So in the fall of 1978, I wound up spending more time helping my dad campaign for his legislative seat than cracking open my three-inch thick law books. I really enjoyed the dynamics of campaigning. In some respects, it's like a sporting event. It's a competition with plenty of strategy involved. And, of course, there's a winner and a loser with a ballot box functioning like a scoreboard.

My dad won that election, and I made the decision to quit law school. It just wasn't for me. I was 23 years old and still hadn't plotted a career path. So, I cobbled together some jobs broadcasting local news at WLVL in Lockport during the week and at WJJL in Niagara Falls on weekends. I was making next to nothing at those jobs. So to make ends meet, I'd also tend bar at Danny Sheehan's Steak House in Lockport.

Sportscasting didn't really enter the picture until around 1980, when WLVL started broadcasting high school football and basketball games. They needed some help. So I pitched in. It was fun, and I enjoyed it, and that's when I thought this was the path for me. I had spent about two years at WLVL when I heard there was a news job opening at a much larger station, WBEN, in Buffalo. I wound up getting the gig and began working weekdays from 3:00 in the afternoon until 11:00 at night. Some of my newscasts would air during Stan Barron's *Free Form Sports*, which ran from 7:00 until 11:00. That's how I got to know Barron. He would do nightly commentaries and often would run them by me for feedback. I really appreciated that and eventually began suggesting topics for him to commentate about, some of which he pursued and some of which he rejected.

Barron was also sharing Bills broadcasts with Miller at the time. Barron took a liking to me and suggested to WBEN station manager Larry Levite that I would be a good choice to produce the Bills three-hour pregame show. That was a lot of fun and a lot of work. I would cut up highlights from the previous week's game, do interviews with upcoming opponents, and come up with historical features, too. This was all in addition to me doing the 3:00-11:00 newscasts.

My timing couldn't have been better because this was a great, albeit brief era of Bills football. Coach Chuck Knox's rebuilding program was taking hold. Not only did Buffalo win the AFC East and make the playoffs two years in a row, it also did so in highly entertaining fashion. Quarterback Joe Ferguson was at the top of his game, throwing to the likes of Jerry Butler, Frank Lewis, and Joe Cribbs, who was kind of like an early version of Thurman Thomas, a dual-threat running back who had a three-, four-year stretch as dynamic as any back in Bills history. Thanks to them and an opportunistic defense led by new-blood players like nose tackle Fred Smerlas and linebacker Jim Haslett, the Bills finally halted that ignominious losing streak that had seen them lose all 20 games to the hated Miami Dolphins during the 1970s.

Around this time, the Buffalo Chamber of Commerce had sought to boost flagging spirits with an ad campaign that included a catchy jingle titled "Talkin' Proud." Yes, it was hokey, but there was no denying those Bills teams had rejuvenated the region's collective psyche and provided a salve, a distraction from the recent closing of the steel mills in Lackawanna. In retrospect, I don't believe that era of Bills football has been appreciated enough. It really did set the stage for what would come in the late 1980s, early 1990s. It was a fun time, a reminder of the Bills' power to boost us, especially in difficult times.

Around this time, Levite was looking for ways to expand coverage and take advantage of the Bills' popularity surge. He added a weekly coach's call-in show with Knox and wanted to do a players' show, too. I immediately suggested Smerlas and Haslett. I had gotten to know them a bit during our weekly media scrums at Orchard Park, and they seemed like fun-loving guys whose zaniness would play well on radio. Levite liked my suggestion, and we made arrangements to do a weekly, one-hour show that would air Monday nights just after Knox's.

To say Smerlas and Haslett were wild and crazy would be an understatement. They were unfiltered guys who said what was on their minds often without thinking about the repercussions, which made for good and sometimes controversial radio. There was rarely a dull moment with them, and my producer and I had to be at the ready to hit the bleep button because you never knew when those two knuckleheads might spout a word that could get the radio station into trouble with the FCC.

Some of the more memorable shows aired during the 1982 season, when the players went on strike for seven weeks. Fans were quite upset that athletes making significantly more than the average American had the audacity to sit out for more money. During one show, Haslett tried to explain why the players were striking and wound up stepping on a hornet's nest. He made the point that NFL players weren't like the "greedy autoworkers' union; we're just trying to get our fair share."

The instant the words came out of his mouth, I thought to myself, *Oh. My. God. I can't believe you just said that.*

Haslett had forgotten that Buffalo was a big union town at the time, and there was a huge General Motors plant and other auto industry spinoffs in the area. Talk about sticking your size-12 cleats in your mouth. The phone console in our studio lit up like a Christmas tree. Haslett never stood a chance. Caller after caller after caller laid into him and Smerlas. By the time we finally went to commercial break, I was exhausted, and Haslett was ready to throw the phone console through the window. We tried to calm him down to no avail. He needed to vent. And boy did he ever.

In rapid-fire succession, Haslett pressed each of the lighted buttons on the console and screamed into the phone at each of the callers on hold.

"F--- you!"

Click.

"F--- you!"

Click.

"F--- you!"

Click.

Once, he cleared the board, the console immediately lit up again, and Haslett quickly repeated his obscene routine. Fortunately, we weren't on the air at the time. Otherwise, WBEN would have had to declare bankruptcy after paying all the FCC fines Haslett would have incurred. He eventually calmed down, and Bills fans eventually forgave him. All these years later, he, Smerlas, and I still have a chuckle over the night he went temporarily insane.

# CHAPTER 3

## VAN WAS THE MAN

Perhaps the biggest break of my career occurred during the summer of 1984, and unfortunately it happened when a person who had opened doors for me and had become a friend, suffered a horrible, tragic break. Stan Barron had been diagnosed with a virulent form of cancer and was courageously soldiering on despite being in immense pain. The disease had severely weakened his bones, and while getting out of bed that August, he shattered his leg. Somehow, he managed to drag himself into the booth for a preseason Buffalo Bills game inside the then-brand-new Hoosier Dome in Indianapolis, but I could tell from listening to him back in the WBEN studio that he was hurting. He didn't sound good at all. As it turned out, Barron never worked another game after that one and died about two months later.

WBEN's general manager Larry Levite immediately called me and told me, "We're in a serious bind, and I need you to work with Van Miller and do the games." I was shaken up about Barron and nervous about trying to do something I had never done before, but Levite told me I would be able to ease into it because they had a three-man booth with Paul Guidry, a linebacker from the Bills AFL championship days, there to provide color analysis from a player's perspective. Van did his best to carry the broadcasts, but it was awkward because I really didn't know what my role was, and Guidry was extremely uncomfortable behind the microphone. No one was blaming Guidry. He gave it an honest try, but he just didn't have a knack for broadcasting and quit after about four games.

Just like that, it was going to be me and my idol, the man I had grown up listening to.

I was excited—and very, very nervous.

Fortunately, I couldn't have picked a better person to break me in. Van's kindness and sense of humor immediately put me at ease. Most color analysts are former players or coaches. I was neither, so I couldn't bring that perspective of what it's like to be out there on the field or the sidelines. But I had followed football very closely for years and had picked the brains of countless participants while putting together the pregame show and while moderating the Smerlas and Haslett show, so I had a feel and a viewpoint that others didn't. I had paid rapt attention. I had some expertise. I figured if I did my homework on the Bills and the opposing team and continued talking extensively to players, coaches, general managers, scouts, scribes, and other broadcasters, I could relay to the listeners the intel I had learned. Van told me that approach would work perfectly.

My first game as Van's solo sidekick came on the road in St. Louis against the Cardinals in Busch Stadium on September 9, 1984. The minute I boarded the elevator to the visitors' broadcast booth, I noticed a taped, handwritten piece of paper that read, "John Murphy, road rookie" with an arrow pointing up. I wondered, *What the heck is that all about?* When I got off the elevator, there was another sign with the same words and an arrow pointing to the right. Every 10 feet or so, there was another sign with another arrow, leading me to the booth. There had to have been at least a dozen of them. When I finally reached the booth, I saw Van standing there with an incandescent smile big enough to light up Busch Stadium. "Glad you were able to find the place, Murph," he said, as I flashed a smile big enough to match his.

I couldn't have been more grateful. Van had loosened me up. I was at ease and in great hands. Looking back, I realized how truly blessed I was to learn about this crazy broadcast business from a master craftsman and a genuinely good and funny guy. That day would be the official start of a beautiful, fun-filled relationship.

I guess, in an ideal world, I would have been walking into a job where I was providing analysis for a team that was good. But the 1984 Bills were anything but good. In fact, they were bad. Historically so. Joe Ferguson was on his last legs, and the quarterback of the future—Jim Kelly—was playing in the United States Football League and had no desire to sign with Buffalo, the team that had drafted him a year earlier. Under head coach Kay Stephenson, who had taken over the season before because Chuck Knox bolted for the Seattle Seahawks, the Bills opened the year losing their first 11 games. An upset of the heavily favored Dallas Cowboys at Rich Stadium would be the highlight in a campaign that saw the Bills finish with a 2–14 record, the worst in the NFL.

Despite that dreadful campaign, I wanted to continue on as Van's color man because—as bad as Buffalo was—this still was the NFL. That said, I didn't hold much hope of being back for a second season. I figured I was one and done, and the team would hire someone new, someone with much more experience. It wasn't until about February of 1985 that WBEN's Levitt and our program director, Bob Wood, gave me the great news that I would be doing color again. Besides providing analysis on Bills broadcasts, they asked me to host the nightly, four-hour sports talk show the late Barron had done for years. My news days were over. They wanted me to devote all my energies to sports.

The funny thing is that they told me they weren't going to pay me anything extra to do the Bills games, but I didn't care about being given a heavier workload for the same salary. So what if I was making no more than $30,000 a year? I was young and living the dream. I was happy as hell being back in the booth with Van, even though we were about to live through another 2–14 campaign.

Van undoubtedly had played a big role in me returning. If he had told the Bills and Levitt that he didn't want me back, I would've been gone. But he clearly put in a good word for me, and I'll always be grateful. Through the decades Van would become more than a mentor and a broadcast partner. He would become a wonderful, caring friend who never ceased finding ways to make me chuckle. There were indeed times, especially in the early years, when I was in awe of just how good he was, times when I'd catch myself looking at him on gameday and thinking, *Holy mackerel! I'm working with Van "Freaking" Miller.*

Van's sense of humor always kept things grounded. He was very smart and very wise in that way. That's not to say he didn't take his job seriously because he did. He worked incredibly hard at it. I learned so much about the importance of preparation from him right down to the name-and-number spotter boards he used to identify players, which I wound up copying and tweaking and still use to this day. He realized how much the Bills meant to people and how important the broadcasts were to them. Van figured if people were going to invest three to four hours of their lives listening to us each week, then we should do our best to make sure they had a good and informative time. One of the things I also admired about Van was the way he managed to keep things in perspective, especially during the low times of Bills history. "Murph," he'd tell me, "this isn't life or death; this is football. This is entertainment. We're describing games here, not wars."

Van loved inviting fans up to the booth. They might be total strangers he'd just met an hour or two earlier. It didn't matter. Van just enjoyed sharing the joy of Bills football with people. He would deadpan to visitors to the booth that this was serious, serious business up here, a ton of work. He'd show them his legal pad filled with pages of notes he had compiled during the week and then he would turn the pad over and show them the words he had written in large letters on the back. They would be readying themselves for some sage words of wisdom from the great Van Miller, and then he would reveal in large, black letters: "It's all bullshit!"

And his guests and I would laugh uproarishly each time he delivered that punch line.

In addition to being hilarious, the skit served as another reminder that this stuff was important, and you should work hard to put on a good show, but you shouldn't go overboard. Entertain and inform people. "We're describing football games here, not wars."

There's no question Van Miller loved being Van Miller. He reveled in his role as the soundtrack of Buffalo sports history and maybe even the soundtrack of Buffalo for that matter. He broadcast just about everything there was to broadcast in sports in Western New York: the Bills, the Braves when we were an NBA city, minor league baseball, college basketball, high school sports, professional wrestling, and bowling. Everything, really, except the Sabres. He also broadcast non-sports stuff, too: news and weather, big band shows, farm reports, a weekly show devoted to Polish music and culture, and that high school show called *It's Academic*.

I know he enjoyed hanging out in the hotel lobby on Sunday mornings before Bills road games and having people come up to him and ask for his autograph or a photo with him. And, invariably, there'd be times I'd show up in the booth, and one of those strangers he had just met would be there, taking a little tour. He'd joke, "Hey, Murph, I'd like to you to meet my long-lost cousin, so-and-so," or "my long-lost Uncle so-and-so."

Had he not made it as one of the greatest sportscasters of all time, I think he might have tried to make a living as a stand-up comedian because he enjoyed nothing more than making people laugh. When Van was in Canton, Ohio, to receive the Pete Rozelle Award for a lifetime of football broadcasting excellence, they presented it to him at a huge banquet the night before the Pro Football Hall of Fame inductions, and many of the Hall of Famers were in attendance, wearing their gold jackets. Van was on the top of his game while delivering his acceptance speech. Only, it wasn't really a speech but rather a monologue worthy of Johnny Carson, David Letterman, or one of the other late-night talk shows. I swear, for a good 15 to 20 minutes, Van had the audience in stitches. Although I'd heard many of the jokes many times before, I couldn't stop roaring, and neither could those who didn't know Van Miller from Von

I could not have picked a better mentor or broadcasting partner than the great Van Miller. (John Murphy)

Miller. His comedic timing was impeccable. After he was through, I had Hall of Famers like John Elway and Barry Sanders come up to me and say, "That guy was unbelievable. He ought to take that act on the road."

Fortunately, for Bills fans, the only time he took his act on the road was for away games.

Looking back, much of the stuff I learned from Van was by example. And he proved to be a great role model. He gave me a lot of creative leeway. He allowed me to carve my own niche, to be myself, to make mistakes and learn from them. I really appreciated that. Van was always encouraging. During commercial breaks he'd often compliment me about some comment I had just made while analyzing a play or a situation. And that was his subtle way of boosting my confidence while also nudging me in the right direction.

One important thing I learned from Van was that, unlike baseball, basketball, or hockey, there were only 16 (now 17) games during the NFL regular season, so each one takes on greater significance, has greater ramifications than they have in those other sports, where the schedules are much, much longer, and the games much more frequent. I learned from him that if you blow a call, you just keep moving on; you don't dwell on it. And if you have a bad broadcast, which every crew has from time to time, you try to learn from it just like the players and coaches try to learn from bad games. "Murph," he would say, "we get another shot to do this all over again next week, and we'll try to fix things and do better."

Again, preparation was big with him—and me. Bills fans are among the most knowledgeable in football, so you better know your stuff forward and backward. And you better be honest. Although I've never believed in turning a game broadcast into a talk show commentary the way some play-by-play guys do, Van taught me that you need to tell it like it is. You can't sugarcoat it when something bad happens or else you'll lose credibility with your audience. By the same token, when things go well, you need to convey that enthusiasm, share in the excitement.

Van became known for several signature phrases. He loved telling people to "Fasten their seatbelts" just before a big game kicked off, and I liked that phrase because it kind of set the tone that we were about to take you on an amusement park ride filled with unpredictable ups and downs. Perhaps the most memorable word he ever uttered was "fandemonium," which, of course, was a clever play on "pandemonium" and a wonderful description for the euphoria fans were feeling.

Although I loved those expressions and felt they worked extremely well for Van, I think many announcers become overly reliant on catchy but contrived phrases, many of which they plotted out days before big games. I'm more into spontaneous reaction and description rather than creating something you've concocted beforehand. Go with your gut in the heat of the moment. Again, that's by no means meant as a criticism of Van because the words he used were genuinely expressed and born of the moment and became a fun part of Bills lore. I just think too many broadcasters have become preoccupied with trying to be cute and clever rather than doing their jobs of describing the action, the sights and sounds, the down and distance, time remaining, and—most importantly—the score.

One of Van's greatest strengths was his ability to be in the moment and capture the moment. Listen to some of his descriptions of big plays and big games in Bills history and you realize and appreciate how good he was. Although many people didn't truly discover Van until the Bills' Super Bowl run of the early 1990s, believe me when I say he was brilliant long before that. When I was cutting up highlights of his calls for the pregame shows back in the early 1980s, I was reminded how great he was. Listening to those broadcasts was like taking a graduate course in sportscasting. He was so good at not only describing the action, but also setting the scene and providing context. Those definitely are things I've attempted to do, too.

In retrospect, one of the big things I learned from Van is knowing—and remembering—who your audience is and what they want and need to know. When things are clicking on a broadcast, the listener feels as if he or she is at the stadium, seeing and feeling what you're seeing and feeling. I try to think of the guy who's maybe driving on the New York State Thruway or the nurse who's at work and might not have access to a television. They can't be there, so you are their eyes and ears. You need to make them feel like they are there in the stands at Highmark Stadium. And Van was so good at that. Describe the scene. Set the scene. Keep that guy on the Thruway and that nurse in the hospital in mind when you are broadcasting that game.

Van also taught me to have fun with the broadcast whenever possible. And man did we ever have fun. We would joke around when appropriate, commiserate when appropriate. We realized how lucky we were to be broadcasting football games and we had a blast even in some of the lean years. I'll never forget the game in Cincinnati when the Bengals provided us with a spotter to help us quickly identify their players. Well, it just so happened that it was a night game, and the guy they gave us was wearing sunglasses, which we thought was kind of strange. Before kickoff he removed the sunglasses, and we saw he was wearing a huge patch over one of his eyes. And to make matters worse, the poor guy told us he was experiencing a little blurred vision with his good eye. During the first commercial break, the one-eyed spotter apologized to Van, "I'm sorry, I've got this patch on my eye and I'm seeing the jersey numbers double."

An exasperated Van told the guy, "Well…just divide by two."

Needless to say, it wound up being a long, long night.

Van hailed from Dunkirk, a small town about an hour south of Highmark Stadium, just north of the Pennsylvania border and he liked to tell the story how as a 10 year old he had prepped for his future job by pretending to announce Notre Dame games into a hose, an eggbeater, or a spoon—anything he could use as a make-believe microphone. "I must have called about 150 of the Fighting Irish's games for an audience of one—me," he said. "And you know what? Notre Dame won every one of those games I broadcast. They were undefeated with me at the mic."

He became the first "Voice of the Bills" in 1960 after general manager Dick Gallagher had listened to him doing high school games—and everything else for that matter—on local radio. Gallagher told Bills owner Ralph Wilson, "You've got to get this Miller guy to do our games."

That started a beautiful relationship between announcer, owner, and team. "It's probably one of the best personnel decisions we've ever made," said Mr. Wilson, who often played tennis with Van and once gave the broadcaster an all-expenses paid trip to Wimbledon. "Van has done as much to spread the word of Bills football and contribute to their popularity as anyone. Players came and go, but Van was our constant."

He definitely was one of the Bills' all-time great ambassadors. In all, Van spent 37 years providing Bills play-by-play—a total of 752 games if you tack on the preseason and postseason games. That's a record neither I nor anyone else is ever going to equal. And he would have done more than 800 games had WBEN not lost the Bills radio rights for a few years in the early 1970s.

When he was gone during that stretch, there was definitely a void; something definitely was missing. I remember going to a Bills game with friend and longtime college basketball coach John Beilein in 1979, and it just happened to be Van's first game back. We're listening to the action on the radio, and Beilein turned to me and said, "Murph, that's what Bills football sounds like." And he was right. So many of us had grown up with that voice and this football team. It was like Van became a member of every fan's family.

Though Van was still on the air, working as a sports anchor for one of the Buffalo television stations during those years, it really hurt him not being able to call Bills games. Years later, I would come to understand what that had been like for him because when WBEN lost the Bills broadcast rights for four years in the early 1990s, I briefly lost my gig as a color analyst. And, yes, my absence just so happened to coincide with the four years the Bills went to the Super Bowl. Fortunately, I was still covering the team extensively during that era, doing my radio talk show, and also working as a sports anchor/director for a Buffalo television station. That kept me fully engaged, but it was strange to be sitting in the press box rather than the announcer's booth on game days.

Covering Super Bowls is exhilarating and exhausting. You go nonstop, especially the week of the game. You're on the run often from early in the morning until late at night. And that certainly was the case for me during the week of Super Bowl XXV in Tampa, Florida, in late January of 1991. Interestingly, you finally get a chance to exhale the morning of the game because kickoff doesn't take place until around 6:30. Because I had been working at a break-neck pace that week, I didn't have time to feel sorry for myself about missing out on being next to Van for what would be the biggest moment in Bills history. When I woke up the morning of that first Bills Super Bowl, it really hit me that I wasn't going to be doing the game, and I was bummed out that entire day. Once I got to the stadium and got involved in providing pregame coverage, I had no choice but to snap out of it. But it was depressing for awhile.

And I'd be dealing with that depression off and on for the next four years as Buffalo made its unprecedented run. In retrospect, I wish I could have provided live color on the 51–3 annihilation of the Los Angeles Raiders in the 1990 AFC Championship Game or the "Wide Right" loss to the New York Giants in Super Bowl XXV or the "Comeback Game," in which Frank Reich engineered that stirring, historic victory after the Bills fell behind by 32 points early in the second half.

I obviously was grateful that I was immersed in coverage of those teams and those games through my radio shows and television work, but I badly wanted to get back in the booth on game days, and fortunately that happened before the start of the 1994 season. I can't tell you how happy I was to be reunited with Van, and the feeling was mutual. Just before kickoff of our first regular-season game that season, we began our pregame, scene-setting comments, and Van opened with the line: "As Murph was saying before being rudely interrupted four years ago."

What a great set-up line. He had a knack for saying just the right thing, a knack for injecting humor and making me and others feel significant.

Before the 2003 season, Van told me it was going to be his last year in the booth. I respected his decision but couldn't help but feel sad. We had been together for 16 years and had shared so many moments. He became so much more than a broadcast partner. I couldn't help but feel nostalgic as his career wound down. That season, I made sure I took time to savor the moments not only in the booth, but also on the plane rides to and from road games and the dinners we often shared the evenings before games.

I was hoping the Bills would give Van a season to remember on the field, and it sure started out that way as they shellacked the New England Patriots 31–0 in the season opener at sunny Ralph Wilson Stadium. One of the big plays featured a tipped pass that was intercepted by mountainous nose tackle Sam Adams, who returned the pass for a touchdown. Van's call on the play was so picture perfect. I remember thinking at that time and in the games that followed that Van shouldn't be retiring because he's still at the top of his game. Unfortunately, the same couldn't be said of the team he was describing. After that thrashing of New England and a rout against the Jacksonville Jaguars, the Bills fell apart, losing seven of their next nine on their way to a 6–10 record.

During Van's last home game, the Bills appropriately honored him and his wife, Gloria, on the field at halftime. I remember him telling me that it might take him a little extra time to get back to the booth, so I should be prepared to do the play-by-play at the start of the second half. And that's what happened. And when he finally did return to the mic, he told the listeners, "Well, folks, Murph just gave you a taste of what the future of Buffalo Bills football is going to sound like, and all I can say is that you're going to be in really good hands." Van was such a thoughtful guy.

His last game was on the road against the Patriots, and that was apropos because he had called his first Bills game against the then-Boston Patriots on July 30, 1960. It's customary for media members covering the team to get together for dinner the Saturday night before road games, and a bunch of us decided to take Van out for his "last supper" at a restaurant across the street from the team hotel in Providence, Rhode Island.

Van was in a joyous mood that night, regaling us with funny stories from his old AFL days right up to the present. Unbeknownst to us, this upscale restaurant also was home to an escort service, and as the evening wore on, some very attractive women noticed our table of about a dozen men and soon came over in hopes of drumming up some business. A couple of them wound up sitting on Van's lap, as he continued his comedy routine. It was all quite innocent, and I can assure you that Van and I returned to our hotel rooms alone.

As the night unfolded, I couldn't help but notice that the escorts were having such a good time listening to Van tell humorous story after humorous story. In fact, they were having such a good time that they stuck around our table even after they realized no one was interested in doing any business with them. They actually were costing themselves money by not seeking out other potential customers at other tables. I guess you could say that spoke to just how entertaining and charming Van could be when he was on a roll.

There was an assumption on the part of just about everyone but me that I would be Van's successor. After the season ended, I mentioned to Scott Berchtold, the Bills' longtime vice president of media relations, that I obviously was interested in the job. Berchtold said we'd talk at some point, and I didn't read anything into that. I understood that team president and general manager Tom Donahoe was preoccupied with a much more important succession plan: replacing coach Gregg Williams following such a disappointing season.

I was confident I was the leading candidate, the most qualified candidate to replace Van, but, still, you never know. There are only 32 of these play-by-play jobs in the NFL, and I'm sure the Bills were inundated with inquiries and audition tapes for the position. And I was thinking if the

Bills ever wanted to make a clean break from the past after a retirement of a legend like Van, this would be the ideal time.

Many teams' play-by-play gigs paid handsomely, making it unnecessary to work any other jobs. Not so with the Bills. They played in the second smallest media market in the NFL, meaning the money they made from local broadcast rights was miniscule compared to New York, Dallas, Chicago, or L.A. People forget that for years Van's main job had been as sports anchor/director of a Buffalo television affiliate. His work as "Voice of the Bills" didn't pay his…um…bills.

During my years as the team's color analyst, I continued working full time as a sports director and radio host of my own local talk show. Later, I would make the transition to television, eventually becoming the sports director/anchor at WKBW and WIVB. So, as I waited to hear back from the Bills about succeeding Van, I wasn't desperate. I had a primary job that paid decently. I had something to fall back on, something I'd continue to do regardless of what transpired with the Bills.

That said, I badly wanted that play-by-play job. There's such great prestige that goes with the job. And the fact I was from Buffalo and would have the opportunity to become the voice of my hometown team placed a personal value on it that went beyond the dollars. The longer I went awaiting the call, the more unease I felt. And it didn't help that people kept inquiring, even though most of them were well-meaning and encouraging. I tried my best not to let any uncertainty or negative thoughts creep into my head. But it was tough. And I wasn't taking it for granted that I automatically was the guy.

Finally, one Saturday morning after dropping my son, Mark, off for high school crew practice, I received a call from Berchtold. He said Donahoe wanted to see me and was wondering if I could head over to the stadium right away. I was grungy and unshaven at the time—heck it was like 7:00 in the morning when he phoned—so I asked Berchtold if I could swing home and wash up. But he insisted Donahoe wanted to see me right away, that I shouldn't worry about my appearance. So I showed up at his office, looking like something the cat just dragged in, and Donahoe gave me the great news that I was the new play-by-play man of the Buffalo Bills. I thanked him and Berchtold and walked out of there feeling euphoric. I reflected on just how fortunate I was and how I had never plotted this path. It all just kind of fell into place along the way. I was truly blessed.

I didn't need any fans or newspaper columnists telling me I had some awfully big shoes to fill. I was fully aware. Heck, I'd grown up listening to Van, he'd been my idol, and I had spent a decade and a half as his gameday sidekick. I damn well knew what I was getting into. I guess in some respects it wasn't all that different from those poor quarterbacks trying to replace Kelly. Van was that big, that beloved.

My mind-set, though, was to suppress those thoughts as best I could because they do you no good. It was inevitable I would encounter critics who would say, "He's no Van Miller." Much of that had to do with Van's longevity, which had been the longest run by a broadcaster with the same team in NFL history. He had been a presence in Bills fans lives for 37 seasons. That's an eternity.

You'll get no argument from me that Van was and will forever be considered *the* "Voice of the Bills," in the same way that many hockey fans regard Ted Darling as the all-time "Voice of the Buffalo Sabres," even though he's been gone for nearly three decades, and his successor, Rick Jeanneret, became so beloved that in 2022 the team honored him with his name on a banner, hanging from the arena rafters right next to those honoring iconic players Gilbert Perreault, Dominik Hasek, and Pat LaFontaine. At the time of those ceremonies, Jeanneret himself said Darling would always be the guy.

During those seasons immediately following Van, I tried to keep my approach pretty simple. I wasn't replacing Van; I was succeeding him. There's a big distinction there. I realized I couldn't be Van Miller even if

I wanted to. Nobody could. And it would have been foolhardy to try to change myself to imitate him. That never works, whether you're a broadcaster, a quarterback, or anything else.

The only way you can succeed is by being yourself. And that's what I tried to do. That's not to say there wasn't stuff I had learned from Van that I could and would use. I'd be a fool not to. But to try to be Van would have made me an even bigger fool and would have doomed me to failure. People would have seen through that immediately. I needed to have laser focus. I needed to block out the criticism that inevitably is directed at those who follow icons. I needed to be me.

# CHAPTER 4
## MY PARTNERS IN CRIME

Not only would I be following in the footsteps of the legendary Van Miller, I also had to make the switch from color analyst to play-by-play for the Buffalo Bills. That's like going from receiver to quarterback. Two totally different positions. Two totally different roles. Although I didn't have extensive play-by-play experience, I clearly had paid attention to what made Van so good. He had set an example of what I should do and needed to do as far as the basics go.

A play-by-play broadcaster needs to paint pictures with his or her words, needs to always remember that he or she is the eyes and ears of the listener. You want to provide not only vivid descriptions, but also context and perspective. The basics are important, essential really: down and distance; direction the ball is moving (east, west, tunnel-side, or scoreboard side of the stadium); time remaining on the clock; and—most importantly—the score. There's nothing that drives listeners battier than an announcer who doesn't keep you apprised of the score. You can't give it enough as far as I'm concerned.

A good play-by-play announcer also understands the importance of setting the scene and setting up your color analyst to flesh out the broadcast. The play-by-play announcer provides the bricks. The color commentator provides the mortar. I see my role, metaphorically speaking, similar to that of a quarterback or point guard. I need to get the ball into the hands of my playmaker and let him run with it. Hopefully, over time the play-by-play person develops chemistry in the booth with their partner. The goal is to make the listener feel as if he or she is there in the stands, enjoying the game with you and your color analyst. I try to help them not only see the game, but also experience it, too: what it looks like, what it sounds like, what it feels like.

Van allowed me to be myself, and that's the approach I've tried to take with the four guys I've been privileged to share the booth with these past 19 seasons. I've been really fortunate to have had great copilots. Alex Van Pelt, Mark Kelso, Steve Tasker, and Eric Wood all played for the

Bills. And they played different positions in different eras for a variety of coaches with varying degrees of individual and team success. So, it's not surprising that each would bring something unique to the microphone. Clearly, each of them has different areas of expertise and interest, and that in turn affects their perspective, subject matter, and approach. Each of them obviously has a unique personality, and that, too, affects what they offer and how they offer it. I've worked with guys who were more analytical and serious, as well as ones who leaned toward being fun-loving and loose. Different strokes for different folks.

The good thing is, that like Van and I, those four guys don't need to be told what the Bills mean to Buffalonians. They learned all about that passion during their playing days. So, the passion they brought to the booth on gameday was genuine and real. It's my job to set them up so they can do their thing, make their points. And it's also my job to bring out not only their football knowledge, but also their personalities and, hopefully, their sense of humor.

## Alex Van Pelt (2004–2005)

Alex was my first color man, and what's interesting about that is that he was coming directly from the playing field to the booth. He had spent the previous nine seasons as a Buffalo Bills quarterback primarily in a reserve role, though he did start a number of games during that dreadful 2001 season, when Buffalo went 3–13 after Rob Johnson bombed following the jettisoning of Doug Flutie.

Alex was very smart and was able to analyze the game as a quarterback would, which was great for our listeners. He'd look at the defensive alignment before the snap and know immediately what the Bills should do to attack it. He'd immediately chime in before the snap and say, "Murph, the Dolphins are playing press coverage and have extra defenders on such-and-such a side, so Drew Bledsoe should go to this spot with his throw." It was really educational for our listeners—and for me. The only downside was that Alex had never done this before, so he had to learn how to play off me and how to make his points quickly, so I could get back to the play-by-play description. But Alex was smart, and we eventually developed that chemistry you need.

It also helped that Alex still had many contacts on the team. He was especially tight with Bledsoe, whom he had backed up the year before. So, in addition to knowing the gameplan and strategy, Alex also had his finger on the pulse of the team.

When Alex left after just two seasons to join new Bills coach Dick Jauron's staff, I was disappointed but not surprised. You could tell by his analysis that he really, really knew the game and would become a great mentor for quarterbacks and an excellent play-caller.

Alex also was a fun guy to be with on the road. He had this strange habit of ordering two different entrees when we went out for dinner the night before away games. I asked him what that was all about, and he said that he had learned that from Jim Kelly. I just chuckled.

He also enjoyed adult beverages. I do, too, but there were nights before road games when he was going strong, and I had to call it a night and head back to my hotel room. Alex told a funny story of one Saturday night that spilled over into Sunday morning before a game against the Dolphins in Miami. Alex stumbled into the hotel lobby about 6:30 that morning and crossed paths with Bills general manager Tom Donahoe. "Hello, Tom," Alex said.

"Hello, Alex," Donahoe responded as he headed for breakfast, while Van Pelt headed to his room for a few hours of shut eye and several aspirins that he hoped would mitigate his hangover a bit before heading to the stadium. Good thing Alex hadn't still been playing or he'd definitely been fined for blowing curfew big time.

I remained good friends with him after he became a coach. A few years into his job as quarterbacks coach, the Bills suffered an embarrassing end-of-the-season loss, and it was apparent that some heads were going to roll. I was working at Channel 4 in Buffalo at the time and was worried Alex might be one of the fall guys, so I called him around 8:30 that Sunday night and asked him how he was doing. He was pretty down, but he managed to keep his sense of humor. "That was an awful, awful loss, Murph," he said. "And what makes it worse is that we have no more Crown Royal in the house."

We both burst out laughing.

After I got off the phone with him, I called my wife, Mary, and asked if she could deliver a bottle of Crown Royal we had to Alex's house, which was only a few streets away from our house in Orchard Park. What's funny is that Mary was town supervisor at the time, so she had an official town car at her disposal. In order to have a little fun, she put the flashers and siren on when she pulled into Alex's driveway. He came barreling out of the house to see what the heck was going on. Once he saw Mary standing there holding the bottle of his favorite whiskey, he realized he had been pranked. The three of us still get a chuckle out of that memory.

Alex remains a good friend, and I'm happy to see the success he's enjoyed in his 13 seasons as an NFL assistant with five different teams. He was a good analyst, but I could tell that he longed to be in a booth calling plays rather than analyzing them. I can see him being a head coach someday.

## Mark Kelso (2006–2018)

My history with Mark runs deep, going all the way back to 1987, when he was moved to the free safety position. He, of course, had a distinguished playing career with the team, manning the back end of the Bills secondary during the Super Bowl years. Mark will be the first to tell you that he wasn't the most physically gifted player, but he what he lacked in brawn he made up for in brain.

He is one of the smartest human beings I've ever encountered. And one of the nicest, too.

A graduate of the College of William & Mary, Mark might be the most cerebral player I ever met. Fans tend to forget that he ranks third all time in interceptions by a Bills player with 30. And most of those picks were the result of him outsmarting quarterbacks and receivers. He was another of Bill Polian's many diamond-in-the-rough finds.

So, when I heard that Mark was going to replace Alex Van Pelt, I felt good. I had a familiarity with him and I figured his understanding of the game was going to translate well to the booth. I also knew there was going to be another break-in period, as Mark learned the ins and outs of the job. Early on, he might have been a little wordy and a little too esoteric, but he quickly got the hang of things in his new job. It didn't take long for me and him to adjust and click. One of the things that enabled Mark to develop into an outstanding analyst was not only his intelligence, but also his work ethic. It was one of those things that had set him apart as a player, too.

When Marv Levy came back to the team as a general manager, he asked me how Mark was doing. I told him, "Marv, he's been amazing. He works so hard that he's forced me and the producers and the spotters to all step up our games."

Levy smiled and said: "Now you know why he was on our roster all those years. The example he set forced us coaches and all of his teammates to emulate him."

In order to prepare himself for something he'd never done before, Mark asked if we could do some practice broadcasts before doing the real broadcasts. So that July and August, we went to the stadium and put on a tape of a game from the previous season. We had our longtime producer, Greg Harvey "Wallbanger," in the booth and even had our sideline reporter down on the field. It was a great idea by Mark and great preparation for all of us. And it's something we did again when Eric Wood came aboard.

Whereas Van Pelt brought an offensive expertise to the booth, Mark's specialty was defense. He could immediately diagnose what an offense was trying to do and how to shut it down. And he was particularly good at diagnosing the passing game, which is such a huge part of the modern NFL.

There's no doubt in my mind that, like Van Pelt, Mark could have become a hugely successful football coach had he chosen that path. He was so smart, so dedicated, knew the game inside and out. I know he did a little coaching at a high school in our area, and those kids were so lucky to be mentored by him.

Mark, like many of his teammates, has made Buffalo his home after retiring as a player. But after his kids were done with high school, he began spending part of his time in North Carolina to work with his NASCAR race team. During those years he remained the Bills analyst, even though he was no longer in the Buffalo area. He continued to work exceedingly hard and even had the Bills overnight him their coaches' tapes. After he finished his NASCAR work, he'd spend his evenings breaking down tapes from Buffalo's previous week game as well as their upcoming opponent.

For home games he'd usually arrive in town on Friday afternoons and would join me at the stadium and sit in while I interviewed the Bills head coach for segments that would run on the pregame show. After I finished up with Rex Ryan, I'd often sit there with him and Mark and just listen as they talked defense for hours. It was like a getting a master's degree in football for me. Despite Ryan's reputation as a defense savant, there would be times when he'd be picking Mark's brain about coverages and strategy. It was fascinating to listen to and observe.

Unlike Van Pelt, Mark was a super serious guy. He was much more strait-laced, much less fun-loving. He wasn't a drinker, so there weren't any concerns about him stumbling into the booth hungover after a night of revelry. That's not to say Mark didn't have a fun-loving side to him. He did. I just had to work a little more, especially early on, to get him to loosen up a bit on the broadcasts and elicit his dry sense of humor.

One of the best pranks I ever pulled involved Mark. We were doing a game at Lucas Oil Stadium in Indianapolis several years ago, and as we were going through security, the guards had us open our bags for inspection. Now, I'm not going to say Mark was cheap, but he didn't like spending money, so he had loaded up his bag with a bunch of cookies so he wouldn't have to buy any concessions. I guess they had a rule there where you couldn't bring food into the stadium. Mark was not a happy camper and started going back and forth with the guards. I had to get to the booth to get my stuff set up, so I left him there. About an hour later, Mark finally gets to the booth—sans cookies—and he's seething. Later, after we wrapped up the broadcast, he was still bitching about the cookies he couldn't eat.

I managed to get a blank piece of stationery with the Indianapolis Colts logo on it. The next day, I concocted this fake letter to Mark. I pretended to be a Colts official who wanted to apologize to Mark on behalf of the organization. I told Mark that in the future he would be allowed to bring cookies of any kind into the stadium. I signed it, "Elvin Keebler, Director of Security," and sent it to Mark in an official Colts envelope. Kelso took the bait, hook, line, and sinker. He thought it was real.

The following Sunday I fessed up, and Mark, being the good sport he is, got a good chuckle out of it. We had other interesting interactions at road games, too. Bills fans probably don't want to hear this, but my favorite road venue is Gillette Stadium in Foxborough, Massachusetts, home of the hated New England Patriots. I like it because the booth affords a great view of the game, which isn't the case any more in many of the new and renovated stadiums. We're at about the 40-yard line at the top row of the first level. The fans, like in Highmark, are seated close enough where you can literally stretch out and touch them. This proximity can lead to some interesting interactions.

We were doing a game there once, and Mark became agitated after Patriots tackle Vince Wilfork drilled Trent Edwards in the knee, knocking the Bills quarterback out of the game. We both thought it was a cheap shot and said as much on the broadcast, but the applauding Patriots fans obviously didn't agree with us. During a commercial break, Mark got into it with a guy seated in front of us. They're jawing back and forth, really going after one another, and I start panicking because I had to get Mark refocused in a hurry. "Mark," I shouted, "we're going back on the air in three…two…one." He wound up commenting again about what a dirty play it was and said it loud enough for the guy to hear. I can chuckle about it now, but I was worried at the time that I'd have to referee a wrestling match between Mark and the fan while simultaneously trying to broadcast the game.

We also had some good experiences in Foxborough. One of the fans outside our booth had this big bucket of chicken wings. And during a commercial break, I said, "Mark, those chicken wings smell really good."

Mark nodded at the guy and said, "Yeah, and they look really good, too." Well, the guy must have heard us. At halftime he went out and bought another bucket of wings and handed them up to us.

I had a long, good run with Mark. I learned a hell of a lot of football from him. He remains a good friend.

## Steve Tasker (2020)

Steve's another whip-smart, salt-of-the-Earth, funny guy with whom I have a long history. I began covering him when he joined the Buffalo Bills during the 1986 season. (He actually was the first player signed by Marv Levy after Levy replaced Hank Bullough as head coach midway through the 1986 season.)

Steve, of course, would go on to become in my estimation the greatest special teams player in NFL history. And during his playing days, the Northwestern University journalism graduate was wise enough to know he wasn't going to be able to play forever. He began plotting his post-playing career, a career that would see him become a respected color analyst for CBS' NFL telecasts and Westwood One's national radio broadcasts.

Those of us who covered the team during the Super Bowl run could tell from our interviews with Steve that he had an analytical mind and knew how to answer questions succinctly and with insight. So, his success in the booth and also as a sideline reporter didn't surprise me in the least. Steve began grooming himself during offseasons by cohosting Buffalo-area morning television shows that dealt with topics beyond football and sports. He was a natural with an easygoing style. His personality and sense of humor always came across on the air. He's an engaging, likeable guy, and that comes across, too.

After Steve's playing days ended, I had the opportunity to work with him on some Bills preseason game telecasts. And in the 2010s, when I was cohosting a daily Bills radio talk show, which was simulcast on the Madison Square Garden television network, we were reunited. By that time, Steve was a seasoned broadcast pro. In fact, I regard him as much as a broadcaster as I do as a former player. Few ex-jocks have made the transition as well as he has. It's always fun working with him.

We teamed up for just one season on Bills radio gameday broadcasts, and that came about in 2020 after COVID-19 threw a monkey wrench into everything. The pandemic had made it extremely difficult to travel, and with Eric Wood being based in Louisville, the Bills thought it would be easier for Tasker to make the drive from the suburbs and join me at the booth at Highmark Stadium than for Eric to try to fly in from Kentucky.

Steve and I wound up working every game—home and away—that season from the booth at empty (until the playoffs) Highmark. That still ranks as the most bizarre season of my career, thanks to COVID. Fans weren't allowed to attend regular-season games that fall so there was almost this feeling that we were broadcasting a scrimmage. A huge part of broadcasting is the adrenaline rush you get from the crowd during the ebbs and flows of a game. Other than the two home playoff games (in which things were livened up when 7,000 spectators were allowed in for each contest), the experience was surreal. And what made that season even worse is that was the year when Josh Allen put up historic numbers, and the Bills finally won the division after two decades of New England Patriots dominance. It's a damn shame Bills fans and players couldn't have shared that experience on gamedays. Steve and I tried our best to convey the excitement, but something definitely was missing. There was little energy, little juice.

The road games were the worst. We're sitting there in empty Highmark with three monitors while being held hostage by the two feeds the networks sent. It was so restrictive. A radio broadcaster is the eyes and ears of the listener. You need to scan the field, check out the sidelines, put your audience there. That was pretty hard to do when I was being limited to two camera perspectives being dictated by a guy in a truck a thousand miles away.

During one of our broadcasts from Highmark, a huge gust of wind blew over one of the monitors. Fortunately, it didn't hit either of us, and we were able to carry on despite having the bejesus scared out of us. In retrospect, that bizarre episode kind of summed up that very strange year. Having a friend and true pro like Steve pinch-hitting on the broadcasts made a rocky ride a little smoother.

## Eric Wood (2019, 2021–present)

Like those before him, Eric brings a unique perspective to Buffalo Bills broadcasts. As a former Bills center (and guard in his early years), he has an intimate, intricate knowledge of line play on both sides of the ball and he knows how to explain it in a manner the average fan can understand. He can tell you how teams are trying to block a certain play and what defenses are doing to try to defeat the blocking. He can show you why the performance in the trenches resulted in a play being successful or blown up.

A former first-round Bills draft pick, Eric spent nine seasons with the team before a neck condition forced him to retire unexpectedly following the 2017 season. The fact he's not that far removed from his playing days and has a strong relationship with head coach Sean McDermott gives him intel that another analyst wouldn't have. The coaching staff will confide in him and even ask his advice once in a while. So, that's clearly an added bonus for us and our listeners.

Eric is really, really good, and we've developed a nice chemistry that I believe is only going to get better as we get more reps together. Looking back, as the quarterback of the broadcast, I needed to do a better job of loosening Eric up a bit during our first year together. And I was fully intending to work on that in our second year, and then the pandemic interrupted things and put everything on hold. Eric and I got back at it in 2021, and I think we started hitting our stride. I got him to joke around more, and we started teasing one another, lightening things up. I've come to learn what Eric's comfortable talking about. The more you work with someone, the better things become.

After calling games with a former quarterback and a former defensive back, working with an offensive lineman has brought a fresh perspective. Plus, there are times on gamedays when you sense Eric feels just like he did when he was suiting up. He gets fired up, and that comes across on air. It's energizing for me and the fans. I look forward to working with him for many years to come.

## Other essential members of the broadcast crew

Though the play-by-play man or woman and the color analysts are considered the so-called stars of the broadcast, the reality is that our success is dependent on the hard work of others. Besides us, our sideline reporter plays a pivotal role, providing injury updates, pointing out things on the bench we aren't privy to, and giving us a feel for what impact the wind and other weather variables are having on the game.

I've been blessed to work with a bevy of talented sideline reporters. My first one was Paul Peck, whom I worked with in television and whom I consider a good friend. He was really, really good, and so well-prepared. Each week, he would come up with about 10 topics we'd get to during the game, and this was so helpful. He would still react to breaking stuff and give us insights and essential information, but it was nice to have him weave in good stories that really added texture to the broadcast. Paul wound up leaving the broadcasting business to become a successful financial advisor, but he didn't leave the industry completely. He is the radio play-by-play voice of University at Buffalo football these days and he does a top-notch job there. He's also married to the daughter of Eddie Rutkowski, who wore many hats during his playing days with the AFL champions. Rutkowski played quarterback, running back, and also punted.

Peck was a thorough professional, as were his successors on the Buffalo Bills sideline: Rich "The Bull" Gaenzler, Joe Buscaglia, and our current reporter, Sal Capaccio. Because they know their stuff from covering the team regularly, they've been able to provide context, insights, and perspective our listeners wouldn't otherwise receive.

Some critics dismiss sideline reporters as window dressing, but I strongly disagree. These guys serve an essential role, especially when there's breaking news or something happens that's out of our view. As a play-by-play guy, I have to follow the ball. So I miss a lot because my eyes can't be everywhere at once. That's where your color analyst and sideline reporter come into play. They fill in the blanks. It's also takes a special talent to be a sideline reporter because you need to provide information in quick bursts, so we can get back to calling the game. They don't have the luxury that I or my color analyst have. We can hammer something over several plays. The sideline reporter has to be in and out. It's not easy.

Other factors that make their job tough include weather and potential injury. It's no fun standing out there when it's raining or snowing hard or when the wind chill is near zero. And one has to be alert at all times on the field because the action is so close—sometimes too close for comfort. If one is not prepared, a player could bowl you over.

A successful broadcast also is aided by behind-the-scenes people. Our producer, Greg Harvey "Wallbanger," is the coach of the broadcast; he's the glue that holds everything together, oversees it all, makes sure we're doing what we are supposed to be doing on time. We're dead without people like him. He and his associate producer Todd Broady makes all of us look good and knows how to solve unexpected problems on the fly.

We're also quite beholden to our spotters. They give us extra sets of eyes, which is essential. The game moves swiftly, and there are 22 players out there along with eight people on the officiating crew. I usually begin memorizing numbers and names of that's week's opponent on Tuesday and feel comfortable by game time. But there's always personnel turnover during a game, so sometimes you draw a blank or sometimes you can't tell who might have caused a fumble or been the first guy in on a tackle. That is when the spotters lend a hand—or I should say—an eye.

One of the perks of my job has been the opportunity to have my sons, Mark and Jack, in the booth as spotters. Mark's been doing it regularly since high school, while Jack fills in on occasion and sometimes will sub as the spotter for the Highmark Stadium public-address announcer. They've both become really good spotters; they know what we need. Mark is much more of a fan than his younger brother, so he tends to take things hard. Jack's the type of person that when the game's over, it's over. He puts his coat on, walks out of the booth, and leaves the game there.

Early on, Mark would react emotionally to every bad Bills play. Ryan Fitzpatrick would throw an interception and Mark would be brooding and lose concentration. Invariably, I'd give him a dirty look and a light-hearted smack during break and tell him, "You have a job to do; you need to be focused every play because we need to have that information immediately and regularly. You can't take any plays off." He got that and has become such an asset to me and Eric Wood.

# CHAPTER 5

## RALPH WILSON: THE MAN WHO PAID THE BILLS

Following Ralph Wilson's death on March 25, 2014, a columnist for the *Buffalo News* opined that he was the most significant sports figure in the history of Western New York. It's hard to dispute that. Think about it. Without him there's no Jim Kelly, Marv Levy, Bruce Smith, Thurman Thomas, Josh Allen, Highmark Stadium, or even the Buffalo Bills. And I can't imagine how much different and poorer my hometown and my life would have been without this NFL franchise.

Mr. Wilson always encouraged people he met to call him "Ralph," but for some reason, I never felt comfortable doing that. It just felt more respectful to me to call him "Mr. Wilson."

In retrospect, I guess you can say his legacy and his relationship with Bills fans, players, coaches, and front-office staff was occasionally fractious, occasionally complicated. He became beloved during the Super Bowl years and he truly reveled in that. He always had a good sense of humor, and it often was self-deprecating. During that glorious run, he liked to joke that "people used to throw their programs at me; now they want me to sign them."

I find it interesting that his original plan back in 1959 was to locate his charter American Football League franchise in Miami, but he couldn't procure a lease to play in the Orange Bowl because a previous South Beach pro football team had failed to pay its bills. (Imagine that: the Bills in Miami. On second thought, given our intense rivalry with the Miami Dolphins, I don't want to imagine that.)

Buffalo had always drawn extremely well in the old All-America Football Conference, and there was a strong feeling that when it came time for the established NFL to absorb several AAFC franchises, the Queen City would be chosen, along with the Cleveland Browns and San Francisco 49ers. Alas, in yet another Buffalo sports snub, it was not to be. We got shafted. Again. Turned down by Miami, Mr. Wilson was forced to find another market, and the story goes that Buffalo was highly recommended by several respected pro football people, and after meeting with the editor of the *Buffalo Evening News*, he brought his new team to town. Mr. Wilson and the other original AFL owners became known as the "Foolish Club" because only a fool would have invested $25,000 in a league that was destined to fail. We all know who got the last laugh on that one. *Forbes* estimated the current Bills to be valued at more than $3.4 billion.

Mr. Wilson would play an integral role in helping keep the league afloat, including subsidizing the floundering Oakland Raiders in addition to the Bills. Without him the AFL surely would have folded instead of forcing the merger that contributed to pro football's explosion in popularity.

Owners of the American Football League known as the "Foolish Club" pose for a group photo in 1961. Seated from left to right are: Bud Adams (Houston Oilers) and AFL commissioner Joe Foss. Standing left to right are: Bill Sullivan, (Boston Patriots), Cal Kunz (Denver Broncos), Ralph Wilson (Buffalo Bills), Lamar Hunt (Dallas Texans), Harry Wismer (New York Titans), Wayne Valley (Oakland Raiders), and Barron Hilton (Los Angeles Chargers).

I remember Larry Felser, the late great columnist for the *Buffalo News*, once sent me scrambling for the dictionary because he had used the word "mercurial" to describe Mr. Wilson. One definition read: "A person subject to sudden or unpredictable changes of mood or mind." Felser was spot-on. Mr. Wilson definitely was unpredictable.

He liked to meddle, which as owner he had every right to do. It was, after all, his team. He was the man who paid the bills and the Bills, so he had a right to know everything that was going on and have final say in monetary decisions. But there were times when his micromanaging wore people down. There were numerous occasions when coaches and general managers told me they couldn't take it anymore, so they left. And once the word got out, which it usually does in the close-knit world of pro football, several coaches and general managers with proven track records of success in other places refused to entertain Mr. Wilson's lucrative offers to come to Buffalo.

Mr. Wilson occasionally would be accused of being too cheap to go the extra mile to sign players that would help the Bills reach that next level. And while there were instances when this might have been true, there also were several occasions when it just wasn't true. After all, he did make O.J. Simpson and Kelly the highest paid players in league history during their respective careers and he reportedly tried to entice former Pittsburgh Steelers Super Bowl–winning coach Bill Cowher out of retirement with a $10 million offer.

As is usually the case, an owner's popularity directly correlates with the team's fortunes on the field. And when things weren't going well, Wilson, who lived in Grosse Pointe, Michigan, next door to the one of Henry Ford's heirs, was vilified as an absentee owner. The thinking was that since he didn't live in Buffalo, he didn't care. I never subscribed to that theory. I think he cared, maybe sometimes too much, which led to the meddling into the football end of the operation and beating down some very bright people who knew their stuff.

Mr. Wilson was always a good and accessible interview. He didn't have a filter. He said what was on his mind. Many reporters had his home phone number and he often would pick up when they called him. This really irked the Bills public relations department because they were worried there would be some fire they would have to put out after Mr. Wilson sounded off about something.

I remember interviewing him in 1998, while the Bills were scrambling to sell a number of luxury suites in order to satisfy league demands and keep the team in Buffalo. I asked him, "How are you going to sell those? How are you going to market the team?"

He got fed up with my questioning. "The only way to market pro football is to win," he grumbled. He was right, and I had my sound bite.

In the years leading up to his death, Mr. Wilson kept us in the dark about the Bills' future and any succession plan. Word was out that neither his wife, Mary, nor his daughters were interested in taking over the team. This understandably made fans very uneasy. As his health declined, he turned over more and more of the day-to-day decision-making to Russ Brandon, who was kind of like the son he'd never had and whom he had named team president. Brandon would attend the owners' meetings and make decisions on behalf of the Bills. Mr. Wilson had total faith in him.

I just so happened to be at the league meetings in Orlando, Florida, in late March 2014 when news of Mr. Wilson's death broke. We had no inkling whatsoever he was ill and was going to die. I was working full time for the Bills then, cohosting a team-sponsored daily radio show, and we felt being at the league meetings would give us access to numerous pro football people—owners, GMs, coaches, sportswriters, and broadcasters. The first morning we were in Orlando, we received a text from Brandon saying there would be a mandatory staff meeting at 1:00 PM. I remember Bills head coach Doug Marrone coming up to me in the hotel lobby, where our radio equipment was set up, asking me if I knew what this was about. I didn't know. I knew that Jim Kelly was really sick with cancer at the time, and I told Marrone I was worried that maybe it had something to do with our former quarterback.

Not long after that conversation, the Bills made the announcement that Mr. Wilson had died. Brandon rounded up me, my producer Jay Harris, team capologist Jim Overdorf, and three or four other people, and brought us into a side room. NFL commissioner Roger Goodell came in shortly after that and was shaking our hands and telling us how sorry he was to hear the news. Later on, I went to this packed hotel bar to have a few beers, and it was amazing the number of NFL people who walked up to us to offer condolences and sing Mr. Wilson's praises.

It struck me just what a positive impression he had made on people throughout the league, particularly several longtime owners and the commissioner, who hailed from Jamestown, New York, about an hour south of Buffalo. Although Mr. Wilson had operated a team in the second-smallest market, he was a respected and influential voice. Some even referred to him as the conscience of the league, particularly after he took an unpopular stand and voted against Browns owner Art Modell's decision to move his franchise from Cleveland to Baltimore. It was nice to hear all the respectful comments about Mr. Wilson that day and it made me think that many powerful NFL people understood the importance of having cities like Buffalo and Green Bay in the league.

I'll always be grateful to Mr. Wilson for bringing pro football to Western New York and keeping it there. He had a great ride as an owner. But his lasting legacy is what he ensured following his death. That clause he helped craft, which made it economically unfeasible for his successor to immediately move the franchise, was indeed a fabulous parting gift. But the philanthropy of the foundation he established is a gift that will wind up having an even greater impact. Mr. Wilson decreed that the money his family made from the sale of the team go to charitable organizations in two New York cities (Buffalo and Rochester) and

Detroit. And, so, arguably the most significant sports figure in Western New York history will also go down in history as one of the region's most generous benefactors, pouring more than a billion dollars back into the communities that helped make him a billionaire.

There's a tendency, often justified, among fans and media to be skeptical of sports owners. The feeling is the people who run these teams just want to bleed as much money as they can from fans and taxpayers. But Mr. Wilson turned that skepticism on its head. The positive influence of a man once criticized for being an uncaring, absentee owner will be felt for years and decades to come. That's a rich legacy for a man foolishly labeled cheap. Mercurial, maybe, but definitely not cheap.

# CHAPTER 6

## BILL POLIAN:
## FOOTBALL'S
## FRANK LLOYD WRIGHT

At the press conference announcing his promotion to the Buffalo Bills' general manager position, Bill Polian opened things up by joking, "Let me introduce myself. I'm Bill *Who?*" Funny line. And not that far off-base because to most Bills fans and media he was a no-name, an anonymous figure many regarded as a totally underwhelming candidate to replace Terry Bledsoe.

Critics—myself included—grumbled that Polian's promotion was just another indication of Ralph Wilson being parsimonious, of not wanting to spend the big bucks to bring a big-name GM to town to turn things around. But sometimes you unwittingly find an incredible bargain. Sometimes you luck out. And Mr. Wilson and the Bills lucked out big time here. It wouldn't be long before Bill *Who?* wound up becoming one of the most recognizable and respected general managers in National Football League history.

I'd had very little contact with him up to that point. I might have chatted with him a couple of times in 1984 and 1985 and observed the job he did filling in while Bledsoe was out convalescing from a heart attack. But that was it. He was anonymous to me, too. It seemed like once again Mr. Wilson had made an accounting decision at the expense of his football team.

Unlike his predecessor, whose background was as an award-winning sports columnist in Wisconsin, Polian was a football guy through and through. Once I started interviewing him, it quickly became apparent he knew his stuff. He had football and street smarts honed while growing up in the Bronx. And he was driven and passionate about what he was doing. That motivation no doubt was fueled by the fact he was forced to claw his way up the football ladder. Nothing was given to him. He talked about times early in his scouting career in the Canadian Football League and USFL when he wasn't even allowed into the press boxes during major college games. Polian definitely paid his dues and then some.

His work ethic and attention to detail would catch the eye of Montreal Alouettes' pro personnel director Bob Windish and Marv Levy. Levy was the general manager and coach of the CFL team at the time and he asked Windish to line up some part timers to scout NFL training camps in search of cast-offs they could sign to play north of the border. One of the guys Windish contacted was Polian, an aspiring scout who was scraping out a living selling advertising for a farm journal in rural counties north of New York City. The scouting reports Polian filed were rich in detail and filled with astute observations. Their thoroughness and thoughtfulness blew Levy away. He told Windish, "We need to hire this guy full time." And they did.

That was the big break Polian needed and the start of a fortuitous football partnership and friendship with Levy. Polian would work with Levy at the Alouettes, the Kansas City Chiefs, and the Chicago Blitz of the USFL. Polian wound up joining the Bills as the head of scouting in 1984, and when it came time for him to make his first head coaching change as GM two years later, he didn't hesitate to strongly recommend the hiring of Levy. He went to Mr. Wilson and told him, "There's only one man I believe can turn this around, and that man's name is Marv Levy."

Some may have perceived this as cronyism, but it really wasn't. Polian was smart enough to realize that if he bombed out in his first try as GM, he might never get another shot. He wasn't going to make a move based primarily on friendship and mentorship. He truly believed that Levy was the best person for the job, and that was based on what he had observed while working for him in Montreal, Kansas City, and with the Blitz. He greatly admired Levy's organizational and leadership skills and his concepts for building a winning football program. He believed the two of them could devise and execute a shared plan to revive the franchise, which, of course, they did.

Hiring Levy was arguably Polian's most important move, but Polian also deserves credit for putting together one hell of a front-office staff. Just look at his general manager tree. John Butler, A.J. Smith, and Bob Ferguson all would go on to run NFL teams. Their teamwork with the Bills played right into Levy's philosophy that organizations win. And Polian had constructed a superb organization from top to bottom.

In retrospect, the drafting and signing of Bruce Smith in 1985 was a no-brainer, but people forget there was a vocal minority of disgruntled fans who wanted the Bills to take quarterback Doug Flutie instead of Smith. Fortunately, Polian, who was filling in for the recuperating Bledsoe at the time, saw through the lunacy of that suggestion.

Polian was a football guy who placed a great deal of trust in his fellow scouts. When he took over for Bledsoe, he was smart enough to retain a number of the veteran scouts, many of whom had followed Chuck Knox and Norm Pollom from the Los Angeles Rams to Buffalo in the late 1970s. And they would wind up playing an integral role in building the Bills' Super Bowl teams.

One of them, former Buffalo all-time great Elbert Dubenion, was extremely high on a quarterback-turned-wide receiver from tiny Kutztown University. During meetings Dubey kept singing the young man's praises, mentioning how hard he worked and how tough he was. Polian decided to check the kid out and was sold. And during the fourth round of the 1985 draft, Buffalo selected the kid from Kutztown. It wound up being one of the best picks in franchise history. The guy's name was Andre Reed.

The signing of Jim Kelly, following the demise of the USFL in the summer of 1986, required some deft and firm negotiating. Kelly, of course, didn't want to come to Buffalo and demanded he be traded to Oakland, Pittsburgh, or some other contending team. Polian met with Mr. Wilson to see what he wanted to do, and to the owner's credit, he was insistent on signing Kelly. The quarterback wound up landing the biggest contract in NFL history—$7.5 million over five seasons. It's kind of a laughable total compared to today's megabucks. To put things in perspective, the cumulative total of that deal is roughly what Josh Allen makes in a quarter of a season.

During the Kelly negotiations, one of his agents, A.J. Faigin, started to really get under Polian's skin. Polian had no love for agents— I remember him calling one of them a "charlatan" and a "fraud"—and he especially didn't like agents who knew little about football. At one heated moment with Faigin, Polian reportedly leapt out of his chair and got into a three-point stance while demonstrating a blocking technique. Fortunately, that's as far as it went because I'm sure Polian would have loved to have pile driven Faigin through the wall.

General managers ultimately are gauged on the success of their high-round picks, but Polian also had a knack for mining free-agent gold. In addition to Kelly, he plucked Kent Hull, the best center in team history, kicker Scott Norwood, linebacker Ray Bentley, and reserve defensive back Dwight Drane from the USFL. Polian's fingerprints were all over the 1987 draft, which yielded six starters: linebacker Shane Conlan, cornerback Nate Odomes, fullback Jamie Mueller, defensive end Leon Seals, tight end Keith McKeller, and offensive tackle Howard Ballard.

Like all great GMs, Bill wasn't afraid to pull the trigger on a huge trade, and his biggest one would occur on Halloween Day of 1987 when he sent two first-round draft picks, a second-round pick, and 1,000-yard rusher Greg Bell to the Indianapolis Colts in exchange for linebacker Cornelius Bennett. The move enabled Conlan to switch to his natural position inside and gave the Bills a superb edge rusher to take some of the extra blocking off Smith. Bennett went on to become one of Buffalo's greatest pass rushers, but I wondered at the time—and still wonder a little bit all these decades later—if Polian paid too much to get him.

Polian didn't appreciate my second-guessing, but his decision turned out pretty well, especially after the Bills found a Hall of Famer in the second round of the 1988 draft. That's when they discovered Thurman Thomas, who had slipped down to the 40th spot because of injury concerns. Polian also selected nose tackle Jeff Wright and linebacker Carlton Bailey in that draft—each of whom became a starter.

Thomas blossomed into the team's all-time rushing leader, supplanting O.J. Simpson. He became what I called a triple-threat back. He also is the Bills third all-time leading receiver and midway through his career became the league's premier blitz picker-upper, saving Kelly's bacon on numerous occasions.

The next year the Bills didn't have a pick in the first or second rounds but discovered speedy receiver Don Beebe in the third round. He would give Kelly the kind of fleet-footed wideout who took the top off defenses and opened things up for the running game and underneath passes to Reed, who became a master at yards after catch (YAC). Polian also added James Lofton to Buffalo's three-wide receiver set. Many thought Lofton was washed up, but Butler and several Bills scouts thought otherwise, and Polian followed through on their advice, signing the future Hall of Famer. Lofton proved he wasn't over the hill, turning in three very good seasons as a complementary receiver.

The building of those teams was something to behold, and Polian was the main architect, the football equivalent of Frank Lloyd Wright. Polian's football acumen was undeniable, and it later would benefit the expansion Carolina Panthers, who reached the playoffs in their second year of existence. He'd also work his magic in Indianapolis, where he drafted Peyton Manning and won a Super Bowl with the Colts. Bill *Who?* wound up winning an unprecedented six NFL Executive of the Year Awards and earned induction in the Pro Football Hall of Fame.

Polian is not only one of the most intelligent people I've met, but also one of the most passionate. He cared deeply about his football teams and would go to the ends of the Earth to defend them. There were times earlier in his career when he pugnaciously directed his ire toward fans, agents, media, and even Mr. Wilson. Like many in the media, I occasionally found myself in his crosshairs. Polian would pull me aside and chastise me if I asked a question he thought was stupid, but he never criticized me publicly, and I never took it personally. We wound up becoming friends.

Polian despised people who didn't put in an honest effort, people who didn't give 100 percent. One player, in particular, that he didn't care for was running back Ronnie Harmon. Drafted out of Iowa in the first round in 1986, Harmon never lived up to the lofty expectations the Bills had for him. And making matters worse, he had become a toxic, divisive influence in the locker room. There were numerous teammates who couldn't stand him. The final play of Harmon's Bills career would be the final straw for Polian. With the seconds winding down and Buffalo trailing by four points in their 1989 wild-card playoff game against the Browns in Cleveland, Kelly lofted a perfect pass to a wide-open Harmon in the back corner of the end zone. Harmon had plenty of room to haul in the toss, but as he was prone to do throughout his career, he short-armed the catch, and the ball slipped off his fingers. Players referred to this as "crocodile arms," a fear of extending your arms because you won't be able to protect yourself if you get hit. The thing here is that Harmon wasn't going to get hit by anyone. There wasn't a defensive back anywhere near him. On the next play, Kelly was picked off by Browns linebacker Clay Matthews, and the game and Bills season were over.

During flights home Polian had a habit of walking up and down the aisles to see how everyone was doing. Van Miller and I usually sat in the back of the plane, and Polian normally would pay us a visit, too, either to make small talk or inquire how the broadcast went. When he got to us on that short hop from Cleveland to Buffalo, I could see that he was really, really agitated. I thought to myself, *Uh-oh, did we say something on the air that pissed him off?* As I quickly discovered, he was really, really pissed at someone else. He leaned over and whispered to us: "That *guy* will never drop another pass for me again." Sure enough, Harmon was released not long after that game. And that might have been the angriest I've ever seen Polian about one of his players.

In perhaps his most famous (or should that be most infamous) blowup, Polian went off on a local radio/television talk show host by the name of Art Wander. He and a few other members of the media suggested some personnel changes, and Polian ranted: "Jim Kelly's still the quarterback, Ted Marchibroda's still the offensive coordinator, and Marv Levy's still the head coach. And if you don't like it, you can get out of town." I joked later to Polian that I was actually a little jealous that he hadn't gone ballistic on me because doing so to Wander made the host into a media celebrity.

In retrospect I think some of those blowups were theater on Polian's part. Yes, he could be passionate and somewhat of a thespian, but he never was crazy or unhinged. I actually think some of it was a case of him perhaps wanting to shield his coaches and players from criticism. It was a way for Polian to divert attention from perhaps what the real issue was. So, he'd create another issue—like the verbal attack on Wander. Polian is a very, very sharp guy. There was always a method to his madness.

And there were plenty of times when we witnessed his softer side. Polian cared greatly about his players and his coaches. I remember press conferences where he'd get choked up, his voice would crack, and he'd be fighting back tears when he was talking about someone who was released, injured, or retiring.

About a month after Buffalo's loss in Super Bowl XXV, I had to race down the highway to Albany because my father had suffered a heart attack during a legislative session and was hospitalized there. One day while I was visiting him, Polian and one of his right-hand men, Ed Stillwell, showed up out of the blue at the hospital. They had been in Albany to receive a proclamation honoring the Bills achievements from that past season, somehow had caught wind of my father's predicament, and decided to take a detour to pay him a visit. I was really touched that they would do that and will be forever grateful for that kind gesture.

I also remember Polian holding a press conference after being forced out by Mr. Wilson, following the third Super Bowl loss. It was kind of strange for an outgoing general manager who had been pushed out the door to hold a press conference at the stadium that had been his office, but Polian just wanted to say thanks to everyone—the media, his players, Bills fans, even Mr. Wilson—and I remember him tearing up. I went back to Channel 7 after the presser. Following the 6:00 sportscast, I got a call from Polian saying, "You want to come over to my house and talk some more?"

So, I went with my cameraman, Bob Dingwall, aka Dinger, and we spoke for about a half hour on camera and another half-hour off camera. The scene at Polian's house was like an Irish wake. Polian didn't have to do that for me, but I think it was a testament to the friendship we had developed.

There were other times in private when he would be talking about something, and his eyes would well up. He's a guy who wears his heart on his sleeve, and I think that just shows how much he cares. I'd rather have it that way than have someone who isn't fully invested.

There's no question he reached a point where he could no longer tolerate Mr. Wilson's interference. As the years passed and Polian mellowed, he and Mr. Wilson made amends. I was glad to see that because Mr. Wilson had given Polian the biggest break of his career, and Polian had given Mr. Wilson a run of success unmatched in team history.

# CHAPTER 7
## MARVELOUS MARV LEVY

When Marv Levy retired following the 1997 season, I wrote him a letter congratulating him for the remarkable run he had in Buffalo and thanking him for making the Buffalo Bills relevant again while being so accommodating to me and other members of the media. He wrote me back a really nice letter, which he signed, "To John Murphy, with best wishes, from a fan of yours, Marv Levy." My wife, Mary, had it framed with a classic portrait photo of Levy, and it hangs in our living room. I don't display too many mementos from my career, but that one has special meaning because, like everyone privileged enough to have covered Levy, I love the guy. He truly was one of a kind.

I could recite his achievements regarding how he won more games than any coach in Bills history, how he transformed a floundering franchise into the only team that ever reached four consecutive Super Bowls, how he has a bust in the Pro Football Hall of Fame and a plaque in the Canadian Football League Hall of Fame. But that wouldn't do his story justice. Levy was remarkable in so many ways on the sidelines, in the locker room, and beyond. Intelligent. Funny, often in a corny and self-deprecating way. And perhaps wiser than any person I've ever met.

The secret to Levy's success wasn't necessarily strategy. You certainly can argue there have been numerous coaches better at X's and O's. But few of them were better at handling people. Levy was a master psychologist. He knew how to read people and get the best out of them. It's easy to say that Levy won so much in Buffalo because he had an enormously talented roster that included five future Hall of Famers and a few others that merit that kind of acclaim. And that's true, though I've never known a great coach who lacked talented players. And that includes the likes of Vince Lombardi, George Halas, Tom Landry, Don Shula, Bill Parcells, and Bill Belichick.

What Bills fans sometimes forget is those Super Bowl teams also featured a roster of massive egos, and occasionally those egos clashed. But Levy had a way of keeping things under control and eventually getting everybody to buy into the good of team over their personal agendas. As someone who devoted a chunk of his life to covering those teams, believe me when I say that was not an easy task. The players from those glory teams will tell you as much all these years later. Their shenanigans could drive one to drink and distraction. With just about anyone else at the helm, there's a good chance that team would have imploded and never realized the greatness it did. Levy held the ship together.

The replacement of Hank Bullough with Levy midway through the 1986 season caught me somewhat by surprise. I knew, though, from conversations with Bill Polian and John Butler, both of whom had worked with Levy while with the USFL's Chicago Blitz, that they had the utmost respect for the guy. I was familiar with Levy's situation coaching the Kansas City Chiefs. It started well but did not end well. His rebuilding program was undercut by the NFL players' strike in 1982. The Chiefs went 31–42 under Levy, and that, along with his advanced age (61), underwhelmed many critics who viewed his hiring as another example of Ralph Wilson's stinginess.

I had a different viewpoint, which was undoubtedly influenced by the rave reviews from Polian and Butler and my own personal interactions with him. I had met him while he was doing color commentary on some Bills exhibition game telecasts following his firing in Kansas City and I couldn't help but be impressed by Levy. He was extremely smart and articulate. I remember him asking me questions about the team. He made me feel as if my viewpoint mattered. He showed a genuine interest in me. And I could see how that interest he showed in others would translate well with his players, coaches, the front-office staff, and the owner.

Levy came across immediately as a great communicator. He knew how to get his points across succinctly and knew what words would produce the actions he desired. This was in stark contrast to his predecessor, whose inability to articulate made him the butt of jokes, sometimes unfairly. Bullough's taskmaster approach had worn thin in the locker room, and many of his players had tuned him out, and some even reportedly took action on the field to get him fired.

Levy realized he was walking into a potentially great but fragile situation. The team had so much upside, but he had to ensure that upside wasn't torpedoed by continued upheaval. The team he was inheriting was demoralized. The euphoria engendered by Jim Kelly's arrival a few weeks before the season opener had disappeared, and there was carping about Kelly's costly interceptions at the end of close games. No doubt realizing he was a dead man walking, Bullough had worked his team extra hard, probably too hard, and his failure to take the foot off the accelerator had backfired. He had lost the team.

As Levy scanned the locker room to address the team for the first time, he couldn't help but realize the abundance of football riches that sat before him, riches that included future Hall of Famers Kelly, Bruce Smith, and Andre Reed. The roster still needed work, but Levy understood those three, along with others like Darryl Talley and Kent Hull, gave him an incredible foundation upon which to build a winner. Levy knew that his predecessor had beaten this team down, so he kept his opening remarks brief. He told them he didn't have many rules. He told them he wanted them to be on time and give an honest effort, and that was that. Meeting over.

That week, Levy made his first big roster move—a move that didn't even register at that time. Having a fondness for special teams, he claimed little-known player Steve Tasker off the Houston Oilers roster.

Practices the rest of the week were shorter, crisper, and more efficient than the never-ending sessions Bullough had put them through. The players appreciated that. They seemed more energized. Their new coach was immediately scoring points with them.

In Levy's debut the Bills hosted the Pittsburgh Steelers in front of 72,000 in Rich Stadium. It was an incredibly blustery day in Orchard

Marv Levy takes the field before leading the Buffalo Bills to a 29–14 road loss against the Washington Redskins in 1990.

Park, so gusty that the marching band's snare drums went blowing down the field during the pregame show. Levy decided the Bills needed to forgo the pass and emphasize the run, and the strategy worked as Buffalo pounded and grounded its way to a 16–12 win. I'll never forget the postgame press conference.

"Thank God for 40 stout hearts and a strong wind," Levy joked.

That blew me away more than the wind. *Wow*, I thought to myself, *we've got a poet*. And Levy was like that his entire tenure with the Bills.

His Marvisms were gold to reporters' ears. He'd tell us, "If Michelangelo wanted to play it safe, he would have painted the floor of the Sistine Chapel." And "World War II was a must-win." Addressing the team after having surgery to remove his cancerous prostate, he said: "My heart and soul will be with you, but my prostate won't." When talking about an aging quarterback's quickness, he told us, "He hasn't lost any speed; he never had any to begin with."

Of course, his most memorable quote—one forever chiseled into Bills lore—is the one he would bellow after huddling up his team just before opening kickoffs: "Where else would you rather be than right here, right now?"

In addition to making us laugh, Levy also would educate us. The guy with the master's degree in English from Harvard loved invoking metaphors and quoting his all-time favorite leader, Winston Churchill. One time he alluded to the German army's overconfidence during World War II. On another occasion he spoke of the importance of "crossing one river at a time, like Hannibal" from Roman days." "To be honest," Levy replied when asked about the analogy, "I don't know how many of these guys even knew what World War II was, and they probably think Hannibal is an offensive tackle for the Jets."

Our knowledge of history wasn't the only thing he enhanced. Our vocabularies expanded, too. Reporters and players were educated and entertained, and I think it was part of Levy's brilliance of relating to people, putting them at ease, and making them feel valued. His extraordinary people skills were a major factor in transforming the Bills from pretenders to contenders.

Levy had a master plan and a vision, and he and Polian worked in perfect tandem to make it come true. Their relationship was crucial to the Bills' success. They had healthy egos, but they never clashed publicly or privately as far as I could tell, and that's pretty remarkable in a high-pressure business, where successful programs often unravel because people haggle over who deserves the most credit. There was no acrimonious breakup similar to the ones witnessed in New York between Bill Parcells and George Young; in Dallas between Jerry Jones and Jimmy Johnson; or in Pittsburgh between Bill Cowher and Tom Donahoe.

I think Polian regarded Levy as a mentor, and he understood and agreed with the grand scheme Levy had devised after decades of coaching on the college and pro level. They both bought into the subjugation of the ego for the good of the team, and I think they convinced the players to do the same, though they endured some bumpy roads before that occurred, particularly during the "Bickering Bills" season in 1989.

Levy understood everyone around him and how he could help them to succeed. *What does my GM need from me in order for us to accomplish our goals? What do my assistant coaches need from me? What do my players need from me? Does a particular guy need a kick in the butt or a pat on the shoulder?* Levy was what I would call a servant leader. He figured out how he could best serve others in order for the team to achieve its goal. Often saying, "Organizations win," he got everyone from the owner to the equipment manager to buy into that.

Speaking of the owner, Levy was a master at handling Mr. Wilson, who could wear coaches and general managers down to a nub. Levy was proactive in preventing Mr. Wilson from doing to him what he had done to other coaches. In fact, he carved out time each week to spend with the owner on phone and in person so he could explain in detailed fashion what he and the coaching staff and front office were attempting to do with personnel moves and strategy. Mr. Wilson greatly appreciated Levy's efforts to keep him totally in the loop. Mr. Wilson had fractious relationships with many of his previous coaches, especially demanding ones like Lou Saban and Chuck Knox, whom he said often treated him like he had no business knowing what's going on, even though he owned the business. Although there definitely was a manipulative method to Levy's madness here, I believe that he and Mr. Wilson developed a genuine friendship that made life much easier for Levy than it had been for his predecessors.

When it came time for Mr. Wilson to hire Levy one thing that really swayed him was a recommendation from Chiefs owner Lamar Hunt. Mr. Wilson and Hunt had been longtime friends, dating all the way back to 1960, when they helped form the "Foolish Club," the group of charter American Football League owners who were "foolish" enough to take on the established NFL. Hunt told Mr. Wilson that one of the biggest mistakes he had made as Chiefs owner was firing Levy. That, I think, was the clincher for Mr. Wilson.

Although Levy won his Bills debut, the rest of his inaugural season was turbulent, as they recorded just one more victory to finish 4–12. He and Polian realized Kelly needed to get better and they could speed up the process by improving the quarterback's supporting cast. The Bills went 7–8 in 1987 and then experienced a breakthrough season the following year, going 12–4 to win the division and reach the AFC Championship Game.

Expectations were sky high heading in the 1989 campaign, but internal strife threatened to ruin everything Levy and Polian had built, as the Bills battled themselves as much as they battled the opposition, while barely making the playoffs. Somehow, Levy managed to hold his bickering team together, and although they lost 34–30 to the Cleveland

Browns in the AFC wild-card game, they would discover the high-octane offense that would power them to four consecutive Super Bowls.

No, they didn't win any of them. And, yes, some of the blame for that, particularly that Super Bowl XXV loss, falls on Levy. But with the passage of time, fans and football historians have come to develop a deeper appreciation of that impressive streak. It's damn hard to get to one Super Bowl—let alone two, three, or four straight. And if we are going to blame Levy for not winning any of them, then we also need to praise him for instilling the will in his players to keep fighting to get back.

It was a sad day when he retired following a 6–10 finish in 1997. It was the end of an era that had seen him win a franchise record 123 games and six divisional titles and reach the postseason eight times in 11-plus seasons. He returned to the team in 2006 for two seasons as general manager during the playoff drought years, but things didn't go well, as the Bills finished with back-to-back 7–9 records under Dick Jauron, the coach Levy hired. There had been some speculation that when Levy took over as GM at the age of 80 that he still wanted to coach. And at the press conference announcing his hiring, he kind of fueled that speculation. But Mr. Wilson quickly put the kibosh on that, saying he hired Levy to be the general manager of the team. End of discussion.

Not long after Levy retired as Bills coach, my cousin informed me that my uncle had been diagnosed with prostate cancer similar to what Levy experienced and endured during the 1995 season. My cousin wondered if I could contact the legendary Bills coach and ask him to send a letter of encouragement to my uncle. Levy was only too happy to do that and wound up writing a heartfelt correspondence, which greatly boosted my uncle's spirits. That was not an isolated incident. I learned that Levy had written scores of letters and made numerous phone calls to cancer patients after he recovered from surgery to remove his prostate. It spoke to the generosity of Levy's spirit. He was always leading by example, always serving others.

Levy received his sport's ultimate honor on August 4, 2001, when he was inducted into the Pro Football Hall of Fame. I was thrilled to be there and listen to his acceptance speech. Not surprisingly, Levy knocked it out of the park. His 14 ½-minute oratory on the sun-burned steps in Canton, Ohio, was almost Churchillian in eloquence and delivery. He'd always been inspired by the beauty of the British premier's words. "To me, Churchill is the greatest orator that I've been able to identify," Levy told my coauthor Scott Pitoniak beforehand. "I think he was the most prominent historical figure of the 20th century. He was rarely wrong. All through the 1930s, he was warning us about Hitler and he was considered a voice in the wilderness. He rallied a totally defeated people in World War II. He made a great statement at the end of the war when he said, 'It was the British people who had the heart of a lion. I was fortunate enough to provide the roar.'"

When I look back on that incredible era of Bills history, I realize it was Levy who provided the roar. It really was an honor to cover him. There will never be another coach like him.

# CHAPTER 8
## OTHER BILLS HEAD COACHES

If you count my years doing pregame shows before entering the booth full time, I've covered 14 different head coaches. (That includes two interim head coaches—three, really, if you add in the three games Elijah Pitts pinch hit for Marv Levy, when Levy was recuperating from prostate cancer surgery in 1995.) I detailed my joy covering Levy in the previous chapter and I write about current Buffalo Bills boss Sean McDermott in a later chapter. This chapter is devoted to the others. From Chuck Knox in the early 1980s to McDermott today, I got to know all of these men to varying degrees and liked each of them, though, I admit I liked some more than others. Regardless of how many games they won, they were dedicated men who truly loved football and had devoted their lives to the game.

## Chuck Knox

I didn't know Knox well, but I respected the hell out of him. He was an authoritarian figure, which was common back in the 1970s and 1980s. The old-school, cigar-smoking coach was straight out of central casting. There was just something about Knox. He carried himself like a head coach. And he obviously knew his football. That someone of his stature would wind up coaching the Bills was a shock in Buffalo—and beyond. Before coming to Western New York, Knox had led the Los Angeles Rams to five consecutive NFC West titles. He was one of the most respected coaches in the game and probably could have wound up leading any number of teams after experiencing a falling out with Rams ownership.

An L.A. sportswriter named Melvin Durslag played a role in helping Knox go from the City of Angels to the City of Good Neighbors. Durslag knew Knox well and he also knew Ralph Wilson well and the scribe wound up putting the two in touch. Still, few expected anything to come of it. Most thought the notoriously cheap Mr. Wilson wouldn't be willing to pay the king's ramson Knox would demand. But every so often,

Mr. Wilson would surprise you. Every so often he would do something that made you go, "Whoa!" in a positive way, and this definitely wound up being one of those moments.

He signed Knox, and within two years, the Bills were the toast of the town. Knox and Norm Pollom, who he brought with him from the Rams, engineered some of the best drafts in Bills history. In 1979 Buffalo selected seven guys who became starters: wide receiver Jerry Butler, nose tackle Fred Smerlas, linebacker Jim Haslett, guard Jon Borchardt, defensive tackle Ken Johnson, and safeties Jeff Nixon and Rod Kush. (Although they squandered the first overall pick of that draft on Tom Cousineau, they eventually received a first-round pick from the Cleveland Browns for him that they would use to select Jim Kelly in 1983.) In the 1980 draft, they added Joe Cribbs, who for four seasons was a dynamic dual-threat running back, and guard Jim Ritcher, who would be a mainstay for nearly a decade.

Quarterback Joe Ferguson was in his prime during those seasons, as the Bills finally ended their 20-game losing streak to the Miami Dolphins and won the division. And it all couldn't have come at a better time because our community was reeling. The steel mills had shut down, the economy had tanked, and people were leaving the city in droves. We were hurting, but our team was flourishing and provided a much-needed distraction. And Knox's imprint was all over that team.

I still think those 1980–81 teams don't get their historical due. I was putting together the pregame shows in those days and also was cohosting the Smerlas–Haslett show, so I got to deal with Knox a little bit and with those players. Those were some fabulous teams, but sadly they also played into our narrative of being good but not quite good enough. We are left with what-ifs. What if Fergy hadn't suffered that late-season ankle injury in 1980 that left him hobbled during the postseason? What if the NFL didn't go on strike in 1982? We'll never know.

Sadly, the Knox era lasted only five seasons. The strike, and career-altering injuries to stars like Butler and Nixon, derailed the Bills. They finished the truncated schedule 4–5 and out of the playoffs. Knox had had enough by that point and wound up bolting for the Seattle Seahawks, where he would build an expansion franchise into playoff contenders.

## Kay Stephenson

Stephenson had been on Knox's staff and was promoted to the head job before the 1983 season. If Jim Kelly, who the Buffalo Bills picked in the first round that April, and Joe Cribbs, the engine of the offense, hadn't bolted for the USFL, perhaps Stephenson's fate might have been different. Unfortunately for him, that didn't happen. Instead, he wound up inheriting a flawed, aging team on the decline.

The Bills showed some signs of life during Stephenson's first season, winning five of their first seven games before stumbling to the finish line with an 8–8 record. The following season, the wheels fell off, as Fergy threw more interceptions (17) than touchdown passes (12) in his last hurrah, and Buffalo plummeted to a 2–14 record. In 1985 the writing was on the wall, and after starting 0–4, Stephenson was fired.

Reportedly, on the Monday following a 27–20 loss to the Minnesota Vikings on a Statue of Liberty play, Stephenson received a phone call from Ralph Wilson that he was being let go. Stephenson went to his secretary, Nancy Hermann, and told her, "I've got to go to the bank." He then walked out of his office and never returned. He was a good man, a humble guy. But he wasn't a great communicator. And I think that hurt him as a coach.

I did a radio show with Stephenson while he was there and, though he was pleasant, he was a bland and guarded interview. He didn't tell you anything, and that was intentional. That didn't lend itself to great radio. Later on, Bill Polian lectured me that Stephenson was actually a very good football coach despite the poor record. And the man who built the

Bills Super Bowl teams confided in me that one of his great disappoint-ments "was that we didn't give Stephenson a good team to work with. He deserved better. He was a good football man."

## Hank Bullough

Bullough had a solid reputation as a defensive coordinator, and when Ralph Wilson hired him before the 1985 season, there was strong specu-lation that Bullough was the head-coach-in-waiting. If Kay Stephenson didn't get off to a fast start, people figured he would be replaced by Bullough, which is what happened after the Buffalo Bills opened 0–4.

Unfortunately, the Bills fortunes didn't improve much under Bullough, as they won only two of their next 12 to finish 2–14, secur-ing a spot in the NFL basement for the second year in a row. Before that season Buffalo signed quarterback Vince Ferragamo in hopes he might recapture some of the magic he had shown six years earlier when he almost led the Los Angeles Rams to a Super Bowl upset of the dynas-tic Pittsburgh Steelers and their vaunted Steel Curtain defense. But Ferragamo was washed-up by the time the Bills got him and he wound up being released late in the season after throwing 17 interceptions and only five touchdown passes. The forgettable Bruce Mathison replaced him in the lineup and added four touchdowns tosses and 14 more picks as the Bills quarterbacks combined to lead the league in interceptions.

The most entertaining thing about that team may have been Bullough's interviews. The man, to put it nicely, had a way with words. After a long pass play led to a Bills loss against the New York Jets, Bullough told reporters, "That's the play that took sails out of our winds." While discussing the NFL draft, he said "you got that Bo Jackson kid out of Auburn and that Napoleon Bonaparte out of the Naval Academy." We think he meant to say Napoleon McCallum, but perhaps Bullough was making a history allusion the way his successor, Marv Levy, occa-sionally did.

My friend, Vic Carucci, an author and longtime, highly respected football scribe for the *Buffalo News*, recalled a time when he brought his cousin to practice and introduced him to Bullough. Carucci's cousin was wearing his Air Force uniform, and Bullough began serenading him with a pretty bad rendition of "Anchors Aweigh." When another reporter mentioned to Bullough that was the theme song for folks in the U.S. Navy, Bullough chuckled and quickly corrected himself by singing, "Off we go into the wild, blue yonder."

Following his first win as Bills head coach, Bullough recounted how he told his players in the locker room that "We finally put one in the L column." Another time he actually said: "We keep beating ourselves, but we're getting better at it."

I think many of us in the Buffalo media welcomed the malapropisms because they provided comic relief from the bungling play on the field.

The night before a road loss that season, a friend of mine named Mark, who was an attorney, joined me for dinner and drinks at a restaurant in the hotel where the Bills were staying. He was a huge, huge Bills fan and he was very upset with Bullough's coaching. On and on he complained. "If I ever meet that asshole, Bullough, I'm going to tell him off," my friend boasted. "I'm going to tell him he doesn't know what the hell he's doing."

A little later that evening, we were standing by the elevator, and I was still listening to him rant, when the doors opened, and lo and behold, out walked Bullough. I couldn't resist. "Hank, this is my friend, Mark, and he's one of your biggest fans."

Bullough smiled and shook his hand, and Mark looked like he just had the wind knocked out of him. He was taken totally by surprise. After a few speechless moments, my friend extended his hand and said, "Um, nice to meet you, Coach."

After Bullough moved on, I couldn't stop laughing.

"Mark," I told him, "I thought you were going to give him a piece of your mind."

Mark just stared daggers at me.

There was a great deal of optimism before the start of Bullough's second season, and it had nothing to do with him. The news of the USFL's demise brought Jim Kelly to the Bills, and expectations were through the roof. Unfortunately, Kelly needed time to develop, and Buffalo needed to greatly improve his supporting cast. Following a 2–7 start, the coaching carousel continued spinning. Bullough was gone and replaced by Levy.

I know many of the players despised Bullough, especially Bruce Smith and Fred Smerlas, who cruelly referred to Bullough as "The Brain Cell." I didn't share their anger. Bullough was not a good head coach. His teams were a reflection of that. The miscues were many, but I thought he was a decent guy. He'd had success in numerous other stops as a bright defensive coach, but as often happens in football and most other endeavors, the Peter Principle comes into play. Just because you are a fine coordinator doesn't guarantee you'll become a fine head coach. It didn't happen with Bullough and many other highly regarded coordinators-turned-head-coaches in Buffalo and beyond. In fact, many more fail than succeed when faced with that transition. Bullough was a down-to-Earth guy who probably was promoted above what he could handle.

The Monday night after he was fired, I took a chance and asked him if he wanted to do his radio show one final time. I was shocked when he said yes. I don't know too many coaches who would have done that, but Bullough did. He was great that night. Clearly, he was unhappy he'd been fired and disappointed things hadn't worked out. But he told me he was looking forward to being able to watch his son's high school games and spend a Thanksgiving at home with his family for the first time in years.

It was a reminder that these guys are just like the rest of us in many ways. There was a humanity to that moment, and I was grateful that Bullough had taken the time to do something that I don't think I and most other people would have done 24 hours after losing our jobs.

## Wade Phillips

Several years ago, before a Buffalo Bills home game, I ran into Phillips in one of the private suites near the radio booth and gave him a big hug. I told him, "Wade, we miss you here. We had some good times when you were here."

He smiled and said simply, "29–19."

That was his won-loss record during his three seasons as Bills head coach, which computes to a .604 winning percentage, trailing only Marv Levy, Sean McDermott, and Lou Saban in franchise history. Phillips also led Buffalo to two playoff appearances, and if the replay officials hadn't blown the call in what will forever be known as "Home Run Throwback"—or as it's known in Buffalo, "Home Run Throw *Forward*"—his team might have reached the Super Bowl in January 2000 and perhaps even won it all. To think the Bills could have hoisted a Lombardi Trophy that year is not a stretch when you consider the Tennessee Titans—the team that beat Buffalo in the "Home Run Throw *Forward*" game—wound up coming within three yards of beating the St. Louis Rams in that year's Super Bowl.

The bottom line is that Phillips did a pretty, damn good job of succeeding a Hall of Fame coach in Buffalo, and I think longtime Bills fans tend to forget that and don't give him his historical due. Looking back, I feel bad for the way fans and several media critics treated Phillips. Because he was from the south and had an accent and a folksy way of explaining things, some people cast him as some sort of country bumpkin. A few even went so far as to disparage him as a Gomer after the simple-minded, fictional character played by Jim Nabors in the popular television sit-com, *Gomer Pyle, U.S.M.C.*

That mean-spirited portrayal couldn't have been more off base. In reality Phillips is a very bright guy and one of the game's better defensive strategists and tacticians. That shouldn't come as a surprise, considering his dad, Bum Phillips, had been a highly successful football coach, particularly with those "Love Ya Blue" Houston Oilers teams of the 1970s. The apple clearly didn't fall far from the tree, as this Son of a Bum proved his mettle in Buffalo as a defensive coordinator and as a head coach.

I always found Phillips to be a fun guy to be around. He has a wonderful personality and a great sense of humor, which he often directs at himself. When Phillips took over for Levy, he was asked to compare and contrast himself with his predecessor. "Marv quotes Homer," he deadpanned. "I quote Homer Simpson."

Phillips loved his job and took it seriously, but he never took himself too seriously. It's easy to see why players wanted to play hard for him. If Phillips had a fatal flaw—and it's somewhat similar to what plagued Rex Ryan more than a decade later—it was his inattention to detail and his failure to spend more time coaching the entire football team, not just the defensive unit. It eventually would come back to bite him.

I blame the negative public perception of Phillips primarily on former Buffalo radio talk show host Chuck Dickerson. After being fired as the Bills line coach by Levy, Dickerson began hosting a local show and he used his forum to poison the waters whenever possible. At one point, Dickerson's vitriol toward Levy became so intense that Levy felt compelled to issue a retort at the beginning of his weekly television show. That was totally out of character for Levy to respond to such garbage, but he felt he had no choice but to stand up to that bully. After Levy retired, Dickerson took aim at Phillips, making him into some sort of cartoonish buffoon.

Phillips' tenure as Bills head coach began bumpily, as his team lost its first three games. That obviously turned up the heat on him, but he remained on an even keel, and I think his players and coaches appreciated that. Good leaders do that; they remain steady during storms.

Although Buffalo was a heavy underdog in Week Four against the San Francisco 49ers, Phillips told me in an interview that aired on our pregame show that he believed the Bills could win that week. Given quarterback Rob Johnson's struggles and the 49ers' status as legitimate Super Bowl contenders, I didn't share his optimism, but Phillips proved me wrong, as the Bills pulled off a 26–21 upset.

They would win their next four games, and during that streak, an unlikely legend emerged—a legend who united and later divided Bills Nation in an ugly quarterback controversy reminiscent of the Jack Kemp–Daryle Lamonica feud during the AFL championship seasons.

A week after beating San Francisco, Johnson was sacked and injured during a game against the Colts in Indianapolis, prompting Doug Flutie to come off the bench. He led the Bills to victory and the following week made a play that would help him become a Buffalo folk hero. On the final snap of the game and with the Bills trailing by six points, Flutie improvised. Instead of handing the ball off to Thurman Thomas, he ran a bootleg around left end for the game-tying score as time expired. Steve Christie's extra point gave the Bills a one-point victory, and Phillips had made up his mind about who was going to be his starting quarterback the rest of the way.

The pint-sized Flutie had achieved national fame 14 years earlier when he won the Heisman Trophy while quarterbacking Boston College, but he had not found success in the NFL and wound up in the Canadian Football League for several years before general manager John Butler signed him as a free agent. Flutie enjoyed a magical run in 1998 as the Bills went 10–6 to earn a wild-card berth against the Miami Dolphins. Although the season ended on a down note with Flutie failing to pull out a late-game victory against the Dolphins in the playoffs, Bills fans had been captivated and energized by his remarkable, improbable run.

Flutie was splashed on the cover of *Sports Illustrated*, earned NFL Comeback Player of the Year honors, and became so popular in Western New York that local grocery stores could barely keep up with demand for his newly released Flutie's Flakes cereal, which raised money for a foundation he and his wife had set up in honor of their autistic son. Flutie's surge couldn't have come at a more fortuitous time as it helped the Bills sell the luxury suites they were obligated to in order to keep the team in Buffalo.

It all looked great.

And then 1999 arrived.

The Bills went 11–5 to earn another wild-card berth that season, but they did so largely on the shoulder pads of their top-rated defense. Flutie Magic waned that season. As his 19 touchdown passes and 16 interceptions indicate, he was rather mediocre. And when Johnson lit it up in a meaningless regular-season finale against the Colts, owner Ralph Wilson intervened and told Phillips that Johnson needed to start that playoff game against the Titans in Tennessee. That week Phillips insisted to us in the media that it was his decision to make the quarterback switch—and his decision alone. Years later, though, he would admit that the call came from Mr. Wilson. Being the good soldier, Phillips had no choice but to fall on the sword for his owner. In retrospect I feel bad for Phillips because when owners make important personnel decisions like that, they essentially undercut their head coaches. Players know what's going on. They know who holds the power. Suddenly, the plug had been pulled on Phillips. He had lost much of his power.

Flutie was none too pleased either, and I get why he might be upset, though I believe the Bills had won that season in spite of him—not because of him. What caught me by surprise was his loud public whining. His team was prepping for a Saturday afternoon playoff game. The last thing it needed, especially in a short week, was a distraction, but Flutie seemed not to care. As my cameraman from Channel 7 and I walked past his locker, we could hear Flutie bitching. He was making his beef to no one in particular but making it loud enough for everyone to hear. So, we turned on the camera lights and began recording, and his rant continued for all the world to hear. His teammates had turned their focus to that week's game, and I felt his focus should be there, too, despite his bitter disappointment and not on himself.

Johnson, of course, started that game and, though he didn't put up memorable numbers, he was gritty and led the Bills on a field-goal drive that put them up by a point with 16 seconds remaining. That go-ahead score by Christie set the scene for one of the most disappointing moments in franchise history.

When we came back from commercial break for the kickoff, Van Miller was quick to tell listeners that it wasn't over yet, that the Bills still had a kick to defend. And it was a good and painful reminder to our audience and to me that it really isn't over until it's over. I would remember that sage advice again 22 years later when the Bills squandered a chance to host the 2022 AFC Championship Game by blowing a lead against the Kansas City Chiefs with 13 seconds remaining in regulation.

Christie's pop-up kickoff wound up being fielded by Titans tight end Frank Wycheck at the 25-yard line. He lateralled the ball (illegally passed it in my mind) to returner Kevin Dyson, who sprinted 75 yards for the dagger-in-the-heart score. No one was more devastated than Phillips, who still refers to the Music City Miracle as "Home Run Throw *Forward*" or "Home Run *Throw Up*."

That botched finish resulted in Phillips being pressured to fire legendary Bills special teams coach Bruce DeHaven, causing a rift between the two that fortunately would be reconciled before DeHaven's death in 2016. The move to start Johnson created a chasm in the locker room and among Bills fans. It would only grow wider and worsen the following season. As it turned out, neither quarterback distinguished himself during the 2000 campaign, and the Bills stumbled down the stretch, losing four of their final five to finish 8–8. Phillips was jettisoned. Interestingly, he finally would win a Super Bowl ring with the Denver Broncos in 2016. His team beat a Carolina Panthers team that featured DeHaven as their special teams coach in that game. I was happy to see that the two coaches had made up long before that game.

I look back fondly on Phillips' time in Buffalo. He was a great replacement at defensive coordinator after Walt Corey's departure in 1995 and was the right choice to replace Levy. He inherited an aging team with quarterback issues and put together some solid seasons. He's a good guy who deserves to be appreciated more by Bills fans.

## Gregg Williams

Tom Donahoe, who reached a Super Bowl with the Pittsburgh Steelers, had taken over as Buffalo Bills general manager after John Butler's departure following the 2000 season, and his first major decision was hiring Gregg Williams to replace Wade Phillips. It seemed like a good choice because Williams was an up-and-coming candidate. He had been the defensive coordinator of a Tennessee Titans team that had allowed the fewest points in the league, a team that came within one play of winning the Super Bowl.

Interestingly, Williams had been on the sidelines for two of the seminal moments in Bills history—the Comeback Game and the Music City Miracle. After he arrived at One Bills Drive, I remember him joking, "I won't bring up Music City Miracle if you don't bring up the Comeback."

He was only 42 at the time and had never been a head coach before, but Donahoe liked his brashness and figured Williams' disciplinary style was just what the team needed after Phillips' loose-ship, player's-coach approach.

The first year, though, was a disaster. Doug Flutie had been released, and there had been hope that Rob Johnson might finally realize his quarterbacking potential, but he didn't and soon played his way to the bench, as Alex Van Pelt got his shot. Buffalo plummeted to a 3–13 record, but Williams was cut some slack because it was obvious the team was undergoing an extreme makeover.

Fans became energized that offseason when the team acquired Drew Bledsoe from the New England Patriots. At first, I was a little suspicious of the deal because I didn't trust that Bill Belichick would trade a veteran quarterback with some gas left in the tank to a division rival. But the more I thought about it, the more sense it made. The Patriots had just won a Super Bowl with their young quarterback, Tom Brady, so why not try to get some value for the guy who won't be playing for you anyway?

I remember Bledsoe's signing was such a big deal that the Bills held his press conference outdoors near the stadium, so fans could be there. A few hundred people showed up, including a guy who put a white strip of tape across the nameplate of his Scott Norwood jersey and had written Bledsoe's name in black marker. (Norwood and Bledsoe both wore No. 11 for the Bills.)

Although Buffalo suffered a devastating loss in the opener in Orchard Park when the New York Jets returned the overtime kickoff for a game-winning touchdown, the Bills opened the season 5–3. They would post the inverse of that record in the second half of the season to finish 8–8. But after the previous 3–13 season, a .500 record looked pretty good. There was a sense of hope. It appeared that Bledsoe could be the guy for the foreseeable future and that Donahoe maybe hired the right coach.

The Bills started the 2003 season with a bang, blanking the Patriots 31–0 in the season opener at Ralph Wilson Stadium and crushing the Jacksonville Jaguars on the road. After dropping three of their next five, the wheels fell off, and Buffalo limped home to a 6–10 record. The Patriots gained retribution with a 31–0 spanking in the season finale.

The 2–7 stretch run was enough to convince Donahoe that he needed to make a change.

In retrospect I'm not surprised it didn't work out for Williams. Not having experience as a head coach at this level really hurt him. He was forced to learn things on the fly and he seemed to spend an inordinate amount of time trying to show his players what a hard ass he was. During practices he'd make players run penalty laps. That's okay if you are coaching high school but not in the modern-day NFL. And some of the team leaders, like eight-time Pro Bowl guard Ruben Brown, would openly defy Williams by walking instead of running his penalty laps. That undercut Williams' standing with his players, and I think there came a point when many of them tuned him out completely.

Sports anchor Paul Peck and I asked Williams if he could get his players, particularly nose tackle Sam Adams, to turn down the music in the locker room after practice because it was making the interviews we taped inaudible and unusable. After practice Williams actually came to our television production truck parked outside the stadium, and we put a tape in so he could hear it for himself. Williams got all fired up. "Don't worry, guys," he said. "I'm going to make sure he turns down the music."

He bolted out of the truck and stormed into the locker room. The next time we showed up for interviews, the music was barely audible. We were grateful, but we couldn't help but notice Adams staring daggers at us because he knew we had something to do with it. That didn't bother me a bit. Adams needed to know that we had a job to do, too.

I think Williams wanted to please people but also wanted to be recognized as an authority figure, and that's a tough road to hoe as a coach. He definitely had a bright football mind, and his aggressive, attacking style defensive strategy would earn him a job with the New Orleans Saints after Donahoe fired him. It would be there that Williams would experience his highest high and lowest low. As a defensive coordinator for the Saints, he would not only win a Super Bowl, but also would wind up being suspended a year for his role in the Bountygate scandal. With head coach Sean Payton's blessing, Williams put a bounty on opposing players. Take one of them out of the game, and there would be a little extra dough in your bank account. Eventually, word leaked out, and after the NFL investigated, both Payton and Williams were suspended for a year.

After it ended, Williams was hired by the St. Louis Rams in 2013, and over the next several years he would work with the Titans, Cleveland Browns, and Jets. While in Cleveland he took over as interim head coach and led the Browns to five wins in eight games but was let go following the 2018 season.

## Mike Mularkey

After firing Gregg Williams, following the 2003 season, Tom Donahoe wanted to hire someone more established, someone more familiar. So, he tapped into his Pittsburgh Steelers connections, choosing Mularkey, who had spent the previous three seasons as the Steelers offensive coordinator after five years as the team's tight ends coach. Mularkey was looking forward not only to being a head coach, but also working with a veteran quarterback like Drew Bledsoe.

I liked Mularkey a lot. He lived about two blocks away, and I probably was as close to him (literally and figuratively) as any coach the Buffalo Bills have ever had. I think he had it in him to be a really good head coach. But it didn't work in Buffalo—where he went 9–7 his first season and came within one brutal game of making the playoffs—or with the Jacksonville Jaguars, where many a head coach has failed.

I think Mularkey got hurt here because he inherited much of his predecessor's staff, especially on the defensive side of the ball. Normally, when a new coach is hired, he brings in his own assistants, perhaps retaining a coach or two. But I believe Ralph Wilson didn't want to eat some

I liked Mike Mularkey a lot. He lived about two blocks away, and I probably was as close to him (literally and figuratively) as any head coach the Buffalo Bills have ever had.

of the contracts from the previous staff, and Mularkey, being a first-time head coach, didn't have much say or leverage in the matter.

Mularkey was a well-respected offensive coach. In fact, he was so respected that each offseason he was asked to go to EA Sports, the football video game manufacturers, to consult with them about what plays and trends to use in their games. He knew his stuff, and they knew they could count on him to help them keep their games current and authentic.

Mularkey's two-year stay in Buffalo did not begin nor end well. The Bills wound up losing the first four games he coached, as the offense sputtered behind Bledsoe, who was starting to show his age. After being spanked 29–6 by the New England Patriots on the road, Buffalo stood at 3–6, and all hope seemed to be lost.

But then Mularkey's offense started to really click. Fueled by running back Willis McGahee, who would finish the season with 1,128 yards rushing and 13 touchdowns, and wide receivers Eric Moulds (88 receptions, 1,043 yards, five touchdowns) and Lee Evans (17.6-yards-per-catch average, nine scores), Mularkey's innovative offense started humming. The Bills averaged 38 points per game and wound up winning six games in a row.

It was their longest winning streak in 14 seasons and set the stage for them to return to the playoffs. In fact, it was all laid out for them on a silver platter. All they had to do was beat the Steelers, Mularkey's former team, in the season finale at Rich Stadium and they were in. And their chances of reaching the postseason were enhanced because the Steelers already had punched their playoff ticket, so they would be sitting the majority of their starters, including star quarterback Ben Roethlisberger and star running back Jerome Bettis.

Sadly, in a scenario that would become all too familiar during Buffalo's 17-year playoff drought, the Bills managed to find a way to fumble the silver platter and lose the game. That defeat definitely struck a nerve with both Donahoe and Mularkey, each of whom had departed Pittsburgh after a falling out with head coach Bill Cowher. All these years later, I still don't know what happened in that game. There was speculation that Bledsoe went rogue and didn't adhere to the gameplan. That's what some—including Mularkey—indicated. Bledsoe definitely wasn't at his best in that game, and his fumble on a sack in the fourth quarter wound up being scooped up and returned for the decisive score. I interviewed Donahoe two days after the defeat and I said, "That was a tough one, especially losing to their backups."

He got really mad. "They weren't backups," he yelled. With all due respect, he was dead wrong. On that day the junior varsity had beaten the varsity, and it was inexplicable.

That marked the end of the Bledsoe era in Buffalo, as Donahoe cut ties with the veteran. The Bills would pin their hopes on J.P. Losman during the 2005 season, and the former first-round draft pick would bomb so badly that Mularkey had to go with veteran journeyman Kelly Holcomb. The Bills dropped six of their final seven games to finish 5–11, and it was apparent Donahoe's days were numbered. Mularkey could have stayed and probably would have been retained because he had a year or two remaining on his contract. But he had grown tired of Mr. Wilson's interference and realized he'd be losing his guardian angel in Donahoe. More importantly, he didn't have a reliable quarterback going forward. So the situation didn't figure to improve.

Those dire circumstances prompted Mularkey to be proactive. In a decision that took me and many others by surprise, he announced he was quitting. I couldn't believe he was really doing that. There are only 32 of these jobs in the NFL—they are extremely rare—and there was no guarantee that Mularkey would ever get another shot at being a head coach at this level. He said he made the decision on behalf of his family, citing the poor treatment of his kids by their schoolmates. I wasn't buying that, and neither was anyone else.

For the third time in Bills history a coach had quit. (Lou Saban had resigned once in the mid-1960s and again in the mid-1970s.) It wouldn't be the last time a Buffalo coach walked away on his own volition.

## Dick Jauron

Ralph Wilson decided to replace Tom Donahoe with Marv Levy. It was a feel-good hire but also a bit of a head-scratcher because, though Levy had enjoyed great success as a coach, he had no experience at this level as a general manager. Levy's first order of business in 2006 was finding a new head coach, and he opted for Dick Jauron, who enjoyed a solid career as a player and assistant coach but who experienced only sporadic success as an NFL head coach. Levy had moved back to Chicago full time after his Buffalo Bills coaching career and had done some television work on Chicago Bears games, so he was familiar with Jauron's five seasons there as head coach. The highlight of those years was 2001, when Jauron led the Bears to a 13–3 mark. But that would be his only winning season in the Windy City.

Jauron's tenure in Buffalo was the epitome of mediocre. Some members of the media sarcastically referred to him as "good, ol' Seven-and-Nine." And, though cruel, the description was accurate as the Bills finished 7–9 in each of his three full seasons. Jauron was as bland as bland could be. Though a Yale graduate and a really bright guy, he never said anything of consequence. At times, you wondered if he had a pulse.

Jauron worked hard, but you got the sense he didn't bleed when the Bills lost. He was always so guarded. And my sense was he was that way with his players. They say a team takes on their coach's persona, and I think those Bills teams took on Jauron's persona. Jauron was a native New Englander, and during a bye week one season, I was watching a Boston Red Sox playoff game on a Saturday night, and there was Jauron on my television screen, sitting a few rows up from home plate at Fenway Park. I wasn't close with him like I had been with some of his Bills predecessors, but the following Monday, I mentioned how I had seen him at the Red Sox game. I was just making idle chit chat, but he quickly stiffened up and said, "It wasn't me."

*Well, yeah, it was you. I witnessed you there with my own eyes, and so had many others.*

He acted as if I had an ulterior motive like I was trying to get him in trouble or something when in reality I was just trying to have a conversation with him about something he loved. Heck, it was the Saturday night of a bye week, so if he wanted to take a break from the stresses of the season for a day or two to watch his beloved Red Sox, more power to him. I was just trying to loosen him up a bit, but he was afraid to admit that he had taken a deserved day off. To me, that was revealing of his character. He guarded his feelings all the time and not just in the presence of the media. From several players I spoke with off the record, he was the same way with them, too. My sense was they wanted more and needed more from their coach and didn't get it, and I think that contributed to those teams being stuck in football purgatory.

It clearly didn't help that Jauron lacked a legitimate quarterback. J.P. Losman wound up being a flop, and the Bills drafted Trent Edwards in the third round in 2007, and he flopped, too. Edwards earned the pejorative nickname "Captain Checkdown" because of his proclivity for dumping off passes to his running backs. Like Losman, Edwards was a good guy. He just didn't have the arm strength nor the confidence to take deep shots.

Levy's reign as general manager lasted just two years before he retired back to his Chicago penthouse. Mr. Wilson decided to replace him with another person who had no GM experience in the NFL, promoting Russ Brandon. He had done a remarkable job on the business and marketing side but had never evaluated playing talent, which obviously is an essential part of a GM's job. Fortunately, Brandon was able to lean on Tom Modrak and John Guy, two lifelong scouts who really knew their stuff.

Brandon wound up retaining Jauron, and, sure enough, another 7–9 record followed in 2008. The next season, after the Bills started 3–6, Jauron was finally cut loose. Perry Fewell was promoted, and the team showed some life, playing hard for him while going 3–4 down the stretch. I liked Fewell a lot and had hoped he would get a shot. He was such a breath of fresh air after Jauron's blandness. But the Bills decided to go with a clean cut in 2010, as Mr. Wilson brought back longtime, well-regarded scout Buddy Nix to become GM. Brandon went back to doing what he did best and eventually was given the title of team president.

# Chan Gailey

After a series of either first-time head coaches or retreads, Ralph Wilson reportedly wanted to make a big splash and sign a big-name coach with a track record for success. There was speculation that the Buffalo Bills owner wanted to lure Bill Cowher away from the network television studio to become not only coach, but also director of football operations. Cowher reportedly would have total control of everything on the football end of things, including all personnel decisions.

Russ Brandon insisted to me the speculation was real. He said he had talks with Cowher, and Mr. Wilson was even willing to ante up the $10 million contract the former Pittsburgh Steelers Super Bowl-winning coach would command. The deal was never consummated, and I never really took it seriously because someone of Cowher's stature and connections was well aware of the Bills' situation—a situation where the owner had a penchant for interfering with football decisions. If Cowher were going to leave his cozy, well-compensated broadcasting job, it was going to be someplace where he was guaranteed to succeed fairly quickly, a place that probably had a franchise quarterback in place, which Buffalo didn't.

The Cowher-to-Buffalo rumor never gained traction. Buffalo was not an attractive destination at the time, so Buddy Nix had no choice but to go the retread route once more and hire Chan Gailey. He was a respected, creative offensive mind who had enjoyed moderate success as a head coach of the Dallas Cowboys and in college at Georgia Tech. Sadly, he had the misfortune of getting off to one of the worst starts in Bills history, dropping his first eight games, before regrouping to go 4–4 in the second half of the season. In retrospect, I must admit it wound up being one of the more entertaining 4–12 teams I've ever covered, thanks to Gailey's pass-happy approach and the Ryan Fitzpatrick-to-Stevie Johnson aerial connection. Fitz would become the NFL's all-time journeyman quarterback, starting for nine different teams during his improbable career. Johnson, meanwhile, would blossom into one of the best seventh-round draft picks in franchise history. The two hooked up 82 times for 1,073 yards and 10 touchdowns that season.

The Fitz-to-Stevie combo was on fire at the start of the 2011 season, as the Bills won their first three games, including a 34–31 victory against the New England Patriots, in which Fitz outdueled the great Tom Brady. We were caught up in FitzMagic at that point, and how could you not be? The Harvard-educated quarterback with the bushy beard and the intrepid, though not necessarily powerful, arm had us thinking that maybe, just maybe this damn playoff drought was over.

After a 5–2 start, the Bills brass was thinking the same thing as Brandon rewarded Fitz with a huge contract extension. Alas, his play wound up being a mirage as Buffalo dropped eight of its final nine to finish 6–10. Fitz threw the ball a franchise-record 569 times, finishing with the schizophrenic stat line of 24 touchdown tosses and 23 interceptions. That kind of summed up the season. A lot of good. A lot of bad. A lot of losses. And another season that ended without a postseason.

Gailey and Fitz would get one more shot at it in 2012, and the results would be identical. Another 6–10 finish. Another coaching change. Another quarterback change. I felt bad for Gailey. He was a really good guy, a fun guy. I loved how innovative his playcalling was. His teams may have been bad, but they were never boring. You can't help but wonder what he could have done had he been calling plays for those Jim Kelly- or Josh Allen-quarterbacked teams.

## Doug Marrone

Dipping into the college ranks to hire Syracuse University coach Doug Marrone to replace Chan Gailey in 2013 was definitely a Russ Brandon hire. Brandon grew up in East Syracuse and actually was a board member of SU's Falk College of Sports Management, so he was intimately aware of Orange athletics. Marrone had paid his coaching dues and had done a masterful job in his four years at Syracuse, elevating a program coming off a 10-loss and a nine-loss season into a two-time bowl-game winner. Although the move seemed to some to smack of cronyism, Marrone came to town with some solid recommendations from Bill Polian and Bill Parcells, each of whom thought he was an up-and-coming coach, and Sean Payton, who had hired him to become his offensive coordinator and offensive line coach with the New Orleans Saints.

I liked Marrone, but I always felt he was a little bit insecure and I think his fractious relationship with the media, some of his players, and a handful of front-office staffers only exacerbated the difficult situation he had inherited. The playoff drought, which had reached a dozen years at the time of his hiring, weighed heavily on him. He desperately wanted to end it, and the incessant questions about it clearly irritated him.

Buddy Nix announced that he would be stepping down as general manager following the 2013 draft and would be replaced by Doug Whaley, a highly respected talent assessor who'd had a good run with the Pittsburgh Steelers before being brought to Buffalo by Tom Donahoe several years earlier. Nix said before he left that he was going to make sure his parting gift was a franchise quarterback and he thought he had found that guy when he drafted EJ Manuel that April. To many NFL observers, the Manuel selection seemed a reach, as Nix selected a quarterback in the first round that many projected as a second- or third-round talent. Marrone wasn't pleased with the pick and reportedly stormed out of the room on draft day.

Though Manuel provided a glimmer of hope by engineering a come-from-behind victory against the Carolina Panthers in Orchard Park in Week Two, the season wound up being another disappointment. Manuel eventually was benched in favor of backup Thad Lewis, and when Lewis was injured, Marrone went with his third-stringer, Jeff Tuel. The Buffalo Bills finished 6–10.

Whaley still had faith in Manuel and thought if he surrounded him with some playmaking receivers he would flourish. In his first draft, Whaley spent two first-round picks in order to move up to select Sammy Watkins, a home-run threat receiver out of Clemson. Marrone felt the price to land Watkins was much too high, an assessment shared by many others. Marrone also felt Manuel would never become what Nix envisioned him becoming and wound up coaxing NFL retread quarterback Kyle Orton out of retirement.

The Bills went 9–7, upsetting a heavily favored Green Bay Packers team featuring future Hall of Fame quarterback Aaron Rodgers. They also knocked off the Patriots in New England in the season finale, though, many have assigned an asterisk to that one because Tom Brady only played a half, and the majority of the starters didn't play at all. It was a strange season, and Marrone seemed irritable and easily agitated throughout much of it. This also was the year that Terry and Kim Pegula purchased the Bills following Ralph Wilson's death, and while the Pegulas' purchase was great news for Buffalo fans afraid the franchise might leave town, Marrone's insecurity seemed to grow because he didn't know if his new bosses would retain him after that season.

The other bizarre thing that happened that year was the blizzard to end all blizzards that dumped nearly seven feet of snow on the suburbs south of Buffalo. As an Orchard Park resident, I can attest that it accumulated so fast and furious that we couldn't keep up with the shoveling and plowing. There was no way Ralph Wilson Stadium would be shoveled out in time for that week's game against the New York Jets, so the NFL made arrangements to play it on a Monday night in Detroit. (A similar situation occurred for a Cleveland Browns game in 2022, which was relocated to Detroit.)

The 2014 game made Marrone a little paranoid. He thought the league was out to get the Bills by moving the game to a neutral site. I remember taping my pregame show with Marrone in his hotel room several hours before kickoff, and he was whining big time. I later ran into Brandon in the hotel lobby and said, "You better get up there and talk to your coach because he's in no state of mind to coach a football game tonight."

So much for losing home-field advantage, as the Bills throttled the Jets 38–3.

Marrone had a great distrust of the media. By that time I had left local television, so I could work full time for the team website, Bills.com. Part of my job included hosting my daily radio talk show, the *John Murphy Show*, which eventually was renamed *One Bills Live* and simulcast on the MSG Network. So, even though I was technically still part of the media, I was under the employ of the Bills, which meant, I guess, that Marrone trusted me at least a little.

As the season wore on, the media criticism toward Marrone intensified and it really bothered his wife. She routinely would call me up on Monday morning to complain about something one of the *Buffalo News* columnists had written, and I would have to explain to her that I have no control over what they write, and that if she had a problem with them, she really should contact them.

I knew that Marrone was miserable, but never in a million years did I think he would quit. On New Year's Eve, my wife and I went to the movies, and when we returned home, the news had broken that Marrone was leaving. We found out later that his agent had shrewdly negotiated a buyout clause that would kick in if he left before his third season. I understood the uncertainty he was feeling about new ownership. Were the Pegulas going to turn the whole thing upside down? I didn't know. And I'm sure the fact that Marrone didn't have a legitimate quarterback also factored into his decision. Still, I was disappointed in him. He joined Lou Saban and Mike Mularkey as the only coaches in Bills history to quit. And Buffalo fans, who never really warmed up to him, will forever be upset with him for walking out on their team.

# Rex Ryan

For many years it was standard practice on Wednesdays before Sunday games to have media conference calls with the opposing head coach and one of his players. We'd all gather in the media room and ask questions and record the audio. It was pack journalism, and the majority of the guys you spoke to were guarded, bland, and said absolutely nothing. There were many weeks when it was almost a waste of time, especially those weeks when New England Patriots head coach Bill Belichick was on the line. He usually was brutal, and I realize it was completely by design.

One guy, though, who was never brutal, guarded, or bland was Ryan. In fact, you could always count on him to provide you with great material during his conference calls and postgame podium appearances during his six seasons as head coach of the New York Jets. He was always entertaining. He often had you in stitches. And he was never, ever boring.

So, I was intrigued when I caught wind that Russ Brandon scheduled a dinner meeting between Ryan and Terry and Kim Pegula. I knew Ryan could be a charmer and I wasn't surprised that he would wind up winning them over.

His introductory press conference in the field house at One Bills Drive was pure Ryan. He was humorous and bombastic, taking shots, telling jokes, making predictions. Buffalo Bills fans were smitten from the start, especially after he assured everyone he wouldn't be quitting on them (a shot obviously at the recently departed Doug Marrone) and that he wouldn't be kissing Belichick's Super Bowl rings. He said the Bills would be taking dead aim at the Patriots. It was music to Buffalo fans' ears.

The apple clearly hadn't fallen far from the tree, as Rex sounded an awful lot like his braggadocio dad, Buddy Ryan. And like his father, Rex had established his football bona fides on the defensive side of the ball. Everyone seemed fired up. I could see why players loved playing for him during his days with the Jets and Baltimore Ravens, where he was the defensive coordinator of a Super Bowl-winning team.

It was a blast covering him, especially after covering so many guys who talked in coach speak and often treated interactions with the media like root canals. Ryan definitely enjoyed having fun. I can't think of too many other coaches who would show up in a Clemson helmet for his press conference because his son was a walk-on there or take a bite out of a dog biscuit at the podium during training camp.

Sadly, we got so caught up in his larger-than-life, fun-loving personality that we ignored the warning signs. After enjoying some success in his early years coaching the Jets, the wheels fell off and they became a train wreck. Ryan's lack of attention to detail and failure to coach the entire team rather than just the defense would derail him in less than two seasons in Buffalo.

Buffalo did go 8–8 his first season in 2015, as former Ravens backup quarterback Tyrod Taylor took over as starter after Ryan convinced general manager Doug Whaley to take a free-agent flyer on him and bring him to training camp. Taylor was serviceable, throwing 20 touchdown passes and only six interceptions while also rushing for 568 yards and four scores. The addition of dual-threat running back LeSean McCoy, whom the Bills traded for before the season, also helped. But the disconcerting thing about that team was the defense. Here was this defensive savant inheriting a very solid defense, and it wound up yielding 30 or more points five times while dropping several spots in the league rankings.

The fact that Ryan liked to have a good time and show the public more of his personality than your typical buttoned-up NFL head coach fed the perception that he didn't work hard at his craft and ran too loose of a ship. In reality Ryan's staff worked hard, and I defended them on several occasions.

The Bills lost their first two games in 2016, but after reeling off four straight wins, including a 16–0 white-washing of a New England team without Deflategate-suspended quarterback Tom Brady, it appeared Ryan might be turning things around. Instead, the streakiness continued. The four wins were followed by three consecutive losses and two straight wins and two straight losses, as the Bills sputtered toward a 7–9 finish and another playoff-less season.

The final straw for Ryan and team ownership occurred in a 34–31 loss to the Miami Dolphins at home in the second-to-last game of the season. There was a reserve Bills linebacker who participated in pregame warmups before the game. None of the coaches told him he was being activated for that day's contest, so about an hour-and-half before kickoff, he showered and headed up to a suite to watch the game with the other designated inactives. But one of the starting linebackers got hurt, and an assistant Bills coach said put so-and-so in the game. Well, so-and-so is nowhere to be found because so-and-so was up in the suite eating wings and watching the game. The coaches finally realized that he hadn't been told he was active for the game, so they contacted him up in the suite, and he had to race down to the locker room and suit up in a hurry.

That incident just underscored how things kept falling through the cracks with Ryan, and he wound up being fired following that loss. He was a fun guy to be around, and I loved doing his television show with him. But Ryan was more interested in the show business aspect of the job. So, it was probably good that he got out of the business of coaching and took that studio job with ESPN.

# CHAPTER 9
## JIM KELLY TO THE RESCUE

No one in the history of Western New York ever received a welcoming like the one Jim Kelly received after his plane touched down at the Greater Buffalo International Airport on the afternoon of August 18, 1986. It was like the Beatles arriving at JFK. It was so over the top and it told you everything you needed to know about the Buffalo Bills' Vise-Grip on the souls of our victory-famished, football-crazed community.

The white knight in shining armor had finally arrived. Only instead of galloping atop a stallion, Kelly zoomed into town in a stretch limo, accompanied by Bill Polian, as police on motorcycles escorted the conquering hero from the airport to the Buffalo Hilton downtown. The overpasses on the Kensington Expressway were lined with people waving, shouting, and carrying signs. Local television stations broke away from soap operas so they could broadcast the insanity live. The city had never seen anything like it. The only thing that might ever top it would be a Super Bowl victory parade.

There had to be at least a thousand people crammed into the Hilton's main ballroom for the press conference announcing that Kelly had signed the richest contract in NFL history—$7.5 million over five years. It was more coronation than press conference. Totally surreal. Bills owner Ralph Wilson and head coach Hank Bullough made a few remarks and then posed for photos next to Kelly, holding his new No. 12 Bills jersey with his nameplate on the back. Kelly was then handed a telegram from governor Mario Cuomo welcoming him to Western New York. Once he hung up, Kelly stepped to the dais and talked about how he hoped to receive a call from the president one day after winning the Super Bowl.

It remains one of the craziest, most joyous scenes I've ever witnessed. And it was a day most of us never thought would happen. Least of all Kelly.

The Bills were the dregs of the NFL at the time. No one wanted to play for Buffalo—with good reason. The team was coming off consecutive last-place finishes and had lost 32 of its previous 37 games. Players regarded it as Siberia, a place to avoid at all costs. And perhaps no player ever avoided coming there more than Kelly. He has said he actually cried when the Bills chose him with the 14th overall pick in the 1983 draft. And they weren't tears of joy.

Kelly did show up in Orchard Park for minicamp and was prepared to sign his rookie contract with the Bills when we experienced another one of those "only in Buffalo" moments that's permanently etched in our sky-is-falling lore. Reportedly, Kelly was about to sign on the dotted line when a Bills secretary put through a call to his agents. Bruce Allen of the United States Football League was on the line and he told Kelly's representatives not to sign anything because the fledgling pro circuit was going to make him an offer he couldn't refuse. Sure enough, the contract went unsigned, and Kelly wound up leaving One Bills Drive and inking a lucrative deal with the USFL's Houston Gamblers. Kelly was gone seemingly forever.

He wound up having great success with the Gamblers, passing for 83 touchdowns and nearly 10,000 yards in just two seasons. Following the 1985 season, Donald Trump purchased Kelly's contract so he could play in metropolitan New York for the New Jersey Generals. I remember seeing Kelly's smiling mug splashed across the cover of *Sports Illustrated* and feeling incredibly deflated. I thought to myself, *That coulda, shoulda been Kelly in a Bills uniform.* Just another case of us being jilted. Only in Buffalo.

In early March 1986, I went with some buddies to the Big East Conference Basketball Tournament at Madison Square Garden in Manhattan, and who do I run into? Kelly. I introduced myself, mentioned I worked in Buffalo media, and did color on Bills broadcasts. He said, "Screw, Buffalo!" He was chuckling as he said it, but I could tell he was serious. We had a beer and talked a bit, but he seemed adamant about not ever wanting to play for the Bills. The funny thing is that I didn't take his comments personally. In fact, I kind of liked his swagger and thought to myself, *This is exactly the cocky, ultra-sure-of-himself quarterback the Bills need.*

Around that time the USFL had filed an antitrust suit against the National Football League, and there were rumblings about the new league hemorrhaging money. If they lost their suit, they might go belly-up. As it turned out, the judge did rule in the USFL's favor but awarded them just one dollar, which was trebled to three dollars. Imagine that? Three measly dollars. The USFL was history, and Kelly would have no choice but to play in the NFL if he wanted to continue his pro football career.

The Bills still held his rights, but Kelly kept up his anti-Buffalo campaign in hopes of forcing a trade. I don't think any of us were convinced Mr. Wilson would load up the Brink's truck to make sure Kelly came here. The more time passed, the more I believed Buffalo would grant Kelly's wishes and deal him to the Los Angeles Raiders. The Bills would get some draft picks and washed-up veterans in return and would wind up drafting another Joe Dufek. (Nothing personal against Dufek; he was a good guy. But you get my drift.)

Polian told me he went to Mr. Wilson and presented the options. They could try to negotiate with Kelly and his agents, who also had publicly dissed Buffalo as one of America's armpits. Or they could trade away his rights and acquire a veteran player or two and some high draft picks. To his credit, Mr. Wilson held firm and told Polian he wasn't trading the rights to the quarterback the team desperately needed.

I'll never forget being in Houston on a Friday night for a Bills exhibition game in mid-August. Kelly lived there and was invited, along with his agents, Roger Trevino and A.J. Faigin, to Mr. Wilson's suite in the Astrodome. As Van Miller described the action on the field, I focused my binoculars on Mr. Wilson's box. That's where the real action was. That's where the game was. There had been talk that Kelly might be signed quickly enough for him to play in the regular-season opener, which was only three weeks away. But when nothing was announced that night, I figured negotiations had hit a snag, and seeing Kelly in uniform by the start of the regular season appeared a pipe dream.

Fortunately, I was wrong. Polian and Kelly's reps got things ironed out the next day, and by Monday, Kelly was on a private jet flying to Buffalo for his coronation. Yes, I was pumped up, but the skeptic in me was hoping this wasn't just another buildup to a dramatic, psyche-wrecking fall. I thought, *Yes, they have a quarterback, but we still really don't know how good he is.* He had compiled those gaudy stats against some good competition, but the USFL was no NFL. I guess the only thing I knew for certain was that Kelly was going to be an upgrade over Vince Ferragamo and Bruce Mathison. I also worried about how little time Kelly would have learning the offense, jelling with his teammates, and getting into football shape. He was going to be taking a crash course, and I was hoping he wouldn't crash.

Kelly's impact on the team's coffers was immediate. The next day thousands of fans showed up for his first practice at the Bills training camp on the campus of Fredonia State. For context, crowds to that point usually were in the hundreds. The excitement was palpable, as fans cheered every pass by Kelly. During that first week, the Bills sold 10,000 season tickets. The combination of Kelly's star power and the fans' ravenous appetite for something positive had created the perfect storm.

His Bills debut took place at Notre Dame Stadium in a preseason game against the reigning Super Bowl champion Chicago Bears. They had a superb defense, one of the greatest defenses of all time, and Kelly was solid, but not spectacular. Unlike today, where starters are lucky to play a few series the entire preseason, they usually played at least two quarters in most exhibition games back then.

The anticipation for the start of recent Bills seasons reminds me of what we felt before Kelly's regular-season debut on September 7, 1986. To say the fans were crazed that day would be a gross understatement.

As 79,951 jacked-up spectators looked on—including some who put up a bed sheet reading "KELLY IS GOD"—Kelly threw three touchdown passes. On one play he spun out of trouble and rifled a bullet for a score. Although the New York Jets prevailed 28–24, you couldn't help but marvel at him. You could tell that this guy was legit, and he was going to be something really special once he got a grasp of the offense and the Bills upgraded his supporting cast.

Success didn't come overnight. In fact, there would be some major bumps in the road those first few years. Kelly would need to learn how to read defenses, deliver in the clutch, and treat his teammates with respect. I had mentioned how cocky Kelly was in his early years, and that proved to be both a strength and a weakness. There were times when he could be off-putting. Early on, he had this really annoying habit of speaking about himself in the third person. *Jim Kelly can't do it by himself. Jim Kelly needs people around him who can block and catch the ball. Jim Kelly needs a better supporting cast.* He wasn't exactly the kind of guy you wanted to go have beers with back then. In fact, he was somewhat of an ass.

Despite his immaturity there was something about him that wound up energizing us. That swagger, that supreme confidence was exactly what a downtrodden franchise and city needed at that time. We had taken so much crap, and it was about time to stick up for ourselves and throw a few punches instead of being everybody's punching bag. Kelly proved to be the right guy at the right time to do that. We needed to start believing in ourselves the way Kelly believed in himself.

We had been in a deep, deep hole for a long time. Something had to change, and Kelly represented change, represented hope. We would grow, and he would grow, too. Teammates would stand up to him eventually and remind him that he wasn't perfect, that he made mistakes, too. And Kelly would mature. He stopped talking about himself in the third person, stopped pointing fingers, and became a true leader, the face of the franchise and the community.

You can make a strong argument that he saved the franchise. He was the missing piece, the essential piece. Once he arrived Buffalo stopped being a football Siberia. Kelly had a pied piper effect. We had a franchise quarterback, and people wanted to join him. Fans wanted to watch him play. Players wanted to play with him. Coaches wanted to coach him. Kelly became the central figure in leading the Bills on their unprecedented run. He established passing records, racked up a ton of wins, and earned a bust in the Pro Football Hall of Fame. And in a wonderful turn of events, the guy who repeatedly and forcefully dissed Buffalo wound up falling in love with the place. He settled here after hanging up his helmet and shoulder pads and is still here. This is home, a place where he was always meant to be.

Bills fans always appreciated Kelly's toughness on the field. He played in an era when quarterbacks weren't protected by the rules the way they are now, which is why I tell people to be careful when you are making comparisons between athletes from different eras. There are too many variables, so it's really impossible to do. Kelly, like many of his quarterback peers and predecessors, endured hellacious hits in the pocket that were celebrated back in the day but would result in suspensions and huge fines in today's game. Kelly definitely was tenacious in the face of such brutality. I recall numerous occasions when he picked himself up off the turf after a bone-crushing sack and retaliated with a big completion. He was remarkably resilient. There were times I don't know how he did it.

Kelly Toughness wound up taking on a whole new meaning in Jim's post-playing life. And the courage he's shown in dealing with life's daunting and often unfair challenges has made him an even more beloved figured in Buffalo and beyond. As a parent of two healthy sons, I can't begin to fathom what Jim and his wife, Jill, were forced to endure after their son, Hunter, was diagnosed with Krabbe disease, a rare, fatal nervous system disorder. The Kellys provided him with love and the best medical care possible, and Hunter wound up defying the odds, living until age eight, nearly five years longer than the typical life expectancy for a child diagnosed with Krabbe.

In 1997, several months after their baby son was diagnosed with the disease, Jim and Jill established Hunter's Hope and wound up raising millions of dollars for research, early testing, and awareness. They traveled the country to lobby state and national politicians about the importance of early detection for Krabbe and scores of other infant diseases. Those efforts resulted in legislation, which has helped save countless lives. Jim and Jill also met and offered support to numerous parents in similar situations. They did their best to turn a tragedy into triumph, and their efforts continue to this day through Jim's Kelly for Kids Foundation. What they've created is a lasting, loving legacy to their son, Hunter.

I've been to Canton for several Hall of Fame inductions, and perhaps the moment that sticks out the most was Kelly's acceptance speech on August 3, 2002. There were about 15,000 in the stadium there that day, and I swear about 14,000 were Bills fans. Near the end of his remarks, Kelly pointed down to the field to acknowledge his son, whom he called "my hero." It was such a poignant moment. I wasn't the only one wiping away tears.

Kelly eventually became a devout, born-again Christian, and his faith has been severely tested. The wear and tear of his football career has hounded him in retirement, and he's undergone multiple surgeries on his neck, back, shoulders, knees, and ankles. But the biggest blow would come several years ago when he was diagnosed with a virulent form of bone cancer that resulted in the removal of his jaw. There were several times when it appeared that Kelly wasn't going to make it, but loving support from relatives, friends, total strangers, and superb cancer doctors and nurses, as well his faith, helped him pull through.

In 2018 Kelly traveled to Los Angeles to receive the Jimmy V Award for Perseverance, named after Jim Valvano, the courageous college basketball coach who inspired a nation when he delivered his unforgettable, "Don't ever give up" speech on national television just a few months before dying of cancer. As about 2,000 theatergoers and millions of more television viewers looked on, Kelly had his Jimmy V moment at the ESPYs. Accompanied to the dais by his daughters, Camryn and Erin, and quarterback contemporaries/friends John Elway and Dan Marino, a frail-looking Kelly spoke from the heart. It was another grab-the-Kleenex moment and a reminder of how lucky I've been to be able to call someone like Kelly my friend.

One of the things I'm most proud of is the way our region has rallied around Kelly during his trials and tribulations. It doesn't surprise me in the least. We really are a City of Good Neighbors. When you're down on your luck, we've got your back. I know Kelly appreciates it tremendously and has said so on countless occasions. And we appreciate all that he has done for us and are thrilled he eventually became one of us. A true Buffalonian.

# CHAPTER 10
## THE COUNTERFEIT AND
## BICKERING BILLS

There had been rumblings before the 1987 season began that a strike was imminent, and that was the last thing I or anyone else wanted to hear after having lived through an NFL work stoppage five years earlier. And what made this latest collective bargaining dispute even worse was the threat by NFL management that the games would continue to be played even if the players went on strike.

I thought it was just posturing on the part of management. I didn't truly believe that such a bright and innovative thinker like NFL commissioner Pete Rozelle would actually carry on with such a preposterous idea, but he did. And so after the Buffalo Bills' 34–30 win in Houston in Week Two, the real players walked out, and the Bills and every other team began scrambling to fill rosters with scabs. I know that neither Bill Polian, Marv Levy, nor their peers throughout the league wanted anything to do with this, but they had no choice because Rozelle decreed that the scab games would count in the standings. It was utterly absurd. So, Polian and his staff began assembling a roster of over-the-hill players and NFL wannabes in order to field a team. Scribes, such as my coauthor Scott Pitoniak, immediately labeled Buffalo's team, the "Counterfeit Bills." It fit.

When the real players walked, the league announced it was canceling that week's games—Buffalo was supposed to travel to Dallas—but would resume with its regularly-scheduled slate of games the following week. That meant the Bills and their counterparts would have less than two weeks to put a team together. Who throws an NFL team together in less than two weeks?

Somehow, the Bills managed to do so, and Levy and his coaching staff installed a playbook on the fly that was Pop Warner football simple. Levy admitted that he and his assistant coaches didn't even know the names of all the guys on the roster—let alone their skill levels. It was just an impossibly ridiculous situation, and in typical Levy fashion, he managed to maintain his sense of humor through it all.

Longtime Bills beat reporter Milt Northrop and I showed up the Friday before the first replacement game, and Levy was telling us about this pint-sized running back from nearby Canisius College named Mike Panepinto that the Bills just signed. "I guess, we'll start him Sunday," Levy deadpanned. "I think he'll be good. In fact, he just got a shoe deal. He got a deal with Buster Brown." Northrop and I started laughing our asses off because Buster Brown sold children's shoes, and Panepinto was rather small in stature.

It was bad enough that we had to cover this team of imposters, but we also had to do stories on the striking Bills, the real Bills. To their credit, unlike during the 1982 strike, the '87 team stayed in Buffalo and held regular practices in Delaware Park. Most of the players attended, though it obviously wasn't nearly as structured as it would have been with real coaches at the stadium.

When I entered One Bills Drive for the first replacement game on the morning of October 4, the real Bills players were standing at the entrance, picketing and harassing every car that drove into the parking lot. Several of the players had consumed their fair share of breakfast beers, which only added to their bravado. There's a story of offensive tackle Will Wolford spitting on the windshield of one of the cars passing through—only to discover the car was being driven by none other than owner Ralph Wilson. I remember when I went through, Fred Smerlas motioned for me to put my window down, and when I did, he started cursing me. "Murph, I can't believe you of all people would cross a picket line," he bellowed. "You're a [bleeping] scab."

It was a mess, but we had a job to do. And it was easy for Smerlas and the others to say stuff like that because once the strike ended, he and his teammates would have their old jobs back with most of them being generously compensated for making a living playing a kid's game. If I, Van Miller, and the reporters covering the team walked out in a so-called show of solidarity, we definitely wouldn't be returning to our old jobs.

We'd be shown the door. That's not to say I didn't believe the players had a legitimate gripe. In many cases they did. I'm just saying they were living in a different world than we were.

Broadcasting that day's scab game and the two that followed was an absolute mess because we didn't know who most of these guys were and had little background on them. We did our best to learn the names of the players and some of the back stories. And we attempted to describe the action as best we could while also realizing the whole thing was a joke. The fans considered it a joke, too. That first game at Rich Stadium drew an announced crowd of 9,860 fans, meaning the stadium was seven-eighths empty.

The games were jokes, too. That day the Indianapolis Colts eviscerated the Bills 47–6, as the immortal Gary Hogeboom fired five touchdown passes to tie the franchise record established by one of the NFL's all-time great quarterbacks, Johnny Unitas. Those Counterfeit Bills were quarterbacked for two games by Willie Totten, whose claim to fame was being a college teammate of pro football's all-time leading receiver, Jerry Rice, at Mississippi Valley State. There's really no kind way to put it, but Totten was rotten in his three games with the Bills. The stats bore this out as he completed only 39 percent of his passes and fumbled nine times. Even simple snaps from the center became adventures for the overmatched Totten.

The Bills wound up winning one of the three games before the strike mercifully ended, and that victory will forever be part of team lore. In front of an announced crowd of 15,737 fans at Rich Stadium, Buffalo eked out a 6–3 overtime victory against a New York Giants team that featured Hall of Famer Lawrence Taylor, one of several veterans throughout the league who had crossed the line. Imagine a high school player going against a Pop Warner player, and you get an idea of just how dominant LT was that day. Will Grant, a former Bills center who had come out of retirement during the strike, was called for something like six holding penalties while trying to block Taylor, and as he walked off the field at halftime, Levy laid into him. "Will, you've been flagged five times already," Levy yelled at him.

And Grant responded, "That's actually pretty good, Marv, considering I've been holding him on every play."

If there was any redeeming memory from that game it's that Todd Schlopy, an Orchard Park kid, wound up kicking the winning field goal from 27 yards out. Levy has called it the worst game in NFL history, and that's hard to dispute. The exhibition of errors saw the teams combine for nine fumbles, five interceptions, five missed field goals, and 48 incomplete passes. Sadly, it counts in the all-time records. We all were just happy it marked the end of the counterfeit schedule. The strike ended with that game. The real players came back. Hopefully, fans never have to go through anything like that again.

Buffalo's first game after the strike was in Miami, and it became a good measuring stick for just how far the Bills had come. South Florida had been a house of horrors for Buffalo, and Miami Dolphins quarterback Dan Marino had established himself as the most dangerous passer in the game. So this was going to be a tough, tough test. In a dramatic back-and-forth game, Jim Kelly led the Bills on the winning scoring drive, setting up Scott Norwood's decisive field goal as Buffalo left Joe Robbie Stadium with a 34–31 overtime victory. Polian looks back on that game as a turning point for the Bills. They had shown they could go toe to toe with their division rivals, and Kelly had outdueled his quarterback classmate.

Six days after that victory, Polian pulled off the blockbuster Halloween Eve trade that brought Cornelius Bennett to Buffalo. Polian definitely was swinging for the fences, and two weeks later, Bennett would make an impact in his NFL debut, harassing John Elway on several occasions as Buffalo knocked off the Denver Broncos at Rich Stadium. It took some time for the linebacker nicknamed "Biscuit" to get his legs under him, but once he did, you could see why Polian and others had salivated over him. In the regular-season ending loss to the Eagles in Philadelphia, Bennett turned in one of the greatest defensive performances in Bills history, sacking Randall Cunningham four times while making 16 tackles and forcing three fumbles.

Despite that scintillating showing, I still questioned whether Bills had given up too much (two first-round picks, one second-round pick, and a two-time 1,000-yard rusher) to acquire Bennett from Indianapolis. I and other skeptics felt a lot better about the trade after Thurman Thomas, Buffalo's second-round pick in the 1988 draft, blossomed into an all-time great. I still contend had they not struck gold with Thomas, history would not have treated that Bennett trade so glowingly.

Thomas became another huge piece of the puzzle for an up-and-coming team that had made progress during that strike-interrupted, 7–8 season. I've come to really like Thomas—much more so than I did during his early years with the Bills when he could become quite feisty with the media. I had my run-ins with him back then, but over time we ironed things out, and I really enjoy being in his company. There's nothing like it when you get Thomas laughing. He has this cackle that becomes contagious. I can see why his teammates loved him.

And, man, what a player he was. He remains the last Bills player to win the NFL's MVP award (back in 1991) and would go on to supplant O.J. Simpson as the team's all-time rushing leader and also establish himself as the Bills' third all-time leading receiver. His fire on and off the field can be attributed to him feeling discounted, especially during that 1988 draft when seven running backs were taken before him, and he sunk to the middle of the second round. As Kent Hull said, "Thurman played with a chip on his shoulder the size of Rich Stadium."

Whenever the Bills played in Miami, Thomas would go out early to do his stretching close to the stands so he could hear the taunts and insults from Dolphins fans. He did this on purpose because he knew those antagonists would get him pissed off and fired up for that day's game. Hey, whatever it takes. Michael Jordan used to do similar things.

He'd find some slight to motivate himself further, and if there wasn't a real slight to latch onto, he'd concoct one. Many times Thomas would find perceived slights in what was written or spoken about him. During training camp in Fredonia, New York, Levy brought in this woman who used to work at CBS sports as a media consultant. I got this brilliant idea of compiling Thomas' greatest rants against the media and playing it for him to get his reaction. There was one clip when Thomas was asked something about the offense after a game, in which the Bills had scored 44 points and he went into a tirade, shouting into our microphones, "Don't you think 44 points is enough mother-bleeping points?"

We sat Thomas down in a dorm room at camp and had him watch that blowup and others from earlier in his career. I asked him how he would react to those questions now that he and his teammates had worked with a media consultant, and he just started laughing. He's come a long, long way since those angry-at-the-world days, and our relationship has come a long, long way, too.

People tend to forget how risky a pick it was because of questions surrounding a knee injury Thomas had suffered at Oklahoma State during his junior year. The Bills did their due diligence, and their medical staff obviously checked him out thoroughly. Running backs coach Elijah Pitts personally worked Thomas out and had a long discussion with his college coach. Kelly—and what would later become the no-huddle offense—benefitted greatly from Thomas' running, receiving, and pass blocking skills. The Thurminator would become an essential cog in that high-octane attack.

In addition to Thomas the Bills picked up nose tackle Jeff Wright in the eighth round and linebacker Carlton Bailey in the ninth round, and those late finds would emerge as solid starters. Such diamond-in-the-rough discoveries were contributing factors to the Bills success, and a credit not only to Polian, but also to John Butler, Bob Ferguson, A.J. Smith, and the veteran scouting staff. Optimism definitely was building going into the 1988 season. Kelly had shown flashes of brilliance the year before, and I felt if Thomas panned out, the offense would be much improved. I also expected Bennett would be strong from the start after having a half season and a full offseason under his belt, and defensive coordinator Walt Corey would devise creative schemes to unleash Biscuit and Bruce Smith on opposing quarterbacks.

Like so many others, I was really looking forward to it, and then a bomb dropped just 48 hours before the season opener. I was working a fan event at the stadium on Friday afternoon when news broke that Smith had been suspended four games for violating the league's drug policy. Talk about taking the air out of the balloon. And talk about horrible timing. I was pissed.

After a disappointing rookie campaign, Smith was starting to come into his own with 27 sacks his previous two seasons. The sky seemed the limit. This was such a huge blow, and I had serious doubts that Leon Seals, a fourth-round pick in 1987, would be able to take up the slack. As it turned out, Seals played solidly, and the rest of the defense stepped up its game. The Bills opened with four straight victories, and three of the wins were by three points or fewer.

Interestingly, Smith returned in time for the Bills much-anticipated matchup against a very good Chicago Bears team at Soldier Field in Week Five. This would be a good test for Buffalo because the Bears still had the core of the team intact from the squad that had won the Super Bowl three years earlier. Mike Ditka's boys proved to be way too much for Buffalo to handle that Sunday, spanking the Bills, 24–3 in Levy's return to his hometown.

That reality check wound up being a good thing for them. They had become a little cocky, and the Bears brought them back to earth with a thud. The Bills regrouped and won their next seven games, clinching the AFC East with a 9–6 overtime victory in front of 78,389 at Rich Stadium. I'll never forget the euphoric scene afterward as thousands of fans poured onto the field and tore down the goal posts. A bunch of us were standing in the tunnel, taking it all in, and it was so surreal because it had been a dank day, and you could see the steam from that mass of humanity rising into the air. It was like a London fog had enveloped the stadium. It was an amazing sight, and as I watched it, I had to remind myself that only three short years earlier the Bills were coming off a second straight 2–14 season, and there appeared to be no hope.

In those days there was this broom closet just off to the right as you entered the Bills locker room, and that's where we would conduct our postgame interviews. I was crammed in there with Fred Smerlas, who had blocked a New York Jets field goal to send the game into overtime. Smerlas joked that he pretended there was chicken wing sauce on the football, and that's why he was able to block that kick. I felt really good for Smerlas, Darryl Talley, Jim Ritcher, and several of the other veteran Bills who had suffered through the thin times. Unbelievably, Buffalo was 11–1 with that November 20th win. I think that was the earliest anyone had ever clinched a division.

Kelly's stats weren't anything to write home about that year. In fact, he threw more interceptions (17) than touchdown passes (15), but I thought he was doing a much better job of managing the game, and he had gotten away from that unnerving habit of throwing bone-headed interceptions near the ends of close games. Thomas wound up being better than advertised, rushing for 881 yards, and dependable Robb Riddick became the Bills' top goal-line threat with 12 rushing touchdowns. Andre Reed continued his upward spiral with 71 catches for 968 yards and six scores. The Bills' most potent offensive weapon, though, wound up being Norwood. He set a club record with 33 field goals and scored 129 points and had five game-winners to earn All-Pro honors as the league's top kicker.

Buffalo would lose three of its final four, but some of that is attributable to Levy resting a number of his starters in the final few games. It would be something he would do in ensuing seasons, and though it cost Thomas a couple of rushing titles, it was the prudent move. Thanks to their sterling record and divisional crown, the Bills wound up hosting their first playoff game ever at Rich Stadium and beat the Warren Moon-quarterbacked Houston Oilers 17–10. That set up a trip to Cincinnati for the AFC Championship Game and the right to go to the Super Bowl. To be honest, I had low expectations. I didn't like the Bills chances. The Bengals were loaded and led by quarterback Boomer Esiason, that year's NFL MVP. The game wound up being fairly non-descript with Cincinnati securing a workmanlike, 21–10 victory.

Though there wouldn't be a trip to the Super Bowl, it appeared the Bills had built a solid foundation. I was cautiously optimistic heading into the following season. Little did I or any of us know that 1989 would wind up being one of the most tumultuous and bizarre seasons in franchise history. When I reflect back on it, it still blows my mind how many crazy things happened that year. And I still don't know how Levy prevented the implosion from destroying what Polian and he had built.

That Bills team was incredibly talented and incredibly immature. There were some massive egos, and that season the moon and the stars definitely did not align. That year was one of the most exasperating and exhausting years of my career. Bizarre stuff occurred seemingly every day. You never knew what you were going to wake up to. All I can say is thank God there wasn't social media back then, or that team would have blown itself to smithereens and almost certainly never would have experienced the ensuing success it did.

The turmoil actually started before the season did. Smith wound up being tendered a contract by the Broncos that the Bills eventually matched despite Smith advising them to take the two first-round picks they would have received. Wide receiver Chris Burkett held out for a new contract, and Riddick never returned after the NFL suspended him for a drug violation the year before.

The season actually kicked off in glorious fashion, as Kelly fooled everyone, including his coaches and teammates and perhaps even himself, by keeping the football and running it into the end zone in the closing seconds to give the Bills a 27–24 victory against the Dolphins in the opener in Miami. A week later, in a *Monday Night Football* game against Denver at Rich Stadium, Kelly went from hero to goat. He tossed three interceptions, and the Bills defense wound up allowing the Broncos to rush for 201 yards in a 14-point loss. That game, though, wound up being more remembered for the sideline confrontation between Kelly and Burkett, a confrontation captured by the television cameras for all America to see. Two days later Burkett, a second-round pick in 1985, threatened to quit the team. Polian saved him the trouble by releasing him.

Buffalo rebounded in grand fashion that Sunday, as Kelly had his best game as a Bills player, throwing for 363 yards and five touchdowns, including the game-winner in overtime to Reed for a 47–41 victory against the Oilers in Houston. After a 21-point win against the New England Patriots the following week at home, it appeared the Bills' troubles were behind them, and they were going to go on a roll like they had the previous fall.

But during and after a mistake-plagued loss in Indianapolis in Week Five, there were more volcanic eruptions. Early in the game, young right offensive tackle Howard "House" Ballard whiffed on his block, and Colts defensive end Jon Hand smashed Kelly onto the Hoosier Dome turf, separating the quarterback's shoulder. Kelly was going to be out at least three games, and when we showed up for the postgame interview, he was loaded for bear. "Four of the five positions [on the offensive line] are very solid," Jim said, launching into his tirade. "I don't have to tell you guys what position they might have to make a change." He didn't name

House by name, but he didn't have to. Everyone knew who the finger had been pointed at.

I could understand Kelly's frustration and anger, but he definitely had crossed the line, and his critical comments did not sit well with his teammates, the fans, and us in the media. Three days later he would back off his criticism, but it was too late. The damage had been done. Something clearly was festering on that team, and you couldn't help but wonder if it eventually might reach the point of no return.

Frank Reich, who hadn't shown much in the few times he had played in previous seasons, replaced Kelly. And his first assignment wouldn't be an easy one as the unbeaten Los Angeles Rams were coming to Orchard Park for a *Monday Night Football* game. The Rams were led by Greg Bell, the former Bills running back who was part of the three-way trade that brought Bennett to Buffalo. Bell had been a very good player for the Bills, but he was somewhat of a prima donna. Smerlas was among those who didn't particularly care for the running back, pejoratively giving him the nickname "Tinker Bell." A few days before the game, Bell gave the Bills some bulletin board motivation by lashing out at his former team. He accused Smerlas and Jim Haslett of being "rednecks" and hinted that they were racists. And he went on to accuse Levy of being a "con artist."

Bell would have been better served had he kept his mouth shut as the fired-up Bills defense limited him to 44 yards on 21 carries. But the big story of the night was Reich, who threw touchdown passes to Thomas and Reed in the fourth quarter as Buffalo upset the Rams 23–20. That game would be a harbinger of things to come with Reich, who proved to be not only a great fill-in for Kelly, but also one of the finest people I've ever met in my decades as a broadcaster. During his three starts that season, Reich would guide the Bills to three victories, completing 61 percent of his passes for 701 yards and seven touchdowns while throwing just two picks. He'd, of course, become best known for engineering one of the greatest comebacks in football history and would establish himself as arguably the best insurance policy in Bills annals.

Six days after the great comeback against the Rams, Buffalo clobbered the Jets 34–3 at home. Calm had returned to One Bills Drive but not for long.

Just when you thought you had heard it all, news leaked out that Bills assistant coaches Tom Bresnahan and Nick Nicolau had exchanged words and punches while reviewing film the Tuesday following the Jets game. Nicolau, the team's feisty 5'9" receivers coach, apparently connected with an uppercut to Bresnahan's chin, knocking the offensive line coach to the floor and opening a nasty gash requiring several stitches. Nicolau then reportedly got Bresnahan, who stood 6'4" and weighed 260, into a headlock and rammed his head through a plaster wall in one of the offices in the Rich Stadium administration building. During meetings with players later that day, Bresnahan wore a turban-like bandage around the top of his head and a Band-Aid on his chin. I was working at Channel 7 at the time and when I heard this latest bizarre incident I threw my hands in the air. *What the hell is going on over there*, I thought to myself. *Coaches fighting with other coaches? You can't be serious.*

I thought the Bills had hit rock bottom, that things couldn't possibly get any worse, but they did. Nicolau and Bresnahan made up and wound up becoming good friends after the incident, but the bickering continued among the players. During an appearance on Talley's weekly television show in Rochester, Thomas was asked what position needed to be upgraded and without hesitation blurted out: "Quarterback."

A week later, while appearing on a local TV show with Paul Maguire, Thomas was asked about the caustic comment and he stood by his remarks, telling the viewing audience that Kelly wasn't perfect and should stop publicly criticizing his teammates. The you-know-what hit the fan, as columnists and talk show hosts had a field day. In an attempt to put out what had become a full-blown firestorm, the Bills held a press conference in which Kelly and Thomas read statements apologizing for their actions. It was awkward as hell.

After Reich led Buffalo to its third straight win—a 31–17 victory against the Dolphins at Rich Stadium—it was announced that Kelly was healthy and would be returning as starter. Many fans and media weren't pleased with that decision, arguing that Buffalo should keep riding the hot hand. Kelly obviously hadn't done himself any favors with the fans or his teammates when he had thrown Ballard under the bus.

This situation had all the makings of a full-blown quarterback controversy, but leave it to Reich to immediately diffuse the situation. On a team full of enormous egos, Reich was without ego. He immediately said publicly that Kelly deserved to be the starter on ability and merit and reiterated that he was just happy to have been able to tide the team over in his absence. It spoke to Reich's humility and character. He's always been a special person, and that team-first approach he took, especially during that tumultuous time, helped calm, at least temporarily, a potentially explosive scenario.

Through the years Reich would prove to be not only a valuable fill-in, but also a wonderful friend to Kelly. Reich was incredibly bright, and I think he played a key role in Kelly's development as a quarterback and as a person. He really was like having another coach on the staff, and it doesn't surprise me in the least that Reich has gone on to have a fairly successful coaching career.

Reich's a devout Christian, and I think his devotion to his faith has kept him grounded, especially during challenging times. Each year he returns to Buffalo in the summer to present an award to someone who has overcome adversity or played a role in helping others, and I've been privileged to have emceed it every year. He's always been somebody you could count on—on and off the field. I love the guy and enjoy seeing him every time he's back in town.

As fate would have it, the Bills were upset by the Falcons in Atlanta in Kelly's first game back and they would wind up losing four of the next six. That only added to the criticism of Kelly in the locker room, the stands, and media. Following an inexplicable loss to a bad New Orleans Saints team quarterbacked by career backup John Fourcade at snowy Rich Stadium in early December, Polian went off on a few reporters in one of his classic eruptions.

I saw what Polian was attempting to do. He was trying to be a lightning rod. He was trying to provide a distraction, take the heat off his players and coaches, and put it on himself, but it didn't always work. The next week, the Bills lost to the 49ers in San Francisco to drop to 8–7. Although they would finish the regular season against a very bad Jets team in the Meadowlands, I was really worried about where things were headed—not just for that season but the future.

Although the Bills wound up crushing the Jets 37–0 in front of only 21,148 fans at Giants Stadium to clinch the AFC East by a game over Indianapolis, I held no hope for Buffalo in the playoffs. They had limped into the postseason, losing four of their last six, and were scheduled to play the Browns in Cleveland. I figured they would be one and done. And given all the self-inflicted turmoil that had occurred, I figured maybe that's what they deserved.

# CHAPTER 11

## THE BIRTH OF
## THE K-GUN OFFENSE

The broadcast booth at old Cleveland Stadium—also known as "The Mistake on the Lake"—was on the roof above the third deck. It was high up for sure, but I loved it because it was on the 50-yard line and offered a bird's-eye view of the action below. It was a great vantage point from which to call a game.

Neither Van Miller nor I were expecting much when we went on the air from there on Saturday, January 6, 1990, for that afternoon's playoff game between the Buffalo Bills and the Cleveland Browns. It had been such a disappointing and exasperating season for the Bills, a season in which too much action—very little of it good—had taken place off the field. I was exhausted, and a part of me couldn't wait for it to be over. I felt like I'd aged five years that season. The Bickering Bills had made the playoffs by the skin of their teeth, and we figured the Browns would put them out of their misery, which they did. But while losing a 34–30 heartbreaker, the Bills discovered a winning formula. In the muck and mire near the shores of Lake Erie, they had struck gold.

That was the day they discovered their revolutionary, fast-paced, no-huddle offense; the day Jim Kelly turned the corner and started living up to all the hype. Jim threw for 405 yards and four touchdowns in that game, and his stats would have been even gaudier and the outcome different had his receivers not dropped several passes. The worst of those butter-finger plays occurred when a wide-open Ronnie Harmon lost track of where he was in the end zone and let the football and victory slip through his fingers. It should have been an easy catch, but Harmon short-armed it.

Although the outcome wasn't what we hoped for, the game was spectacular—a back-and-forth shootout between Kelly and his Browns counterpart and former University of Miami teammate, Bernie Kosar. Until that unbelievable playoff duel between Josh Allen and Patrick Mahomes in 2022 (yes, that one also ended in heartbreak), this might have been the best broadcast I've ever been a part of. That second half was amazing. What's interesting is that neither Van nor I nor anyone else for that matter knew the seed had been planted that day for the three-wideout offense that's now all the rage in the NFL. It wouldn't be until that offseason, when Ted Marchibroda and his staff broke down the film of the playoff game that a siren went off.

Marchibroda knew what made quarterbacks tick. He'd been one himself back in the day for St. Bonaventure University (yes, the Bonnies once fielded a football team) and the Pittsburgh Steelers and had enjoyed success in the NFL as an assistant and head coach. He could see that Kelly was so much better operating at a quick pace, dictating the action rather than sitting back in the pocket and reacting to it. Marchibroda had a good working relationship with Kelly, who really respected him, considered him like a father figure. Marchibroda was confident Kelly would be capable of calling his own plays in the hurry-up attack and flourish doing so.

Marv Levy and Marchibroda also had a mutual admiration for one another. They both had been in the game a long, long time and had a perspective and wisdom that newer, less experienced coaches lacked. So, Marchibroda felt comfortable bringing the idea to his boss. Levy's coaching career was somewhat old school. Running and stopping the run were his main credos, but he was also open-minded, a flexible thinker. He listened to what Marchibroda was proposing and said, "Let's give it a shot. Let's open things up." I give Levy a lot of credit. He was willing to take a huge gamble. He was willing to go against the grain of what most NFL coaches were doing at the time.

Kelly was ecstatic when Marchibroda broke the news to him. The no-huddle offense reminded him of the run-and-shoot attack he operated for the Houston Gamblers in the old United States Football League. But this offense was different in that it also allowed for the running game to succeed. Once he got to the line of scrimmage, it would be up to Kelly to quickly decide, and it should be noted that, though he loved nothing more than throwing the ball, throughout his career he often audibled to a run because he knew he had one of the most dangerous running backs in the game in Thurman Thomas.

Unlike other pass-happy quarterbacks, Kelly was willing to do whatever it took to win even if it meant less spectacular passing stats. I think this sometimes gets lost when comparing Jim's numbers with his contemporaries and those who would follow. That selflessness spoke to his greatness as a quarterback and became a key factor in the Bills' success.

The other thing that made this fast-paced attack work—and this often gets overlooked, too—is the Bills' superb, well-conditioned, intelligent offensive line. The anchor was Kent Hull, a really, really bright guy, who in essence served as the quarterback of the line. Hull could instantly diagnose the defensive front and signal to his linemates the best course of action based on that formation and the play Kelly was calling. It took a lot of quick thinking, and Hull and Kelly usually were in synch.

There were a few, humorous times when they weren't in synch, when Hull would look back at Kelly before snapping the ball and give him one of these *You're not really calling that play, are you?* looks. Kelly would then see what Hull was seeing and often would change the call.

During the Bills' second Super Bowl against the Washington Redskins in Minneapolis, when Kelly was a little woozy out there, Hull actually was calling the plays. Concussion protocols weren't anywhere near as stringent as they are today, so in all likelihood, Kelly was playing with a concussion during the second half of that Super Bowl. Thank goodness, Hull was out there to help out. I think the Bills' all-time great center actually called one play that resulted in a touchdown pass.

Strategically, the K-Gun (with the "K" denoting tight end Keith McKeller and the three wideouts) seemed a perfect match to the skill-sets of Kelly and the Bills personnel. Of course, you can have the best plan of attack in the world, but if the players disliked one another or the guy calling the plays, it doesn't matter. I think Kelly really matured and grew as a person following the Bickering Bills season. He realized he needed to become a better leader, a better person, and I saw a big change in him on and off the field. The finger-pointing ceased, and Kelly began reaching out to his teammates. He started inviting all of them—and their friends and relatives—to his house in Orchard Park following home games. Steve Tasker said that gesture and those parties resulted in healing some of the divisions on the team. The players grew closer and started understanding each other on a deeper, more personal level. And I think that really helped. When you like your boss or leader, you tend to want to work harder to please them and help them out. It's human nature.

Fortified with a new-age offense and a new espirit de corps, the Bills took the league by storm during the 1990 season. In the season opener against Indianapolis, they unleashed their hurry-up attack, and the Colts didn't know what hit them in a 26–10 thrashing.

The following week, the Bills suffered a hiccup in Miami, as the Dolphins rolled them 30–7. It was just one of those games even good teams experience from time to time: a bad day at the office. The loss was so decisive that Levy wisely pulled his starters early in the fourth quarter. The move didn't go over well with Bruce Smith, who grumbled about it to reporters afterward. He said Marv had waved the white flag too soon. Some fans and media members were worried Levy's criticism was an indication the Bickering Bills had returned, but Levy quietly and forcefully put that fire out behind closed doors, and the Bills went on a roll, reeling off eight straight victories in both dramatic and dominating fashion.

The national media took notice, and soon all the networks, national magazines, and newspapers had jumped aboard the Bills fanwagon. They flocked to town to do features on this entertaining, swashbuckling team. Faster than you could say "Machine Gun Kelly," the Bickering Bills had transformed themselves into the Beloved Bills. Although Kelly's stats weren't spectacular that season (2,829 passing yards, 24 touchdowns, nine interceptions), he did a great job getting the ball into the hands of his playmakers. His connection to his favorite target, Andre Reed, continued to get stronger, as the dynamic duo teamed up 71 times for 945 yards and eight scores. James Lofton became the Bills deep threat, averaging 20.3 yards per catch, and McKeller chipped in with five touchdown receptions. The biggest playmaker, though, was Thomas. For the second of what would become four consecutive seasons, he led the NFL in total yards from scrimmage, putting him in the company of the immortal Jim Brown. Thomas rushed for 1,297 yards and 11 scores and caught 49 passes for 532 yards and two scores.

It was such a dynamic offense. It featured an abundance of playmakers and a quarterback who understood how to take full advantage of them. Interestingly, the man who had come up with the idea for the no-huddle offense was quick to divert attention from himself. Marchibroda publicly credited Levy for being willing to take a chance on this new-age offense and he lauded the players who were executing it to perfection. This was so indicative of Marchibroda. He was such a great guy and so low-key and down-to-Earth. So many other coaches would have boasted how they had spent hours in their football laboratories, plotting this offensive scheme that would change the nature of the sport. Marchibroda just said that it kind of happened spontaneously and out of necessity. I was sad to see him leave after Super Bowl XXVI, but I was happy that he was leaving to get another shot at being an NFL head coach. He deserved it.

To have people like Marchibroda, Elijah Pitts, Walt Corey, Ted Cottrell, Wade Phillips, Dick Roach, Bruce DeHaven, and Rusty Jones on your staff was a huge plus. Those men and several others contributed greatly to the Bills success. And that's a credit to Levy. He hired some fabulous coaches who got the best out of their players.

About the only bad hire he made—a hire who would wind up being a thorn in his side—was Chuck Dickerson. The guy was a backstabber, a toxic influence, and Levy had no choice but to eventually fire his ass. Dickerson, who billed himself as "The Coach," became a Buffalo talk show host who sadly made a name for himself through his incessant negativity and personal attacks. Thank goodness his radio show is a thing of the distant past, and we no longer have to listen to his vitriol.

Although the Bills really came into their own in 1990, I look back on that season with mixed emotions. Clearly, I was thrilled with their success, especially considering how awful the previous season had been with all that bickering and upheaval. But the '90 season was a tough one for me personally and professionally because I no longer was in the booth doing games with Van Miller. Before that season my radio station, WBEN, lost the Bills broadcast rights to WGR. I was crushed.

I appreciated the fact that Bill Polian went to bat for me. He even tried to see if they could arrange it so I continue to do the games, even though I would be doing so for a competing station. But WBEN management wasn't going to allow me to do that. I was also working as a sports anchor at our local ABC affiliate, and people were like, "Why don't you just quit WBEN, so you can work the Bills games?" What they didn't understand is that I had signed a no-compete contract with WBEN, so I was legally committed to them. And what people also didn't understand is that in a small market like Buffalo, you didn't get paid much to work the two dozen or so games you might do a year if your team reached the Super Bowl. Mary and I had two young boys at the time, along with the other expenses that many deal with—a mortgage, car payments, etc.—so it just wasn't feasible. Losing the Bills gig was a huge blow to me. The opportunity to broadcast games of the team I grew up rooting for with a man I grew up listening to had exceeded my wildest dreams. And now that opportunity was gone.

Fortunately, I had my television work and radio talk show to keep me busy during the 1990 season, so I was still heavily involved in the coverage of the team. It was just so strange on game days, sitting there in the press box instead of being in the booth commentating on the game with Van. My timing, of course, couldn't have been any worse. After having broadcast so much bad football, I would have had the opportunity to help chronicle the exploits of the Bills Super Bowl teams. Instead, my mic was turned off, so to speak, for four seasons.

Gamedays and nights were so depressing that I often considered not going. There were times when Mary would literally have to push me out the door. I only live about five minutes from the stadium and on occasion I would wait until about 10 minutes before kickoff to head out.

As I said, my radio and television work kept me very busy that season, and it was nice to talk about and produce stories about the special things that were unfolding. Although that team was very, very good, I didn't think the Bills were a shoe-in to reach the Super Bowl. And I was concerned when Kelly was injured in the New York Giants game in Week 15 in the Meadowlands. Yes, I was confident Frank Reich would tide them over for a bit, and he did so, leading the Bills to a victory in that game and victories in two of their final three to finish 13–3. But I knew that Kelly was *the* guy, and the Bills would need him back in the starting lineup for them to have any shot of realizing their dreams.

Fortunately, the Bills' brilliant record had ensured them a first-round playoff bye, and Kelly was back in time for the divisional round game against the Dolphins. On cue, Lake Erie greeted their South Florida guests with a snow-covered field, and Kelly outdueled Dan Marino in a decisive, 44–34 victory. That would set the scene for what would become one of the most memorable games in franchise history, a game that's known in these parts as "51–3."

The Los Angeles Raiders were all that stood in the way of the Bills' first trip to the Super Bowl, and though I was confident Buffalo was the superior team, I was shaped by past disappointments and misery so I wasn't by any means assuming this was a sure thing. The Raiders showed up a day before and went through their walk-through practice at Rich Stadium, and there's a story Polian tells about the Raiders' overconfidence that may be apocryphal, but it is fun nonetheless. There was a pay phone near the bottom of the locker room tunnel, and apparently one of the Bills security men overheard Raiders defensive end Howie Long griping to someone on the other end of the line that he needed to purchase more Super Bowl tickets to accommodate all his relatives and friends who would be headed to watch him play in Tampa. That info was apparently relayed to Polian and Levy, who mentioned it to their players for further motivation.

Again, I'm not sure if it's true or not, but it's a great tale. And what followed is the stuff of legend. The Bills took the opening kickoff that Sunday and rapidly moved the ball down the field. The Raiders had no answers. They looked as if they were trying to stop an avalanche. At one point during that drive, they were sucking wind so badly and so flummoxed that Long called a timeout. It didn't matter. The Bills scored on that drive and stampeded to one of most dominant performance in franchise history. Afterward, Long said: "I don't think anybody could have stopped them. You could have brought back [Pittsburgh's] Steel Curtain, and it wouldn't have mattered."

It was almost as if 31 years of pent-up Bills frustration was released that day, and many of the 80,324 fans, who had stuffed Rich Stadium, couldn't believe their eyes and their good fortune. *Was this really happening? Please tell me I'm not dreaming 'cause if I am, I don't want to wake up.* It was such a surreal scene. The Bills were about to achieve the unthinkable: going to the Super Bowl. But there was a certain somberness to the occasion, too, because the United States had just commenced the Persian Gulf War. There clearly was a patriotic vibe in the stands. Fans waved American flags, and chants of "U.S.A! U.S.A!" reverberated throughout

Jim Kelly, who completed 17-of-23 passes for 300 yards, looks to throw during the Buffalo Bills' 51–3 dismantling of the Los Angeles Raiders in the 1990 AFC Championship Game.

the stadium. Every so often, you'd steal a glance at the television monitors in the press box and notice that the network had broken away from game coverage to provide updates from Iraq. Scud missiles would be exploding in the background as a correspondent gave his report. This would be going on at the very same time this incredible game was unfolding on the field below us. Your eyes would bounce from one scene to the other. War. Football. War. Football. War. Football. It was all so bizarre.

Back in those days, Raiders owner Al Davis would sit in one of the upper rows of the press box, and I remember watching him seethe. He was like a volcano; the pressure was slowly building. He didn't erupt in the press box, but he probably did either in the locker room or on the long flight back to L.A. We were all scrambling to file our reports the instant the game ended because many of us had to catch a media charter the Bills had set up to fly us to Tampa that evening. That was one of the last years where there was just one week between the championship games and the Super Bowl. There was so much going on and so little time to process it all.

I felt really good for Darryl Talley in particular. He had been drafted in 1983 and had lived through the back-to-back 2–14 seasons when the Bills were the laughingstock of the NFL. Talley had a big game with two interceptions, including one that he had returned for a touchdown. He was one of the most respected leaders on the team, a guy everyone shut up and listened to, and I always liked him because he wore his heart on his sleeve. There were no filters with him. He spoke his mind, still does. If the Bills stunk, he told you so. He didn't hold back. And after the blowout victory, he related a story about what it was like during those last-place years. "Guys used to tell me knock-knock jokes," he began. "They'd say, 'Knock-knock.' 'Who's there?' And someone would answer, 'Owen.' 'Owen who?' 'Oh-and-10,' which just so happened to be our record in 1984. Well, people can shove those jokes now. They are ancient history."

It was also cool to witness the trophy presentation in the locker room. The AFC Championship trophy is named after Lamar Hunt, the Kansas City Chiefs owner who, along with Ralph Wilson, were among the original founders of the "Foolish Club," the name given the men foolish enough to think the old American Football League could go toe to toe with the NFL. Hunt was on hand to present that piece of silver to Mr. Wilson. That was pretty special. It wasn't until we were on that plane heading south that it finally hit me: *Wow! The Buffalo Bills are going to the Super Bowl.*

# CHAPTER 12
## A SUPER RUN

When I look back on the Buffalo Bills Super Bowl seasons, I'm struck by how different each journey was. Yes, for the most part, the core group of players and coaches that fueled that run were the same, but each year was unique with so many unexpected plot twists and turns. With each passing year and decade, that era becomes more impressive and more historically significant. How the Bills dug deep into the reservoir of their souls and found the resiliency to bounce back year after disappointing year is truly amazing. And even people who once mocked them for their futility realize there was something truly special about those teams and that time. The Bills' perseverance and relentlessness spoke to the spirit of the city and region they represented. These guys just wouldn't give up.

## Super Bowl XXV

We didn't realize it at the time, but the Bills' best chance to win it all was their first chance. And they blew it. Yes, the outcome would have been different had Scott Norwood's fateful field goal attempt from 47 yards not sailed wide right in the waning seconds. But Norwood didn't lose that game; the Bills did. Just as they had won as an organization, they had lost as one, too. They were outplayed by the New York Giants and outcoached by them, too. There were too many missed tackles. Too many missed opportunities by the Bills offense. And, maybe, too many late nights by a number of players who were too immature to delay their party animal tendencies just one more week.

Just as the AFC Championship Game the week before at Rich Stadium had been played against the backdrop of the war, so, too, was Super Bowl XXV. Reminders that America was at war for the first time since Vietnam were all around us. One Bills player, linebacker Carlton Bailey, had a personal connection to it because his father was an Army combat officer stationed near the front lines in the Persian Gulf. There had been discussions between NFL commissioner Paul Tagliabue and president George H.W. Bush whether the game should be played at all while American troops engaged in what was being called Operation Desert Storm. Bush, like Franklin Delano Roosevelt had done with Major League Baseball during World War II, said it would be good for the morale of the country and the troops in the Middle East for the game to go on as scheduled.

Super Bowls are pack journalism to the nth degree. You're herded around on buses for three media days in which one-on-one interviews with stars and coaches are virtually impossible. The first media session for Super Bowl XXV was staged the Tuesday before the game, and thanks to some wrong turns by Marv Levy's personal driver, Joe Niland, he missed it and was fined. It was actually kind of funny, and Levy made light of it the next day. Poor Niland. These were the days before GPS and Google Maps.

Super Bowls are bears to cover not only because you've already told the majority of the stories about your team, but also because your access is so limited and you're doing interviews in the presence of 3,000-to-5,000 credentialed media. I don't recall many significant stories coming out of those sessions that week other than Bruce Smith announcing that he had supplanted the Giants' Lawrence Taylor as the NFL's best defensive player. L.T. was in the latter part of his career, and Smith was just entering his prime and coming off a 19-sack season, so there was truth to what he was saying. But why poke the sleeping bear? The Associated Press had in fact voted Smith Defensive Player of the Year. It would have been better if he had just kept his trap shut and let his play speak for him.

I was really depressed the morning of the game because that's when the realization hit me like a blindside sack that I wouldn't be broadcasting the first ever Bills Super Bowl game with Van Miller. But I would get over it once I got to the stadium known as the Big Sombrero. When I got off the media bus, I immediately saw what extraordinary measures were being taking to secure America's biggest sporting event. Our military knew this would be an ideal target for a terrorist attack, so the stadium was turned into a fortress of sorts. Barbed-wire fences and concrete slabs circled the periphery of the stadium. That afternoon was the first time I remember going through metal detectors and searches before entering a sporting event. Now, of course, it's the norm.

The airspace within 30 miles of the stadium was closed off, and there were numerous Apache helicopters—capable of engaging fighter jets in combat—buzzing above and around the stadium. It was all somewhat unnerving, but it also gave you a sense of the heightened security that wouldn't let anyone do harm in that stadium that night. As was the case at the AFC Championship Game, you couldn't help but notice the patriotic fervor inside Tampa Stadium. The war in the Persian Gulf had ratchetted up several notches in the days leading up to the Super Bowl, and many noted that it was fitting that two teams boasting the colors red, white, and blue were about to play one another. Whitney Houston's rousing rendition of the National Anthem amid a roaring jet flyover only added to the intensity. Everyone was ready for some football, and what transpired truly was a game for the ages.

The Bills were 6.5-point favorites, and like the oddsmakers, I believed they were the more talented team. They were on a roll, having piled up 95 combined points against Don Shula's Miami Dolphins and Al Davis' Los Angeles Raiders. But being Buffalo born and bred, I braced myself for once more having my heart broken, and it was.

What I've learned from all my years of covering football is that most games usually turn on a handful of plays, and that clearly was the case in this one. I still can't help but wonder what would have happened had Smith got his paws on that errant snap in the Giants end zone. Somehow quarterback Jeff Hostetler managed to prevent Smith from wresting that ball away from him, and the Bills had to settle for a safety that made the score 12–3 midway through the second quarter. Had Buffalo gone up 17–3 at that point, perhaps the Giants would have had to abandon their

Ottis Anderson-centric running attack, and Hostetler would have had to pass more.

Alas, we'll never know. The Bills defensive stalwarts didn't exactly distinguish themselves that game. They missed so many tackles and allowed Anderson to keep moving the chains and keep the ball out of Jim Kelly's hands. And the Bills failed to take advantage of Giants defensive coordinator Bill Belichick's unusual defense, which often featured just two down linemen. Thurman Thomas wound up having a great game, accounting for 190 yards (135 rushing and 55 receiving) on 20 touches. But there were times when they actually should have run him more because of Belichick's exotic formation and the abilities of Thomas and an offensive line that was among the best in football.

It, of course, came down to the Bills asking Norwood to do something he had never done before (kick a 47-yard field goal on grass) in the biggest game of the year and his life. I was heading down to do my live television shots back to Channel 7 in Buffalo when I saw the missed kick on a TV monitor. I was stunned, but I didn't have time to dwell on anything because I was in full-scramble mode to get postgame reaction.

And the first guy I wound up getting was Norwood. In fact, I believe I was the first one to interview him. It was one of the most memorable and painful interviews I've ever done. He was understandably down and despondent, but I had always found Norwood to be a stand-up guy, and on the lowest night of his life, he stood the tallest. He matter of factly took me through every step of the kick that went awry. At one point Norwood got choked up, and I did, too. He had tears in his eyes. I don't remember if I was crying, too, but I do remember having trouble getting through my questions, as my voice cracked several times. I don't think Norwood told me anything different than he said to the other reporters when he held court in the locker room. I just remember it all being incredibly emotional. Norwood is such a good guy, and you just wished you could somehow comfort him. I felt helpless. And so did everyone else

After Scott Norwood missed the game-winning field goal in Super Bowl XXV, I spoke to him, and it was one of the most painful interviews I've ever done. To his credit, on the lowest night of his life, he stood the tallest by answering the questions in stand-up fashion.

who knew him and cared for him, especially special teams coach Bruce DeHaven, who was standing nearby and stuck by Norwood throughout that horrible night. Reporters, who went into the locker room to interview Norwood, told me he stayed there for a good hour, answering question after question after question about the worst moment of his life. I don't think I could have done that. And I don't know too many people who could have either. But that was Norwood, and it spoke to his courage and character.

After playing golf at Kelly's charity tournament the next summer, a bunch of us, including Bill Polian, went out for a few beers. Polian told a story about how he had attended a mass with several of his players the morning of the Super Bowl and how Kelly read an inspirational Bible passage. Polian said he took it as a good omen, a sign that God was about to welcome the Bills to football's promised land. Sadly, it was not to be.

## Super Bowl XXVI

Despite the pain of "Wide Right," fans and pundits near and far were really bullish on the future of the Buffalo Bills. And I understood why. The Bills had a group of star players just entering their primes and they had discovered an offense that figured to become more potent as a result. I knew they had the potential to be very good, but it kind of worried me that the wizards of odds in Vegas, as well as many national football experts, had installed them as Super Bowl favorites. When you're a Buffalonian, you're always fearful of your dreams being shattered, so my optimism was somewhat guarded.

Before that season started something really cool happened to me, thanks to Bill Polian. The Bills general manager valued loyalty above all else and he knew I was down because I was no longer doing the games. So he asked me to come to his office and he handed me a box. I opened it up to find an AFC Championship watch like the ones he had given to all the players, coaches, and support personnel at One Bills Drive. I was stunned, didn't know what to say. I can't tell you how much I appreciated that, and it really picked up my spirits and also gave me hope that when the radio rights came up again in a few years that I would be back with Van Miller in the booth.

The Bills opened the season like a team on a mission, winning their first five games and 10 of their first 11. And what made that start all the more impressive is that it was being done mostly without Bruce Smith, who was battling a knee injury that would limit him to just five games total. Defensively, the linebacking corps of Cornelius Bennett, Shane Conlan, and Darryl Talley took up much of the slack. But the real story was the offense, especially Jim Kelly. He was healthy that season and at the top of his game, passing for 3,844 yards and a team record 33 touchdowns. In the second game of the season, the Pittsburgh Steelers came to town, and Kelly enjoyed the best statistical game of his career, tossing six touchdown passes and accumulating 363 yards as the Bills romped 52–34.

Buffalo's win-streak was interrupted with a 33–6 thrashing by the Chiefs in Kansas City in Week Six in a game in which linebacker Derrick Thomas sacked Kelly twice. But there weren't any lingering effects as Buffalo rebounded to go on another five-game win streak. The Bills finished the year with a 13–3 record that would have been 14–2 had Marv Levy not rested his starters in the season finale. Thurman Thomas became the first Bills player since O.J. Simpson in 1973 to be named league MVP after rushing for 1,407 yards and catching 62 passes for 631 yards.

The Bills seemed unstoppable heading into the playoffs, but being a worrywart, I was concerned. After a bye and a rout of Kansas City in the divisional round, Buffalo hosted the Denver Broncos in the AFC Championship Game. Everyone was expecting a high-scoring affair, with Kelly and John Elway trading spirals. What we got instead was a defensive struggle, and the Bills eked out a 10–7 win thanks to Carlton Bailey's pick-six of Elway and a 44-yard field goal by Scott Norwood.

The Bills were set to face the Washington Redskins in the Super Bowl in Minneapolis. Many figured the Bills would romp because they would have such a huge advantage at quarterback (Kelly vs. journeyman Mark Rypien), but I had watched several Washington games that year, and they struck me as a really good team with big, physical offensive and defensive lines.

This, of course, was the game that saw Thomas miss the first two plays from scrimmage because he couldn't find his helmet. Kenneth Davis, who had been an exceptional backup for the Bills that season with 624 rushing yards, filled in for those two plays. Kelly called his number on one of the plays, which the Bills had perfectly blocked, but Davis misread it and was stopped for little yardage. Though the play seemed inconsequential at the time, it would become one of those what-if moments in Bills history. The feeling is that if Thomas been in there, he would have read the blocking correctly and would have been off to the races because the Washington defense had overcommitted and would have been walled off. Perhaps if the Bills been able to deliver a punch like that early, they might have stunned Washington and got on some sort of roll. Instead, they went three-and-out and the Redskins built a 17–0 halftime lead en route to a 37–24 victory. Rypien was named Super Bowl MVP. Kelly played most of the game woozy with an undiagnosed concussion. He doesn't have many memories of that game. And I wish I didn't either.

## Super Bowl XXVII

There wasn't the same sense of optimism heading into the 1992 season that there had been the year before. It's damn hard making it to one Super Bowl—let alone two in a row—and many of us were wondering if this era was beginning to run its course. Ted Marchibroda, the mastermind of the hurry-up offense, had left to take over as the head coach of the Indianapolis Colts and would be replaced by Tom Bresnahan, who had served as Marv Levy's offensive line coach both with the Kansas City Chiefs and Buffalo Bills. I was a little concerned about the impact that might have because Marchibroda had been a great mentor to Jim Kelly, and Bresnahan, though a highly respected o-line coach, had never been a coordinator.

Those fears were quickly allayed when, like the previous season, the Bills won their first four games. The offense appeared more dynamic than ever, as Buffalo averaged nearly 38 points per victory. The second win in that streak will forever be remembered as "The No Punt Game," in which Kelly outdueled Steve Young and the San Francisco 49ers 34–31. The teams combined for more than 1,000 yards of offense, and for the first time in league history, neither team punted. Kelly and Young each threw for more 400 yards, and four receivers had more than 100 yards apiece. There were 18 plays of 20 or more yards and five plays of 40 or more yards.

The Bills were flying high until the Miami Dolphins came to Rich Stadium and throttled them by 27 points. That was followed by a 20–3 loss to the Raiders in Los Angeles. But Buffalo regrouped by winning five in a row. At 9–2 the Bills seemed in good position to maintain their death grip on the division and secure home-field advantage once more for the AFC playoffs, but they stumbled down the stretch, losing three of their final five to finish in second place. The last of those losses was a 27–3 arse-kicking in Houston, in which Kelly suffered strained knee ligaments. As fate would have it, the Houston Oilers wound up traveling to Orchard Park the following week for the wild-card game. Many of us figured Buffalo would be one and done. No one was thinking Super Bowl. The run appeared over.

Frank Reich had replaced Kelly in that loss in Houston and didn't play well, completing only 11-of-23 passes for 99 yards with two interceptions and a pathetic quarterback rating of 23.6. In addition to Kelly, the Bills would be without Cornelius Bennett, and on the opening drive of the second half of that wild-card game, they lost Thurman Thomas to a hip injury.

Back then, the NFL's television blackout rule was in effect, so despite selling 75,141 tickets—about 5,000 shy of capacity—no one in Western or Central New York was able to watch it legally. Given the ugly way things started out, it was just as well. Oilers quarterback Warren Moon continued the hot hand he had shown the week before, completing 19-of-22 for 216 yards and four touchdowns in the first half as Houston stormed to a 28–3 lead. I remember calling Mary at halftime and telling her to book a hotel room for a getaway in Toronto the following weekend because I wouldn't be working any more games that year. Thousands had left the game at halftime, and when Reich threw that pick-six to increase the deficit to 32 points early in the third quarter, thousands more headed for the exits. I couldn't blame them. If I wasn't covering the game for Channel 7, I would have left, too.

Well, we all know what happened next. The Bills and Reich staged the greatest comeback in NFL playoff history. While the game became known simply as the "Comeback" in these parts, it became known as the "Choke Job" in Houston. All these decades later, I still scratch my head and ask myself, *How in the hell did it ever happen?*

Certainly, a lot of it had to do with Reich's resilience. He had authored the greatest comeback in major college football history while playing for Maryland, and Kelly was aware of that, joking to Reich as they headed out for the second half, "Maybe lightning will strike twice."

One of the reasons it did strike twice is that the Oilers were incapable of playing ball control football and milking the clock. Under the play-calling of Kevin Gilbride, who later became the offensive coordinator for the Bills and the Super Bowl-winning New York Giants, Houston kept passing. Moon's hot hand finally cooled, and Buffalo took full advantage of the clock mismanagement. The Bills caught a few breaks along the way. On one touchdown pass, Don Beebe stepped out of bounds but came back onto the field, and Bills kicker Steve Christie recovered an onside kick that was intended for one of his Bills teammates. Crazy stuff like that happened, and Reich maintained his cool while calmly chipping away at the huge deficit. Mind-bogglingly, Reich brought them all the way back, and Christie's field goal in overtime wound up giving Buffalo a 41–38 victory in a game that became an instant classic. It's funny, but many of the thousands of people who had left the game early wound up coming back. I even heard stories of people who already were on the road back to Rochester or Canada or the Southern Tier turning around. They wanted to be there for history. In the postgame presser, Reich talked about a piece of spiritual music that had inspired him. One of my sharp producers at Channel 7—Brenda Brenon—was able to locate it, and we included it with the video package we put together recounting the game.

It's amazing the impact the Comeback had on everybody's spirits. It was magical what had transpired, and you couldn't help but think that perhaps the Bills were destined to go back to the Super Bowl a third straight time. This journey, though, would be more difficult than the first two because it would have to be accomplished the rest of the way on the road. In the divisional round the following week, they visited Pittsburgh and wound up throttling the Steelers 24–3, as the Bills defense forced three turnovers, Davis rushed for 104 yards, and Reich threw two touchdown passes, including one to Mitch Frerotte on a tackle eligible play.

The AFC road to the Super Bowl would go through Miami, and during the week leading up to that game, there were many Bills fans and some media members lobbying that Reich remain the starting quarterback, even though Kelly was medically cleared to play. I didn't share that opinion. I felt if Kelly was healthy, he should start. I remember during one of the press conferences that week, I asked Jim to comment about what it had been like to have his good friend, Reich, tide the team over in his absence. I was just looking to get a comment on Reich. I wasn't intimating in any way that Reich should be starting. But Kelly, bless his heart, totally misinterpreted my question and wound up giving me a snarky answer and embarrassing me in front of my peers.

To his credit and this was so in keeping with his character—Reich again put the kibosh on any talk of him starting. Jim started that week and played a solid game despite two interceptions, completing 17-of-24 attempts and tossing one touchdown pass. Kelly quickly saw that the Dolphins couldn't stop the running game, so he stuck the ball often into the guts of Thomas and Kenneth Davis, and the strategy worked as Buffalo rumbled for 182 yards and manhandled Miami 29–10. The Bills were going back to the Super Bowl for the third straight year and would be playing a loaded Dallas Cowboys team in the Rose Bowl.

In the weeks leading up to that game, I heard some rumblings that this might be Bill Polian's last hurrah as general manager, but I couldn't pin it down. Apparently, this was something that he and Ralph Wilson had worked out before the season even began. The two had locked horns frequently, and I think Polian was beaten down from all the meddling. Reportedly, it was a blowup that Polian had with one of Mr. Wilson's daughters that was the final straw.

The likelihood of him leaving bummed me out because he obviously had been the architect of this run and had put together such a great staff and had worked so well with Levy. The only saving grace is that I had tremendous faith in John Butler, the guy who was going to replace him. I had gotten to know Butler well and really respected him. In fact, when it came to assessing talent, he might have been even better at it than Polian, and I think many of those acquisitions—big and small—had Butler's fingerprints on them. He knew his stuff.

One of the cool memories I have about that Super Bowl—perhaps the only cool memory—is that the first media day was in Dodger Stadium. I've always been a huge baseball fan, and Van Miller, Chris Berman, and I walked to the mound to have our picture taken. I remember standing atop that hill, looking around the ballpark, and thinking, *Wow, this is the same view Sandy Koufax had when he was striking out all those batters and throwing those no-hitters.*

One of the national media narratives that week was about how America had grown tired of seeing the Bills in football's biggest game. *New York Daily News* columnist Mike Lupica called them the "serial killers of the Super Bowl." People everywhere seemed to be piling on.

Berman, who had been on the Bills bandwagon since their rise in the late 1980s, tried to come to the rescue of his adopted team. That's when he came up with his us-against-the-world line that "nobody circles the wagons like the Buffalo Bills." I didn't like the way the media was treating us because it was reminiscent of all the crap we Buffalonians had dealt with for decades. It evoked bad memories. I was glad to see Bills fans hoisting signs during that AFC Championship Game in Miami that read: "We're Back! Deal With It!"

Sadly, the Cowboys easily dealt with the Bills. The game itself quickly devolved into a disaster. Kelly was knocked out early with a concussion, and Reich came in but had used up all his magic in beating Houston and Pittsburgh. The Bills committed a Super Bowl-record nine turnovers on their way to a 52–17 blowout loss. The critics had a field day.

At halftime Butler grabbed me by the arm, and I followed him and another Buffalo TV reporter, Brian Blessing, out a back door of the press box to a stoop. Butler and Blessing immediately lit up cigarettes to relieve the stress, and even though I'm not a smoker, I said, "Give me one of those," and I began puffing away, too.

The only Buffalo highlight in a night filled with lowlights was when Don Beebe sprinted about 70 yards and knocked the ball out of Leon Lett's hands just as the Cowboys' defensive lineman was going to cross the goal line to make it 58–17. It was a great hustle play, showing there was no quit in Beebe. And after the game, Mr. Wilson came up to him in the locker room, shook his hand, and told him, "Son, that's Buffalo

Bills football." Although it had absolutely no bearing on the outcome, it's been ranked as one of the 50 most memorable plays in Super Bowl history. It did speak to Beebe's hustle and to Lett's showboating. I guess the Dallas lineman took an awful lot of abuse, especially from gamblers who had nines on their Super Bowl boards.

I despised the Cowboys, so that made the blowout loss even harder to stomach. They were such a cocky bunch, starting, of course, at the top with their motormouth owner, Jerry Jones, down to their coach, Jimmy Johnson, and several of their star players, including quarterback Troy Aikman and wide receiver Michael Irvin. Even Daryl Johnston, their marvelous fullback who hailed from Youngstown just north of Buffalo, seemed to have copped an attitude that week. And that was so disappointing because he had seemed to have forgotten his roots. It wouldn't be until years later when he became a network football analyst—and a very good one, I might add—did I come to view Johnston in a much better light.

A few days after being routed in the Rose Bowl, we attended Polian's farewell press conference at Rich Stadium. It was a somber occasion. I had grown close to Polian and I'm still close to him, so it was doubly sad to see him go. Yes, there had been times when he reacted too emotionally and would have been better served had he taken a deep breath and kept his mouth shut. But he did get better at that as he went along. Plus, I really liked the fact he was passionate about his coaches and players and would do anything to defend them. The proof was in the pudding. He had taken a laughingstock of a team and built it into a Super Bowl contender. And he would go on to work similar magic with the expansion Carolina Panthers and the Indianapolis Colts, where he would get the Super Bowl ring he had hoped to win with the Bills. Although he was a New York City guy, I think Polian got and appreciated us. He became a true Buffalonian.

## Super Bowl XXVIII

Though saddened to see Bill Polian leave, I was so happy to see Ralph Wilson promote John Butler to the general manager job. Butler definitely had earned it and, like so many others in the organization, had busted his butt and paid his dues. As good as Polian had been—and he's a deserved Pro Football Hall of Famer—I felt the Buffalo Bills would be in very good hands with Butler. He was a gentle giant of a man with an engaging personality and a self-deprecating sense of humor. I became close to him, too, and miss him a lot.

Butler was quite comfortable with the media and enjoyed shooting the breeze with us. At the previous Super Bowl, he would hang around for half an hour or so after finishing his formal press conference to chat with reporters. After one of those sessions, he talked in great detail about his experience as a Marine in Vietnam. It was absolutely riveting.

We became even closer once he became GM. Early on in his tenure, he would call me up and say, "Hey, Murph, what are you doing for lunch? Meet me at my house, and we'll go to Briarwood Country Club."

It was in the middle of winter, and there was hardly anybody there, and we'd sit around and talk for hours about football and life. He took an interest in me and others. He was always asking me how my kids and Mary were doing. He was such a personable and down-to-Earth guy.

There were times at training camp when he would invite me to his dorm room to watch film. He'd have the air conditioning jacked up so much that you could hang sausages in there; it was freezing. And the place would be filled with smoke from all his cigarettes. I learned a lot from those off-the-record sessions, and it really helped me, when I started doing games again with Van Miller.

Like Polian, Butler had great respect for Marv Levy and worked well with him. Levy and Polian had given him his first break in pro football when they hired him as a scout with the Chicago Blitz of the USFL. After the league folded, Butler went to the San Diego Chargers and spent two seasons there before Levy and Polian brought him to Buffalo in 1987 as pro personnel director. Butler was a master at finding diamonds in the rough. Among his better draft discoveries were defensive end Phil Hansen from North Dakota State, defensive end Marcellus Wiley from Columbia, and massive offensive tackle Howard Ballard from Alabama A&M. Butler also played a role in convincing Levy and Polian to select Thurman Thomas out of Oklahoma State.

Butler was inheriting a talented, but aging team, as well as a team dealing with the bitter disappointment of three consecutive Super Bowl losses. I definitely thought they were trending downward. Not in a million years did I think they would become the first team to play in the big game four years in a row. After opening with wins against the New England Patriots and the Dallas Cowboys, they lost to the Miami Dolphins at Rich Stadium and then stacked five wins in a row. They were sitting pretty at 7–1 and would wind up repeating as AFC East champs for the fifth time in six years. Jim Kelly did not have a great year statistically with 18 touchdown passes and 18 interceptions, but Thomas remained a potent dual threat with 1,315 yards rushing and 48 receptions. Led by Bruce Smith's 14 sacks and cornerback Nate Odomes' nine picks, the defense was stout.

Although they had clinched home-field advantage in the AFC and had a first-round bye, I didn't think I'd be spending January 30, 1994, at the Super Bowl in Atlanta's Georgia Dome. In that year's divisional round playoff game, only 61,923 showed up at Rich Stadium, an indication to me that Bills fans had grown a little fatigued of their team, too, and maybe were hoping subconsciously that Buffalo wouldn't subject itself to another Super Bowl embarrassment. But the Bills wound up knocking off the Los Angeles Raiders 29–23, setting up an AFC Championship Game matchup against the Kansas City Chiefs. The Chiefs had signed Joe Montana in the offseason, and I was a little worried about going up against a guy who led the San Francisco 49ers to four Lombardi trophies.

But Joe Cool wound up getting knocked out of the game by Smith and Co., and the Bills romped 30–13. The moment the final gun sounded, I could hear the national media chirping. "Oh, no, not the Bills again!"

Oh, yes, the Bills again. Deal with it. But the Cowboys were back again, too. And given the way they'd torched Buffalo the year before, I figured the Bills sadly were destined to become the first team to lose four Super Bowls in four years. I continued to feel that way even when the Bills took a 13–6 lead into halftime. It just seemed to me that some self-fulfilling prophecy was at work by this point. I think even the Bills players and coaches had that feeling in the deep recesses of their minds that somehow, some way the shoe eventually would drop—and it did 45 seconds into the third quarter when Thomas fumbled and Dallas safety James Washington picked it up and ran 46 yards for the tying touchdown. Those would be the first of 24 unanswered points. The Bills would not score again.

I think age coupled with mental, physical, and emotional fatigue had just caught up with the franchise. As Steve Tasker pointed out, the Bills postseason run had taken its toll. The Bills had played roughly the equivalent of an additional full season in the past six years when you added up the playoff games and Super Bowls. That's a lot of football. Plus, the advent of free agency was starting to exact a price and led to the departure of Pro Bowl talent like Will Wolford and Ballard. The Bills could no longer could afford to keep together not only their standout players, but also their depth behind them.

The Bills plummeted to 7–9 in 1994, bounced back with 10–6 records the next two years before slumping to a 6–10 mark during Levy's last season as Bills coach in 1997. Kelly, Tasker, and Kent Hull were among the significant players to retire, and following the 1999 season, Butler faced the unenviable task of releasing three Hall of Famers—Bruce Smith, Thomas, and Andre Reed—on the same day.

Wade Phillips enjoyed some success as Levy's replacement, but soon he and Butler would be gone, too. And the Bills would begin that hideous, unfathomable playoff drought. Over time, history has come to judge those Super Bowl teams with great fondness—and deservedly so. What they accomplished was quite remarkable, especially the perseverance and persistence they exhibited. Some had unfairly labeled those teams losers. Nothing could be further from the truth. I liked what Mr. Wilson said about them. He called them silver medalists. They were indeed that. And it was a privilege to be able to chronicle them and get to know them.

# CHAPTER 13
## THE PEGULAS KEEP THE BILLS IN BUFFALO

Ralph Wilson's death on March 25, 2014, was greeted with great sadness. The well-deserved tributes flowed, as did the questions, including the billion-dollar one: was the franchise that Mr. Wilson had brought to town and kept there for 64 years going to leave?

Like many, I felt great trepidation about what lay ahead. I never took for granted how great it had been to have an NFL franchise in my backyard. I fully understood it probably didn't make any sense whatsoever for us to still have a team, considering we were only the 52$^{nd}$ largest television market in the United States and we weren't exactly overflowing with Fortune 500 companies and huge corporate advertising dollars. The league had grown dramatically, and we had shrunk dramatically since Mr. Wilson brought the team to our city in 1960. The NFL and Buffalo no longer looked like a great fit.

My uncertainties and fears only worsened after we interviewed Peter King on our Buffalo Bills radio show the day after Mr. Wilson's death. King had made his mark with *Sports Illustrated*'s highly respected and exhaustive "Monday Morning Quarterback" column. He was really wired into football's biggest powerbrokers. He told me that Buffalo's going to have to find a way to remain viable in the NFL, and it's not looking good. I remember my brother sending me a text with an Irish proverb about how everything changes when somebody dies. I really thought that might be the end of the run. I believed the Bills were about to bolt.

About a month after Mr. Wilson's passing, I attended a Buffalo Sabres game and was sitting in a suite with Hall of Fame goaltender Dominik Hasek, when Mike Gilbert, the Sabres vice president of media relations, walked over to me and began asking me about the status of the Bills sale. Gilbert told me Sabres owners Terry and Kim Pegula were very interested in the Bills and might make a strong bid for them. That got my heart to racing because I saw how Terry had saved hockey in Buffalo a few years earlier by purchasing the Sabres from Rochester billionaire Tom Golisano. I thought to myself, *Wow, they would be the ideal match.*

When I got to work at One Bills Drive that Monday, I told Marc Honan, who was in charge of the Bills multimedia operations, about my conversation with Gilbert, and he said we should go upstairs and tell team president Russ Brandon, who also said he'd heard they might be interested, but he didn't know their level of interest was that high. I'm not saying by any means that I brokered the deal, but I'd like to think my intel might have added some momentum to the process. Brandon took it from there.

After having been so despondent, I was feeling upbeat. The more I thought about it, the more sense the Terry and Kim Pegula ownership plan made. The thing I was most encouraged about was that—unlike the other candidates—they would keep the franchise in Western New York.

A lot of angst had been created by the two highest profile candidates—rock star Jon Bon Jovi and bombastic entrepreneur Donald Trump. But I wasn't overly concerned. Yes, Bon Jovi was fronting a bunch of Canadian billionaires, but I think the Bills experiment playing regular-season games in the fifth largest North American market had been a real eye-opener. The NFL pooh-bahs had to wonder if Toronto truly was an ideal NFL city despite having the requisite population numbers and enormous corporate dollars. Toronto could be an NFL city, but it certainly wouldn't be the same kind of NFL city that places like Buffalo, Green Bay, Cleveland, Kansas City, and Pittsburgh are. It would be more like Los Angeles, where games are more like happenings, events for people to be seen. That's not meant as a knock on Toronto. It is a marvelous, international metropolis that offers so many different entertainment and cultural opportunities. I love the city. In fact, Mary and I have always enjoyed crossing the border and zooming up the QEW (Queen Elizabeth Way) for weekend getaways. I just think NFL football would be kind of an afterthought there. Hockey really is the only sport that stokes Torontonians' passions. They support their other teams—MLB's Blue Jays and the NBA's Raptors—but not to the extent they do their NHL Maple Leafs. The other issue with Canada's largest city—and it's a big one—is it would have to build a new stadium because the Rogers Centre was too small and lacked the spacious luxury suites and seating the league demands.

During that time when the Bills were up for grabs, I remember bars and local radio stations banning the playing of any Bon Jovi songs. They were verboten. I think the ban continues. I know I won't ever listen to any of his stuff again. Hey, what can I say? We Buffalonians have long memories. Anybody who tries to take away our football team is persona non grata in our book.

I never took Trump's posturing seriously. I doubted he had the monetary wherewithal to pull it off and figured he wouldn't even bother subjecting himself to the extensive financial vetting the league would put him through. Plus, he was despised by longtime NFL owners who hadn't forgotten the time in 1984 when Trump convinced other United States Football League owners to launch an antitrust suit against the NFL. The suit fortunately bombed and forced Jim Kelly to come to Buffalo. I didn't see Trump getting the required three-quarters of the votes he would need to gain entry into this most exclusive of clubs. I also didn't want him to purchase the team because I'm pretty sure that he would have moved it. Buffalo was nowheresville as far as he was concerned.

There were other deep-pocketed suitors, but they undoubtedly were scared away by the iron-clad stadium lease Mr. Wilson had signed with New York state and Erie County in 2012. In exchange for more than $100 million dollars in taxpayer money for stadium improvements, Mr. Wilson agreed to a clause that said any owner who broke the lease before 2020 would have to pay the state and county $400 million. Even for multi-billionaires, that kind of penalty has teeth. Owners with designs on relocating the team would be saddled with keeping the franchise in Buffalo for at least six seasons, meaning they would have to be willing to endure huge losses while Bills fans stayed away in droves because they had no desire to support a lame-duck team.

It all made for a perfect storm and opened the door for the Pegulas to purchase the Bills for $1.4 billion. Predictably, when the news broke, Trump told reporters the Pegulas had grossly overspent. He said they got fleeced, and it was a poor investment. Interestingly, that "poor investment" is now worth about $3 billion, according to *Forbes*, and is expected to keep appreciating as the NFL's television network and streaming revenues continue to soar.

In retrospect I credit Brandon's role—not just in courting the Pegulas and holding their hands through the process—but the work he did in prior years that helped put the team on solid financial footing. This was not an easy task given Buffalo's market size and lack of corporate dollars. His decision to move the team's training camp to his alma mater, St. John Fisher College (now St. John Fisher University), undoubtedly was partially motivated by his allegiance to his school, but it turned out to be a brilliant marketing and business development ploy that helped further regionalize the team and ensure more ticket and corporate dollars flowed west from Rochester. His other move: staging a Bills home game every year in Toronto was widely criticized, including by me. Like the fans, players, and coaches, I hated moving a home game to a neutral site even if it was just 90 minutes up the road. But the deal proved to be a financial windfall, enabling the Bills to make many millions more during those Toronto games than they would have playing in Orchard Park. I think Brandon also played a role in negotiating that lease deal with the state and county. He and Jeff Littmann, one of Mr. Wilson's longtime associates, made it a reality with Mr. Wilson's blessing.

Brandon's 21-year Bills career would come to a dramatic end in May 2018. He released a statement saying it was solely his choice, that he was resigning as team president of the Bills and Sabres because it's something he'd planned to do once he hit the two-decade mark, which he just had. But the *Buffalo News* reported Brandon had been subject to an internal investigation regarding inappropriate relationships with female employees, and that was the real reason for his departure. I have no idea what happened. All I know is he helped grow the fanbase, raised millions of corporate dollars that enabled the franchise to remain solvent, aided in the negotiations of that iron-clad lease that ultimately kept the team here, and brokered the deal that helped the Pegulas come on board as owners.

Terry had made his fortune through his oil and gas fracking business, a business he reportedly sold about a decade ago for $4.7 billion. While Bon Jovi, Trump, and others were constantly chirping in the media about their desire to purchase the Bills throughout the process, Terry kept shrewdly quiet. He never went public. The day before the final bids were due, Terry called up the man brokering the sale of the team, and said, "What do you think about $1.3 billion? Would that be enough to do it?"

And the broker reportedly responded, "Well, I think there would be a 90 percent chance of your bid winning."

Terry then said, "Well, what are the odds if I increased it to $1.4 billion?" And the broker told him his chances would increase to 100 percent. And that's what happened.

When the NFL owners unanimously approved the Pegulas' ownership on October 8, 2014, an entire region exhaled. I'll never forget the reaction of one particular caller to a local radio station that day. While fighting back tears, he spent nearly three minutes perfectly summing up what this meant to him—and to us. I don't know if younger Bills fans truly understood what a significant moment this was in franchise history. Since the age of 10 up until that day, I had been dealing with this fear in my mind and my soul that the team might leave. It was like a storm cloud that always hung over the team. And I was not alone in those concerns.

Then, suddenly, that dark cloud had been replaced by sunshine; those fears were allayed. The Pegulas already had invested millions of dollars into commercial development projects in downtown Buffalo. They had put their money where their mouths were. They had saved the Sabres and now they were saving the Bills.

Five days after receiving unanimous approval from their NFL brethren, Terry and Kim Pegula attended their first game as Bills owners. The fans already were fired up because the hated New England Patriots were in town, but the game was secondary that Sunday at Ralph Wilson Stadium. Even a 37–22 loss to Tom Brady's bunch couldn't ruin the welcoming party.

I'll never forget how emotional people—myself included—became when Terry and Kim were officially introduced over the public-address system. As the Pegulas walked across the field with their grown children, the majority of the 70,185 spectators rose to their feet and applauded loudly. It was one of the more memorable days I've witnessed at One Bills Drive. A day of celebration. A day of thanks. A day of great relief.

# CHAPTER 14
## THE McBEANE TEAM

The revolving door wound up revolving again following Rex Ryan's firing with one game remaining in the 2016 season. For the fifth time in eight years, the Buffalo Bills were hiring a new coach, and it appeared there would be a new general manager at some point, too, because Doug Whaley was on thin ice.

It's probably not a popular opinion, but I think Whaley did a decent job given the circumstances. Usually, a general manager gets to pick his head coach, but Whaley wasn't afforded that opportunity. The hiring of Doug Marrone was made by Russ Brandon before Whaley had been promoted to GM, and the hiring of Ryan was a decision by Bills owners Terry and Kim Pegula. A general manager usually gets to pick his quarterback, too, but Whaley didn't really have a final say in that either because that was his predecessor's call, and Buddy Nix did neither Whaley nor Marrone any favors by reaching for EJ Manuel in the first round of the 2013 draft, when many NFL scouts had the former Florida State signal-caller projected for the second round. Manuel was a good guy and perhaps might have developed into a serviceable quarterback had his head coach been a little more committed to him. Instead, he wound up being such a bust that Whaley and Marrone had to convince journeyman quarterback Kyle Orton to come out of retirement early in the 2014 season.

I think the criticism of Whaley was a tad harsh. He came to the Bills with a solid reputation as a talent evaluator for the Pittsburgh Steelers and contributed to one of their Super Bowl wins. People forget that Whaley was the guy who essentially stole Jerry Hughes from the Indianapolis Colts in exchange for Kelvin Sheppard. And he also signed Lorenzo Alexander, who, in addition to being a solid player, emerged as a positive mentor for several young Bills players and helped establish the team's current culture. Whaley also engineered the trade for running back LeSean McCoy in exchange for Kiko Alonso, and the Bills got the better of that deal, as "Shady" turned in several productive seasons. Yes,

I'll admit that Whaley overspent, when he dealt two first-round picks to select wide receiver Sammy Watkins out of Clemson, but I understood the rationale. He was doing all he could to surround Manuel with playmakers in hopes that would enhance his chances of becoming a solid quarterback. But not having a coach or a quarterback of his choosing ultimately doomed Whaley. He became a fall guy for the deficiencies of people he didn't hire.

Despite the playoff drought, the never-ending personnel turnover, and the Bills' sketchy track record of hiring new coaches, I tried to remain upbeat that they eventually would find the right guy. And that finally happened when they hired Sean McDermott. I didn't know much about him, but I liked what I had read and heard. He was an overachieving guy who had played alongside Steelers Super Bowl-winning coach Mike Tomlin at the College of William & Mary. That school obviously has a connection to Bills history. The team's all-time kicker, Steve Christie, and my buddy, safety-turned-color-analyst Mark Kelso, hail from there.

There also were the ties to Marv Levy, and that was kind of cool. At William & Mary Levy coached Jimmye Laycock, who later would coach McDermott. Laycock, who played quarterback under Levy, has a pretty impressive coaching tree. In addition to McDermott and Tomlin, former Bills offensive coordinator Brian Daboll cut his coaching teeth under Laycock as did former University of Maryland head coach Ralph Friedgen and former Atlanta Falcons head coach Dan Quinn, who is best known for coordinating the Seattle Seahawks' Super Bowl-winning "Legion of Boom" defense.

I like the way McDermott had worked his way up the coaching ladder, learning first under the tutelage of Andy Reid with the Philadelphia Eagles before heading to the Carolina Panthers, where he worked under Ron Rivera and eventually became the defensive coordinator for a team that reached the Super Bowl in 2015. So, there were some pluses there. And I felt even better about the hire after I heard the

Pegulas had sought Bill Polian's counsel during the search process, and he had given McDermott a strong recommendation.

Still, you never know how these things will work out. McDermott had never been a head coach, so that was a concern. Would he be able to go from managing a defense to managing an entire team? Or would the Peter Principle come into play, as it had numerous other times with these types of hires? Some were skeptical because McDermott was a bit of a no-name. They viewed this as the Bills going the cheap route once more and also as a sign that no big-name coach wanted to come to Buffalo because things were in such disarray. Although there may have been some truth to those perceptions, I was of the opinion that maybe a no-name, no-nonsense, organized, highly disciplined, super hungry football guy would be just what the doctor ordered following the disorganization that was "big-name" Ryan. I wanted to give McDermott the benefit of doubt and see if he could be the man to finally turn things around.

They say you only get one chance to make a first impression, and McDermott made a good one on me. I was working for the Bills at the time—broadcasting games, hosting their talk show, and writing for their website—and I remember being invited to meet McDermott in the lobby of the administration building when he first showed up. A ton of people—everyone from the owners down to the receptionists—were there. I went over to introduce myself to McDermott, and he shook my hand, smiled, and said, "John, I know who you are." He said he listened to me on the Bills daily talk show, and I thought maybe he was just saying that to be nice. But then he started referencing interviews I had conducted with various players in prior weeks, and I realized he wasn't blowing smoke; he really had listened.

The fact he was familiar with what I did told me a lot about how much homework he had done in preparation for this job. It revealed an attention to detail of all aspects of the organization, not just the football side. It was in stark contrast to his predecessor's lack of attention to detail and it also reinforced to me that McDermott, like Levy and Polian long before him, subscribed to the theory that organizations win. I think Levy and Polian knew what everyone in the organization did right down to the janitor, and they tried to make every employee feel as if they played a role, no matter how small, in the Bills' overall success. McDermott feels the same way.

One of the first things McDermott did was invite some of the core players from the Bills Super Bowl years to dinner. This wasn't like that publicity get-together Ryan had with them, when they did a *Sports Illustrated* photo shoot at the Big Tree Inn just down the road from the stadium. McDermott's dinner with them was much more low-key and was out of the sight of the media glare. He just wanted to meet with Jim Kelly, Steve Tasker, Thurman Thomas, and Bruce Smith, who flew up from Virginia, so he could pick their brains about what made those teams successful and why the Bills were so important to Buffalo. I think he also wanted them to know that they were welcome at practices and games. Kelly, of course, has formed a tight bond with Josh Allen. And McDermott has invited Smith on several occasions to work with the defensive linemen. I think this all speaks to how McDermott is one of those people who leaves no stone unturned.

He talked a lot at the outset—and still does—about the importance of having a solid culture. Some cynical media types and fans immediately dismissed such talk as a bunch of hooey, but I truly believe it makes a huge difference, and one of McDermott's strengths has been the culture he's built at One Bills Drive. These guys genuinely care for one another and also hold one another accountable. That's a winning combination.

A culture, like a successful football team, isn't built overnight. And there can be plenty of pain a team must endure to get there. McDermott's a smart football guy. He did a brutally honest assessment of the team he was inheriting from Ryan and realized he needed to do a massive make-over of the roster. He needed to fill it not only with more talented guys, but also guys who could lead by example. Arguably, the most important personnel move McDermott made was hiring Brandon Beane to replace Whaley as his general manager following the 2017 draft. Some criticized the move as cronyism. (Remember how we heard similar complaints when Polian hired Levy?)

McDermott and Beane had become friends while working together with the Panthers. They would go jogging together and undoubtedly occasionally talked about their aspirations of one day running their own show. During that time McDermott developed a huge respect for Beane's ability to assess talent. And he no doubt liked the fact that, like him, Beane had paid his dues and had put in the hours and hard work, climbing up the ladder from his days as a media intern for the Panthers. McDermott wanted someone as committed as he was and someone who thought like him. He found that guy in Beane.

The GM/coach relationship can be crucial to the success of a team. Sure, there will be disagreements on personnel matters or strategic approach, but the two positions need to share the same vision. And McDermott and Beane clearly have been on the same page every important step of the way. They are joined at the hip, and the "McBeane" moniker is a perfect symbol of their shared leadership style. Over time Beane may have leapfrogged McDermott on the list of most influential people in the organization's success—behind only Allen. And that doesn't seem to bother McDermott in the least. I've never caught wind of any strife or credit envy between them like you do in other successful organizations.

One thing I really like about the makeup of the current Bills roster is the number of hard-working leaders. And this clearly was by design. It's part of the culture McDermott and Beane established. In that first season, McDermott immediately identified veteran players like Kyle Williams and Alexander. They were guys who played hard all the time, no matter the situation, and also were great mentors to the younger players. They set the example McDermott desired.

He understood completely that leadership needed to come not only from the coaching staff, but also from the players themselves, which is why he was intent on adding people who had the work ethic and drive that Williams and Alexander had. And what impressed McDermott even more about those guys is how they rose above the losing and didn't let it drag them down.

When you look at the construction of the current Bills roster, you notice it is filled with guys who lead by example. It helps immeasurably when your team's pace-setter just so happens to be your best player. That's definitely the case with the Bills and Allen, who works as hard as any player I've covered. His teammates see Allen putting in the extra time at practice, in the weight room, in the film room and they figure they better ramp up their work schedule, too.

Early during the McBeane era, the Bills added guys like safeties Jordan Poyer and Micah Hyde, who proved to be hard workers and good mentors. You get enough of these types of talented, high-character guys on your team and you don't have to worry as much about holding players accountable because they'll hold themselves accountable. It makes a coach's job 10 times easier.

McDermott talks a lot about the importance of having one another's backs when adversity inevitably strikes. One of the team-building exercises he implemented, which I really loved, was having individual players get up in front of the team to talk about their life journeys. I think this has contributed greatly to the closeness of this team. Everybody has a different story. Some players have come from difficult backgrounds. Some players have come from privileged backgrounds. If you know where people are coming from and the things that have influenced and shaped them both good and bad, you develop a greater understanding and empathy for them. You get them to metaphorically walk in someone

Buffalo Bills head coach Sean McDermott (left) and general manager Brandon Beane (right), who visit prior to a Week Two game in 2018, have formed a great partnership.

else's shoes—or in this case someone else's cleats. I think this was a brilliant initiative by McDermott.

The McBeane Team clearly has done a masterful job of making over this roster. One can't say enough that the key to success, especially in the modern NFL, is finding the right quarterback. Ultimately, GMs are measured by whether they get this right, and Beane always will have near the top of his resume the fact that he picked Allen with that seventh overall pick in the 2018 draft. Yes, there's a certain amount of luck involved, but Beane and McDermott must have seen some attributes in Allen that made them believe he had the potential to be *the* guy and succeed at the highest level. Beane's ability to move up in that year's draft was brilliant. It was all very measured, no panic. And he wound up not only landing Allen, but also highly-regarded linebacker Tremaine Edmunds in the first round.

Like Polian, Beane has shown a capacity for making blockbuster deals that have made a difference. Before the 2020 season, he traded a first-round pick to the Minnesota Vikings for wide receiver Stefon Diggs, who immediately became Allen's go-to guy, leading the league with 127 receptions for 1,535 yards while scoring eight touchdowns his first year in Buffalo. And, then there was the huge free-agent signing of Von Miller from the Super Bowl champion Los Angeles Rams. There was plenty of risk signing a superb but 32-year-old edge rusher to a six-year, $120-million contract, but it told me that Beane was willing to take a gamble on a move he believed would put the Bills over the top. He knew how close his team was to winning it all and he also realized how quickly opportunities can disappear, so he put all his chips in the middle of the table.

I think the expansion of the analytics department under Beane also has played a role in the Bills' revival. He definitely is a 21st century GM, and it's been interesting to see how the team has incorporated the data it gathers not only for strategy, but also in their scientific approach to training, conditioning, and recuperation from injuries. They know things like the number of steps and the amount of exertion each of their players goes through in a practice and they can use this information to determine if certain players need to back off a bit or ramp it up. All the tools and data they use to measure players and help them achieve their peak performance really is fascinating. It's a brave new world and one that I suspect will continue evolving under Beane.

McDermott is big on messaging and shortly after arriving he began using the phrase, "Trust the process." He said it repeatedly as a reminder to Bills fans, media, and, most importantly, his players that he had a plan and that people needed to keep believing in that plan. McDermott beat the phrase to death, and that led to some snark, particularly during those first two years when the team hit some turbulence. But he stayed the course, blocked out the noise, and kept listening to his inner voice. And his process has worked—probably more rapidly than even he might have expected. I don't think he believed the Bills would be making the playoffs in his first year, but there was some good luck involved there. The Bills finally caught some breaks that had gone against them in previous seasons. And after dropping to 6–10 that next season, as Allen took his lumps and honed his craft, the Bills turned the corner.

One of the things I really like about McDermott and Beane is that they have a vision and the ability to weather the storms, but they aren't intransigent thinkers. They are flexible, willing to admit mistakes and adjust. That occasionally can lead to some difficult personnel decisions, but they don't strike me as guys who are willing to hold on to or keep playing guys simply because they are high draft picks, the way some teams do. They do their best to give players the best chance to succeed, but this is a highly competitive, results-driven business, and sometimes you have to cut your losses and move on—even if it means taking some abuse from fans and media.

When McDermott first came here, I don't think he was keen on going to St. John Fisher College (now University) for training camp. The NFL trend had moved toward staying home at a team's training facilities usually next door to their stadiums. Football coaches are creatures of habit. They don't like to disrupt routines. But McDermott began to see the benefits of going away to camp for a few weeks. Yes, it wasn't fun sleeping in hard beds in tiny cinder-block dorm rooms with occasionally faulty air conditioning. It wasn't easy being away from family. But there was something about having the team gathered together in a place away from the potential distractions of home that facilitated team building and bonding. So, McDermott had a change of heart, and it appears the Bills will continue to go camping for a few weeks each summer.

At the end of each season, McDermott and Beane assess not only their players and coaching staff, but also themselves. It's a healthy, positive endeavor that has enabled them to grow and get better at their jobs. Instability was a contributing factor to the playoff drought. There were times when it felt like we were changing coaches and GMs as often as we changed socks. But the revolving door finally has stopped revolving. The Bills wisely signed both McDermott and Beane to long-term contract extensions. For the first time since the Polian/Levy era, we have stability at the top. I think the sentiment of most Bills fans can be summed up thusly: "in McBeane we trust."

# CHAPTER 15
## ENDURING THE DROUGHT

It became an annual ritual, a standing joke, throughout his retirement and much of the Drought. From 2004 until his death in 2015, Van Miller would call me up before the playoffs began and tell me, "Well, Murph, the Bills almost made it. If only they had won 10 more games." I would chuckle, as I listened to the ice cubes clanging in his glass, as he nursed a vodka gimlet, his drink of choice.

There were a few years during that 17-year Buffalo Bills playoff famine when they came a lot closer than 10 games, including one really, really painful season in 2004, when the Bills missed the playoffs after dropping their season finale at home against a Pittsburgh Steelers team that sat most of its starters.

I tried at times to make light of it. You laugh, lest you cry. I still tell people that Van was the Voice of the Super Bowl run, while I was the Voice of the Drought. In retrospect there was little funny about this way too long period of Bills mediocrity. It was wearing on me, the players, coaches, fans, and owners. Some equated it to the Bill Murray movie, *Groundhog Day*, and it's a somewhat fitting comparison because the games and the years all started to blur together and repeat themselves. Every season, regardless whether the record was 3–13 or 9–7, ended the same way.

I'm optimistic by nature, a glass half-full kind of guy. So, I always held out hope that this quarterback, this coach, this general manager, this team was going to be different. I always held out hope that this was going to be the year and I even made that prediction on several occasions.

My good friend, John Beilein, the highly successful college basketball coach and die-hard Bills fan, would email me and bust my chops. He'd write things like, "Well, Murph, how many games do you have the Bills winning this year? Fifteen? Sixteen?"

I never got that carried away. I just thought a particular year might be *the* year. How was I, or anyone else for that matter, to know it would drag on for almost a generation. Before the Drought ended, my son,

Mark, and I moved an old TV out to the street and he told me, "You know, Dad, we've never watched a Bills playoff game on this TV." It really put the duration of the misery into perspective.

I always tried to remember what Van had told me about how every game matters and how you owed it to the listener to be prepared to tell the story of that week's game to the best of your ability. So, just like the players and coaches who suffered through those games and those seasons much more than I or the fans did, I needed to try to get up for every broadcast. Still, I must admit there were plenty of Decembers during that stretch—after the Bills had been eliminated—when it was tough to be at the top of your game. By that juncture fans lose interest and enthusiasm; they're already looking ahead to the offseason and the replacement of coaches, general managers, and players.

I treated each game individually and with as much enthusiasm as I could muster, but you can't sugarcoat things; you can't paint a picture that this game means more than it does. Bills fans are among the most knowledgeable and passionate in all of sports. You can't BS them, and if you try to, you lose credibility. What you can do during those types of games is highlight any glimmers of hope. For example, a young player may have developed during the course of the season and might have a legitimate future, or one of the veteran players, like a Fred Jackson, Kyle Williams, or Brian Moorman, might have risen above the mediocrity.

As a fan I lived through the Miami Dolphins' decade-long dominance of Bills during the 1970s. But this stretch was more difficult. By season's end it would wear you down, and you'd often have the feeling of: *here we go again.* New quarterback. New coach. New general manager. Same old Bills. And then hope would spring eternal. And you would have teases like the 5–3 start with Drew Bledsoe in 2002. Or the eight wins in a nine-game stretch under Mike Mularkey near the close of 2004 season. Or the 5–1 opening with Trent Edwards in 2008. Or the 5–2 beginning with Ryan Fitzpatrick in 2011. And then—thump!—it would come crashing down again.

It all started with that heartbreaking loss to the Tennessee Titans in that AFC wild-card game on January 8, 2000. That, of course, was the game that finished with the Titans throwing an illegal forward pass (not a lateral!) on the kickoff, which Kevin Dyson returned for the winning touchdown. Music City Miracle, my arse. That was highway robbery. I was doing color with Van on that game and I actually was feeling pretty good about the chances of the call being overturned when it went to replay review. But the longer they took to review what looked and still looks to be an illegal lateral to me, the more concerned I became that they were actually going to let the touchdown stand. And when they did, I was crushed and angry and let that anger be known on the air.

Replay had been instituted for the express purpose of preventing things like this from happening. It was meant to get it right. My feeling was that if they couldn't get something like this call right, then why bother? And it's a feeling I still express today. Let's just get rid of replay because this stuff still happens. They can't get it right. I think one of the reasons "Home Run Throw *Forward*" still stings is that it very well may have cost the Bills a chance of not only making it back to the Super Bowl, but also winning the whole damn thing. Think about what transpired. The Titans went on to reach the Big Game and came within one tackle of winning the Lombardi Trophy.

Ironically, Dyson, the same guy who put the dagger in Buffalo's heart just a few weeks earlier, caught a pass and was tackled around the three-yard line as time expired, preserving the St. Louis Rams' 16–13 victory. The Bills had the league's best defense that season—a stout unit featuring Bruce Smith, Ted Washington, Phil Hansen, Sam Cowart, and Henry Jones. And maybe, just maybe, Rob Johnson might have shaken off the rust from that surprise start over Doug Flutie and played like he had in the regular-season finale when he threw for 287 yards and two scores. We'll never know because the Zebras couldn't get it right.

The Flutie–Johnson quarterback feud would rage into the next season, tearing the team and the fanbase asunder, and following an 8–8 finish, Wade Phillips was jettisoned. Tom Donahoe came to town from the Steelers to take over as general manager, and one of his first moves was releasing Flutie. I don't subscribe to curses, but some would wind up citing the "Curse of Doug Flutie" as the reason for the Bills' prolonged woes. And that narrative gained some legs when Flutie led the San Diego Chargers to a come-from-behind, 27–24 victory the following season—a loss, by the way, that really irked Ralph Wilson. But I think such talk is a bunch of baloney. There are many explanations for the Bills' sustained ineptitude. They went through a busload of coaches, general managers, and players. They botched drafts. They signed the wrong free agents. They suffered some bad bounces and inopportune injuries to key players here and there. And during those times when they still were in playoff contention in December, they inexplicably came up small.

All that said, the No. 1 reason for that lost generation of Bills football is simple: they didn't have a true franchise quarterback. That was in stark contrast to the AFC foe who would torment Buffalo for two decades. The New England Patriots obviously found not only a franchise quarterback, but also perhaps the greatest quarterback of all time. And Tom Brady would wind up dominating the Bills like no quarterback had dominated an opponent in NFL history. That combination of Brady and his coach, Bill Belichick, also played a role in denying the Bills a postseason berth. If that combo was not in New England all those years, Buffalo definitely would have ended its streak much earlier.

When I look back on that era—and believe me I try not to look back very often—I focus on the several Bills players who distinguished themselves. Near the top of that list is Jackson, one of the truly great success stories in franchise history. Steady Freddie was the consummate professional and was a huge find by Marv Levy during his brief and rather forgettable two years as Bills GM. Like Levy, Jackson had played at Division III Coe College in Iowa. From there the running back worked his way through pro football's bush leagues, playing in the Arena League and NFL Europe before the Bills took a chance on him.

He wound up having a career in Buffalo that exceeded anyone's expectations. In fact, you can probably stump a lot of fans with this trivia question: who is the franchise's third all-time leading rusher? That's right. Jackson's 5,646 yards rank third behind leader Thurman Thomas and runner-up O.J. Simpson. He was not only a player you could count on, but also a person you could count on, a really nice human being.

Brian Moorman was another guy you could count on—on and off the field. He was a superb punter—the best in team history—and, sadly, he got plenty of work. He also was an exceptional athlete, one of the best on the team. In addition to being an All-American football player at tiny Pittsburg State in Kansas, he earned All-American honors as a hurdler, establishing several school records. That athleticism would come in handy on the several faked punts Moorman executed during his career. Five times he ran for first downs and he also tossed two touchdown passes on fake field goals. While he was playing, Moorman and his wife established the P.U.N.T. Pediatric Cancer Collaborative, a collaboration with the Roswell Park Comprehensive Care Center in Buffalo that helps kids facing serious illnesses. Moorman was another really good guy.

A player who kind of gets forgotten from that era is wide receiver Lee Evans. He was a legitimate deep threat for the Bills during his seven seasons. He had two 1,000-yard receiving seasons, averaged better than 15-yards-per-catch six times, and scored 43 touchdowns. And what makes his numbers even more impressive is that he did so while playing with six different starting quarterbacks—none of whom exactly set the world on fire.

There also was Fitz, who was so down-to-Earth and provided us with some magical moments before continuing his historic, nomadic quarterback journey through the NFL. He's still beloved in these parts.

Eric Wood and Williams are two other near-and-dear guys who also shone during those dark times. Before Wood became my broadcast partner, he established himself as one of the best centers in team history. He was a first-round pick out of Louisville. Though drafted as a center, he started a few seasons at guard before the Bills moved him over to his natural position. Unfortunately, Wood's career was cut short by a neck injury.

Williams, meanwhile, was a defensive tackle described as the "heart and soul" of those Bills teams, and it's an apt description. Though undersized for his position at 6'1", 303 pounds, Williams had great quickness, great moves, and knew how to beat blockers with his feet and brain. He wound up earning six Pro Bowl selections—not an easy thing to do when you are playing for teams with sub-.500 records—and he ranks eighth all time in Bills history in tackles and sacks. I was so happy that both Wood and Williams had opportunities to be on the team that ended the Drought. They got a chance to experience a playoff game, and I'm sure it's an experience neither will ever forget.

A bunch of fortuitous events came together in order for the Bills to sneak into that final playoff spot on the last day of the 2017 regular season. It made Andy Dalton part of Buffalo sports lore, which is pretty cool, considering he never took a snap in a Bills uniform. When Mark Kelso and I signed off, following the Bills victory against the Dolphins in Miami that day, we had no idea Buffalo was going to make the playoffs. We just talked about how the Bills had ended on a positive note in Sean McDermott's first season, and a 9–7 record gave them something to build on. We knew Buffalo had a slim chance to getting in even if the Cincinnati Bengals somehow upset the Baltimore Ravens.

We wound up watching on a television in the booth and were soon joined by a couple of the Dolphins broadcasters. They were good guys and they were pulling for us because they knew how long it been since we had tasted the postseason. And, lo and behold, it happened thanks to Dalton's 49-yard touchdown pass to Tyler Boyd. Kelso and I hugged each other and we high-fived the Dolphins broadcasters. I received texts from a bunch of people, including several of my play-by-play peers, including Dan Hoard of the Bengals and Bob Socci of the Patriots.

It was a joyous mood on the charter flight back and it was heartening to see how Williams' teammates kept coming up to him. Many were much younger and only had been around for a few seasons of the Drought, so they couldn't even imagine what he had been through during his 13 seasons with the team. And the fact that Williams had announced this would be his last year of pro ball only made the circumstances sweeter.

At that time Wood had no idea about the seriousness of his neck condition. He was ecstatic that he was going to the playoffs for the first time in his nine-year NFL career and obviously figured he had many more games to play before he joined Williams in retirement. And that made the news that Eric received after the playoffs ended all the more shocking and difficult. He still wanted to play but couldn't because of the nature of his injury. It ended rather abruptly for him, but he's such a bright guy, and I'm glad that he's been able to remain connected to the game as my partner.

I'll never forget arriving back at the Buffalo Niagara International Airport that night and seeing several thousand fans waiting to greet the team after the Drought ended. A bunch of the players headed immediately to the fences near the parking lot and began high-fiving the fans. I remember trying to drive out of the lot and having people high-fiving me when I put my window down. It was such a joyous scene and yet another reminder of what the team means to so many.

The Bills wound up losing their Drought-ending playoff game 10–3 to a Jacksonville Jaguars team led by Doug Marrone. The game was almost an afterthought, though Buffalo fans clearly had hoped to stick it to the guy who had quit on them as coach. The game was ugly—especially offensively. And it served as a reminder that the Bills really needed to address the quarterback position in a big way that offseason in the draft. Tyrod Taylor, though serviceable, clearly was not the long-term answer. There was much work to be done in revamping the roster. But McDermott and Company would be able to do so without having to answer incessant questions about the Drought. There was a sense of relief in Bills Nation. I, like most Buffalonians, couldn't be happier that it's over. Time and memory can be funny. Thanks to Allen and the great things that have occurred for the Bills in recent years, the Drought now seems like a thing of the distant past.

# CHAPTER 16
## THE DEVELOPMENT
## OF JOSH ALLEN

After those serendipitous series of events on the final day of the 2017 regular season, we could all exhale. What an incredible relief it was not having that damn playoff drought weighing us down anymore. (Thank you, thank you, thank you, Andy Dalton—and thank you to the football gods who for too long had forsaken us.) In a way it felt like the weight of Highmark Stadium had been lifted from our collective shoulders.

Though the famine was history, there still was much work to be done. And first-year coach Sean McDermott and his hand-picked general manager, Brandon Beane, knew that. The Buffalo Bills had taken some positive steps, but by no means had they turned the corner. The extreme makeover of the roster began shortly after Beane replaced Doug Whaley as general manager following the 2017 draft. All but 12 of the 28 players Whaley had drafted in his four seasons as GM were jettisoned by the time Buffalo kicked off McDermott's rookie season.

I know a lot of people wanted to pile on Whaley, but it should be noted that the last draft he and his scouting staff were heavily involved in produced a few gems, including cornerback Tre'Davious White in the first round, offensive tackle Dion Dawkins in the second round, and linebacker Matt Milano in the fifth round. Interestingly, the Bills had entered that draft with the 10th pick overall and could have selected Patrick Mahomes. But this was before quarterbacks like him and Josh Allen had proven the more-wide open college offenses could not only succeed, but also flourish in the NFL. Hindsight is 20/20, and it's convenient to forget there were question marks regarding Mahomes coming out of Texas Tech. He wasn't a slam-dunk choice by any means, and some even criticized Kansas City Chiefs coach Andy Reid for trading two first-round picks to Buffalo in order to move up into that 10th spot. They're obviously not questioning Reid anymore, as Mahomes has garnered two Super Bowl rings and two NFL MVP awards while establishing himself as one of the top quarterbacks in the game.

Also, word was out that the following year's draft was going to be stacked with quarterback talent, so I'm sure McDermott instructed Whaley to move down and stockpile some draft picks, which he masterfully did. Picking in the Chiefs 27th spot, the Bills landed White, the kind of shutdown corner that's a focal point of a McDermott defense and they also picked up the rights to Kansas City's first-round pick the following year. It would be a pick Beane would parlay into one of the most monumental selections in franchise history.

So, priority No. 1 in the 2018 draft was no mystery. The Bills needed to find their franchise quarterback. They needed to swing big. Tyrod Taylor had been a decent signal-caller for them for a few years, but it was apparent he wasn't going to be the guy who could make them legitimate contenders for years to come. He was a stopgap quarterback. As his lackluster playoff performance in the Jacksonville Jaguars loss underscored (Taylor completed just 17-of-37 passes for 134 yards), it was time to move on.

Some scouts were calling that year's draft the deepest quarterback class since the bountiful one that yielded Hall of Famers John Elway, Dan Marino, and Jim Kelly in 1983. So the Bills would have some opportunities to land a guy who might finally stop the game of quarterback roulette Buffalo had been playing since Kelly's retirement following the 1996 season.

The top-rated signal-callers on most mock drafts included Baker Mayfield, who had won the Heisman Trophy at Oklahoma; Sam Darnold out of USC; Josh Rosen from UCLA; Lamar Jackson from Louisville; and Josh Allen from Wyoming. The problem for the Bills would be moving up the pecking order high enough to get their man. By lucking into the playoffs, they had dropped to the 21st pick overall, but the trade they made with the Chiefs a year earlier gave the Bills the 22nd pick of the 2018 draft as well. So, they had some draft capital with which to wheel and deal. Beane wound up maneuvering with the skill of a professional poker player. About a month before the draft, he traded Buffalo's 21st pick and veteran offensive tackle Cordy Glenn to the Cincinnati Bengals in exchange for Cincinnati's 12th overall pick. As part of a deal that sent wide receiver Sammy Watkins to the Los Angeles Rams the previous August, Beane had picked up a second-round pick. Then, on draft day he sent the pick he'd received from Cincinnati, along with two second-round picks, to the Tampa Bay Buccaneers in order to move up to No. 7. By this time two quarterbacks were off the board— Mayfield first overall to the Cleveland Browns and Darnold third overall to the New York Jets.

In retrospect I believe the Bills might have drafted Darnold had he slipped down the board a bit more, but as it turned out, they wound up getting Allen. The pick was far from universally hailed. In fact, a number of national pundits—and many local ones, too—pilloried the move. Some bemoaned this as another example of the Bills not knowing what the hell they were doing. On the plus side, Buffalo was getting a huge (6'5", 245-pound) athletic guy with a cannon for an arm. But the rap on Allen was that he was an erratic thrower who had played against inferior competition in college. I thought the criticism at the time was unjust. By no means, am I saying I knew Allen would blossom into an MVP candidate and put up historic seasons like he has, but I liked a lot of what he brought to the table—size, arm strength, and athleticism. You can't teach those attributes. I was more than willing to give him the benefit of the doubt and trust what Beane, McDermott, and their scouting staff had seen in him.

I think the Bills' inability to find even a reasonable facsimile of Kelly for nearly two decades contributed to the unfair criticism of Allen early on. There was no doubt he was raw and tried to do too much, which led to turnovers and losses. But I also thought about how it didn't happen overnight for Kelly either. One of the problems with modern sports and maybe modern society for that matter is that we want instantaneous results. We don't allow people ample time to develop and make mistakes and learn from them. Whether it's building a football team or a franchise quarterback, you need some patience. You really do need to—as McDermott preaches—trust the process.

In retrospect Allen couldn't have walked into a better situation, even though the Bills still were far from being a contender and needed to make huge upgrades at numerous positions, especially on offense. The stability of having the same offensive coordinator for his first four seasons played a huge role in his success. Brian Daboll, a Buffalonian and a former player at the University of Rochester, proved to be the perfect coach for Allen. Daboll had worked for two of the most brilliant coaches in football, having won Super Bowl rings with Bill Belichick with the New England Patriots and a national championship ring while calling plays for Alabama's Nick Saban. Daboll and Allen bonded immediately, and the offensive coordinator brought his young quarterback along at a perfect pace. The more comfortable Allen became with the playbook and with reading defenses, the more Daboll put on his plate. The Bills offensive coordinator realized he was working with a generational type talent—a talent capable of doing things no quarterback had done before. Daboll was intent on taking full advantage of Allen's unique skills. Allen appreciated Daboll's creativity and willingness to take the quarterback's suggestions to heart. It was a perfect combination and reminded me a bit of the relationship between Kelly and Ted Marchibroda, though Marchibroda was much older.

When you look back at that much-hyped quarterback class of 2018, it's interesting to note that the two guys with the most question marks—Allen and Jackson—are the ones who have experienced the greatest success, while each of the others have really struggled. The other Josh—Rosen from UCLA—was, according to some, the brightest and most NFL-ready quarterback coming out, but he wound up bouncing from one bad team and coach to the next and is out of football. Darnold had the misfortune of trying to live up to the impossible expectations of playing in metropolitan New York for a dysfunctional Jets team and wound up in Carolina, where he continued to flounder. Mayfield landed some huge national endorsements right off the bat but couldn't produce the wins for another dysfunctional organization, the Browns. Ironically, Mayfield wound up in Carolina, where he tried to resurrect his career there at the same time Darnold was trying to do the same thing with the Panthers. Jackson earned an NFL MVP award and is extremely talented—probably the greatest running quarterback of all time—but I think Allen is a much better passer and a much more complete quarterback.

So, Allen was lucky from the perspective that he was chosen by a team that had a solid coaching staff and front office. Had he been drafted by someone else, who knows what might have happened? You'd like to think that Allen is such an extraordinary talent and has such a great work ethic and drive that he would have overcome any obstacles anywhere, but there are no guarantees. He was fortunate to wind up where he did, and I think he knows that and is grateful for that.

After Allen's up-and-down rookie season, Beane went to work at shoring up the Bills pass protection and surrounding his young quarterback with some weapons. He signed wideout John Brown, and the veteran was in synch with Allen from the start, catching 72 passes for 1,060 yards and six touchdowns. Although Brown wound up suffering several injuries during his second season with the team and was never again the threat he had been, I believe he played a big role in Allen's development.

Of course, the biggest gift Beane gave Allen occurred in 2020, when the GM dealt a first-round pick for Minnesota Vikings wide receiver Stefon Diggs. There had been reports that Diggs was disgruntled and perhaps somewhat of a diva with the Vikings to the point that maybe he could be a toxic influence. But he and Allen hit it off immediately. Their connection resulted in an NFL-leading 127 completions for 1,535 yards and eight scores, as Allen established himself as one of the league's best quarterbacks in 2020. That Allen-to-Diggs combo—which has been celebrated with red, white, and blue, election campaign-type lawn signs throughout Western New York—had a Kelly to Andre Reed vibe to it. But Diggs did raise some concerns with his cryptic comments about the Bills postseason woes after they laid an egg in that January 2023 loss to Cincinnati.

I think Beane's signing of veteran slot receiver Cole Beasley before the 2019 season also aided Allen's development. Allen took full advantage of Beasley's ability to get open and move the chains. In their three full seasons together, they combined for 233 connections for 2,456 yards and 11 scores. Beasley was released and re-signed late in 2022, but wasn't nearly as effective.

So there were many people who played a role in Allen's success, including receivers, coaches, and a general manager committed to helping him succeed. Still, when I reflect on his development, I believe the most important person in Allen's development was Allen himself. His size and physical skills are as obvious as the nose on one's face. As we've seen in his first five seasons, he is a freakishly gifted athlete. One of the first things people notice when they meet Allen in person is his size. The guy is enormous. You can see why defenders have a difficult time bringing him down. It's not only Allen's stature that makes him tough to tackle; it's his temperament. He's not afraid to dish it out. Just ask those poor cornerbacks he's stiff-armed into oblivion. And when you watch Allen throw, you realize that he's been blessed with a rocket launcher. To paraphrase the description once used for legendary baseball pitcher Sandy Koufax, Allen boasts "the right arm of God." I've seen a lot of superb riflers of the football through the decades—guys like Kelly, Dan Marino, John Elway, Randall Cunningham, and Warren Moon—but I don't think I've seen anyone with a stronger, more powerful arm than Allen. And that's such a huge plus, considering he has to play half his games in a place where Lake Erie's gusts occasionally wreak havoc with passes.

There are throws I've seen Allen make that no one else can. I mean, no one. There are times when you just shake your head at how fast and true his passes travel, which enables him to fit the ball into the tightest of windows. These are passes that would be picked off if thrown by anyone else. Allen's combination of size, speed, leaping ability, and fearlessness has enabled him to become the Bills most dangerous runner, especially near the goal line. His dual-threat skills have contributed to him scoring more rushing touchdowns in Buffalo history than anyone not named Thurman Thomas or O.J. Simpson. And that's insane when you consider he's a quarterback, not a running back, and he's only played five seasons.

Because he's so big and physically gifted, I think we tend to overlook the amount of work Allen has put in to become arguably the most potent offensive force in the NFL. Sports is filled with stories of sublimely talented athletes who relied mostly on their talent, didn't work hard at their crafts, and therefore came up short of fulfilling their potential. That clearly hasn't been the case with Allen. Every year he's busted his ass to get better physically and mentally. His drive to become the best version of himself has been relentless. The term "offseason" has mostly been a misnomer in Allen's case. In fact, the work he's put in during football's down times has enabled him to become this otherworldly football player.

After each season he sits down with quarterback guru Jordan Palmer, and the two men assess areas of Allen's game that need improvement and then develop a specific gameplan of how to make that happen. Thanks to Palmer's tweaks to Allen's throwing motion and footwork, Allen has gone from being a guy who completed just 52.8 percent of his passes his rookie year to one of the NFL's most accurate throwers. His completion percentage has reached the low 60s in recent seasons. Their collaboration also enabled Allen to go from one of the least successful deep throwers to arguably the best.

The interesting thing—and Bill Polian has talked about this—is that it's very, very difficult for a quarterback to significantly improve his accuracy. It's almost something you're born with. Hardly any quarterbacks with low completion percentages in college go on to record consistently high completion percentages in the pros. So, in that respect, Allen is somewhat of an outlier. It's a credit to him and all the hard work he's put in under Palmer's tutelage. The unlearning of bad habits can be extremely difficult. For example, a coach might work on improving the throwing motion or footwork of his quarterback, and that quarterback might see significant improvement. But what often happens is that when that quarterback is under duress, he reverts to his old, bad habits. That, too, hasn't happened with Allen. I think that speaks to his football intelligence. He's practiced and absorbed the new techniques to the point where they are second nature, so it's rare for him to revert to the old Allen. Not saying it never happens. But it's rare. He's also put in the time on the mental and strategic aspects of the game. He's watched thousands of hours of film and extensively picked the brains of Daboll and Daboll's successor, Ken Dorsey. As a result of that homework, Allen clearly has become much quicker at diagnosing defenses and identifying mismatches and getting rid of the ball.

Sure, much of this is attributable to experience—the more you practice and play, the more familiar it becomes—but a lot of it has to do with the time Allen has devoted to the process. And he's at a stage now where the Bills offense has become *his* offense. And he has much more latitude audibling into a different play or having input in the gameplan itself. The other thing that sets Allen apart is his ability to make those around him better. He has elevated his teammates. His athleticism and elusiveness enables him to extend plays and cover for protection breakdowns. And his powerful, pinpoint passes put his receivers in the optimal positions to make plays. He plays with supreme confidence, and his teammates and coaches feed off that. There's a belief that somehow, some way, Allen will find a way, no matter the deficit. There have been numerous games when he has put this team on his broad shoulder pads and carried it to victories that would have been losses with quarterbacks less talented and driven than him.

About the only concern people have about Allen these days is his health. He's such a superb runner that you want to keep his legs as part of your attack. But the Bills coaching staff has been more judicious in the number of designed quarterback runs in recent seasons, and I think Allen has learned that discretion can be the better part of valor, that sometimes it's better to slide, run out of bounds, or just toss the ball away and live to play another play, so to speak.

In that AFC playoff game that the Bills frittered away to the Chiefs with 13 seconds to go in 2022, Allen gave it everything he had, occasionally battering forward like a pile-driving fullback on some plays. He took quite a pounding in that game and admitted he needed to take a few weeks off after the season to let his body heal. I think that was a reminder of the toll the sport can take, especially now with a 17-game regular-season schedule, and I think Allen, the fiery competitor, has become smarter about the pounding he subjects himself to. It is a fine line, a tough balancing act. He's always going to go the extra yard for the extra yard and do whatever it takes because that's who he is. But I think he's become wiser about such things.

And I think it was great that unlike previous offseasons he took some time to restore his physical and mental batteries. I know that was one of the concerns McDermott and Beane had about him. They wanted him to take some time off, to get away from football occasionally for the good of his mental, physical, and emotional health.

The thing we have to keep reminding ourselves is that Allen is just 27 years old, so he hasn't even come close to reaching his ceiling. He's just entering his prime. That's a scary proposition for defensive coordinators trying to devise ways of stopping him. If Allen can stay healthy, the sky's definitely the limit.

Allen's personal popularity and the immense popularity of the NFL was underscored when his No. 17 became the best-selling jersey in the NFL before the start of the 2022 season opener. A few months prior to that summer's training camp, we got another reminder of his arrival as a megastar when he joined Tom Brady, Aaron Rodgers, and Mahomes in a nationally televised celebrity quarterback golf match in Las Vegas. Although it was great to see Allen in that esteemed company, he didn't seem comfortable. My sense is that he really doesn't crave the limelight the way some of those guys do. He'd rather just be one of the guys and be with his guys—his teammates on the Bills. When that evening's golf match in Vegas ended, Allen immediately hopped aboard a private jet so he could get back to Orchard Park for a non-mandatory offseason practice the following morning. He didn't have to do that. He could have skipped that OTA, and everyone would have been cool. But that's not who Allen is. He never acts like he is bigger than the team. And I think his teammates really respected that. It's another example of Allen's level of commitment to the Bills. And just another example that despite his $43-million-a-year contract and exploding fame, he remains grounded, hasn't let it all go to his head.

Allen can be a goofball at times at practice, a big kid. He loves keeping things loose, joking around with teammates and coaches. He and his receivers have so many different types of celebratory handshakes after connecting on big passes that I don't know how they keep them all straight. Allen appears to really enjoy the camaraderie as much as he enjoys the competition. I think his fun-loving nature is contagious and contributes to the close-knit nature of this team.

But he also can be driven and super serious. When it's time to work, he's locked in. He goes at it full bore with rapt attention, and his teammates follow suit. It's a classic example of leadership by example.

Allen revels in the success of others. I'll never forgot how ecstatic he was on the field during the Bills blowout of the Tennessee Titans during the 2022 home opener while watching fullback Reggie Gilliam rumble around left end for a touchdown. Allen was happier than if he had scored himself. Gilliam's one of those unheralded, dirty-work guys, and Allen was thrilled that Gilliam got a rare chance to feel what it's like to reach pay dirt. Allen really tries to get everyone involved, tries to acknowledge everyone's importance on the team. That's the type of unselfish leader he is.

# CHAPTER 17
## 13 SECONDS OF PAIN

Most games fail to live up to the hype, especially ones where we're expecting to see two elite quarterbacks duke it out spiral for spiral. And that was true of the January 23, 2022, divisional round playoff game between the Josh Allen-led Buffalo Bills and the Patrick Mahomes-led Kansas City Chiefs.

It didn't live up to expectations. It exceeded them.

It was not only the most electrifying game I've ever broadcast: It was the most electrifying game I've ever seen. It was exhilarating, exhausting, and devastating—all rolled into one. I just wished it had ended differently because if it had, there very well might be a Lombardi Trophy on display at One Bills Drive. The game, of course, will be remembered forever in Buffalo as the "13 seconds" game. And it will hold a permanent, painful place in Bills lore right down there with "Wide Right" and "Home Run Throw *Forward*."

Thirteen freaking seconds is all that separated the Bills from hosting their first AFC Championship Game in two decades. Thirteen freaking seconds—and that damn overtime coin flip—may have robbed them of an opportunity to win their first Super Bowl.

Like two heavyweight champions pummeling each other with haymaker after haymaker, Allen and Mahomes went after each other. Allen threw for 329 yards and four scores and also rushed for 68 yards. Mahomes threw for 378 yards and three touchdowns and rushed for 69 yards and a score. When all was said and done, the Chiefs walked out of Arrowhead with a 42–36 victory.

As exciting as it was, it was a difficult game to keep track of as a broadcaster because there were so many lead changes in those final two quarters, so many momentous plays. Back and forth, back and forth they went, as Allen did things only Allen could do, and Mahomes did things only Mahomes could do. Just when you thought one team had knocked the other one out, the other one would get up and deliver more blows. It was amazing to behold. The game of football at its absolute best.

I was pretty confident when Allen threw his fourth touchdown pass to Gabriel Davis to put Buffalo up 36–33 with 13 seconds to go that the Bills had a great chance of winning the game. And NFL Next Gen Stats backed me up, putting the win probability at 91 percent. Still, you worry because Mahomes is one of those guys you never feel you have beaten until there's no time remaining on the clock. What happened next has been debated to death by Bills fans and reporters, and the second-guessing probably will continue until the end of time.

On the sidelines several Bills were yucking it up after Davis had put Buffalo ahead with his fourth touchdown reception—an NFL postseason record. And I couldn't blame them. There was euphoria in our booth as well as we went to commercial break. It seemed like this one was pretty much over. Like the Miami Dolphins and New England Patriots from earlier years, the Chiefs had become an annoying nemesis—a roadblock to Bills glory—and it felt as if that albatross was finally going to be removed.

A lot of people thought the Bills should have squibbed the ensuing kickoff or pooched it high just short of the end zone because that could take precious seconds off the clock during the ensuing kickoff return. Instead, Tyler Bass wound up kicking the ball through the end zone. No return. No time expired. I might be in the minority on this one, but I didn't have a problem with them kicking it through the end zone. The Chiefs had some dangerous return men—I believe they even had speedy wide receiver Tyreek Hill back deep—so there was risk there. And remember they only had to get into field-goal position to send the game into overtime. What did trouble me—and I didn't notice this until I rewatched the game—was the general confusion on the part of the Bills kicking team. It looked like some of the gunners were thinking Bass was going to kick it short, while others acted like he was going to kick it long. I sensed some miscommunication there. But I don't know if not squibbing it or kicking it high and short was a fatal error.

I did have a problem with what transpired next.

Everyone in the stadium and beyond knew Mahomes was going to try to target his two main weapons—Hill and tight end Travis Kelce. Sure enough, the first play was a short pass to Hill, who caught it at the 30 and raced 19 yards. On the next play, following a timeout from each team, Kelce had a free release off the ball and took a pass from Mahomes to the Bills 31-yard line. Harrison Butker then came on to kick a 49-yard field goal to send the game into overtime.

Two plays. Forty-four yards. No attempts to jam either receiver at the line of scrimmage.

Instead, they were both given plenty of cushion, and Mahomes, who probably couldn't believe his good fortune, quickly took advantage of the loose coverage. It made no sense to me or Eric Wood why you wouldn't try to jam those guys at the line and assign two defenders to each. Instead, the Bills seemed more intent on protecting the sidelines and the goal line, leaving the middle of the field open.

The next pivotal play would be the coin toss, which the Bills lost. You sensed whoever won the flip would win the game because both quarterbacks had been unstoppable, and both defenses were gassed. This game would come down to who had the ball last. Eight plays into the extra session, Mahomes hooked up with Kelce on an eight-yard touchdown for the win.

I was emotionally spent as I wrapped up the broadcast. I felt as if I had just played in the game myself. In the postgame presser, McDermott was grilled extensively about the kickoff and his defense's failure. McDermott's not the type of coach to throw anyone under the bus. He blamed the loss on a lack of execution, but he didn't get specific about who's execution. Was it a lack of execution by the coaches? By the players? Both?

Bills special teams coach Heath Farwell was replaced by Matthew Smiley following the season. Some have speculated that Farwell was made the fall guy and perhaps the real strategy was to squib or pooch the final kick. And no one has explained why Hill and Kelce were allowed to run scot-free on the two plays that set up the game-tying field goal. The reality is that we may never find out what really happened and who's at fault. What we do know is that it will continue to talked about and debated. I was so caught up in the adrenaline rush of the broadcast that the ramifications of the loss didn't really hit me until Tuesday morning. That's when it struck me that we should have been preparing to broadcast the first AFC Championship Game in Orchard Park since 1994. Buffalo would have been playing an up-and-coming but inexperienced Cincinnati Bengals team that would have been underdogs. The Bills would have been favorites to win that game and probably would have been favorites to win the Super Bowl, too, though I wouldn't have taken it for granted that they were going to just show up there in L.A. and beat the Rams because the Rams were a very good team.

Again, as so often has been the case in Bills history, we'll never know. The pain of "13 seconds" carried on for several weeks and months, but once training camp opened at St. John Fisher University, the Bills seemed really focused. They had become the darlings of the Vegas odds-smakers and national pundits. They entered the 2022 season as many people's Super Bowl favorites. That made me a little uneasy. Bills fans have always pined for their team to receive national acclaim, but I think a large segment of them would rather their beloved team be the hunter rather than the hunted.

I thought McDermott and his players did a good job of embracing the enormous expectations. There still was going to be that one-play-at-a-time, one-game-at-a-time mentality, but there was nothing wrong with being confident as long as you didn't become cocky. Lessons had been learned from the previous season, and it wasn't just the lessons learned from those 13 seconds.

They realized if they had taken care of business in the 2021 season opener at home against the Pittsburgh Steelers or in an inexplicable loss to the putrid Jacksonville Jaguars, they would have had home-field advantage throughout the playoffs. And you always have to like the Bills chances when the road to the Super Bowl goes through Buffalo.

As it turned out, 2022 would wind up becoming one of the most emotionally challenging years ever for the city of Buffalo, the Bills, and me. And in the end, I think the stress wound up getting the best of all of us.

Our community was shaken to its core on May 14 of that year when a racist gunman murdered 10 innocent people at a Tops Friendly Market in Buffalo. Sadly, it was the latest in a spate of mass shootings that's become commonplace in America. In true Buffalo fashion, the city and its sports teams rallied during a time of tragedy, as people embraced the relatives of the fallen and raised millions for food banks in the neighborhood where the murders had occurred. Team owners Terry and Kim Pegula, as well as current and former Bills and Sabres players, set up tents in the Tops parking lot to dispense food supplies and decry the massacre and encourage the need for us to love one another. The aftermath of that tragedy was another instance where the City of Good Neighbors lived up to its motto.

More bad news would break a month later when the Bills announced Kim Pegula was "receiving medical care for unexpected health issues." Roughly seven months later, we would learn the severity of those issues. On February 7, 2023, her daughter, international tennis star Jessica Pegula, penned a heartfelt essay for The Players' Tribune revealing Kim had suffered cardiac arrest and was still recovering from what was described as "significant expressive aphasia and significant memory issues." That sad revelation just added to the when-it-rains-it-pours gloom many of us were feeling.

\* \* \*

The Bills seemed focused like I had never seen them focused by the time they arrived at for training camp in late July of 2022. The addition of accomplished pass rusher Von Miller added to the feeling this might be the Bills' year. He was a two-time Super Bowl champion who could be the big-play, defensive closer they'd been missing. In addition to being a great player, Miller was a great teammate and mentor—the kind of guy who could make everyone around him better, especially those young guys on the defensive line.

The Bills didn't waste any time serving notice to the NFL that they would be a team to be reckoned with, throttling the defending Super Bowl champion Los Angeles Rams 31–10 on the road in front of a nationally televised audience in the Thursday night game that kicked off the season. Eleven days later in a nationally televised Monday night contest, they crushed the previous year's No. 1 seed in the AFC, the Tennessee Titans, 41–7 in Buffalo's home opener.

Foolish talk about an undefeated season was put to rest the following Sunday, as the Bills wilted in the 100-degree, field-level heat in Miami and were upset 21–19 by the Dolphins. That forced them to refocus, and they wound up reeling off four straight wins, including a statement victory against the Chiefs in Kansas City. After that things got really interesting, as they dropped two straight games they should have won. One was a loss to the New York Jets, in which Josh Allen injured the elbow on his throwing arm. Western New York held its collective breath and feared the worse, realizing that if Allen was lost for the season, the season would be lost. Fortunately, he didn't miss any time and managed to gut his way through the remainder of the season, as they won seven straight—though many were in less-than-convincing fashion.

In October, our family was shaken by the death of my older brother, Matt. I had always looked up to him and was proud of the things he had accomplished as a judge and the longest-running district attorney in

Niagara County. But I was even more proud of the family man he had become. He was the patriarch not only of his family, but also of all the Murphys. His death, along with my brother Paul's death just a few years earlier, were shocking blows. When you lose loved ones like that, there's a tremendous void that's hard to fill, and you can't help but think of your own mortality. It was difficult to get my mind back on work, but I had no choice, and in some ways, it was good to have something I could focus on besides grief.

Buffalo's reputation for harsh winters would be bolstered during the Bills' stretch run in November and December, as two massive storms led to disruptions and deaths. The first storm, which dumped nearly seven feet of snow on us, forced the Bills to move their November 20th home game against the Cleveland Browns to Ford Field in Detroit. It just so happened that the Bills would have to play in that same stadium four days later on Thanksgiving against the Detroit Lions. That would be followed by a December 1 game in New England against the Bill Belichick-led Patriots, meaning Buffalo had to play three road games in 12 days. That is taxing under any circumstances but even more so when your quarterback is dealing with an injured wing. To their credit the Bills won all three and kept things rolling with consecutive wins at Highmark Stadium against the Jets and the Dolphins.

Enter Mother Nature once more. Another huge snowstorm altered the Bills plans, forcing them to depart Buffalo a day early for their Christmas Eve game against the Bears at Chicago's Soldier Field. In the coldest Bills road game since 1967, they weathered subzero wind chills to throttle the Bears and improve to 12–3. We had all hoped to be home with our families following the game, but the blizzard was so fierce that it had closed the Buffalo airport and forced us to stay an extra day in the Windy City.

We were all disappointed, but Sean McDermott put things in perspective, telling the players that while it was tough being away from your loved ones on Christmas Eve there were many people going through much worse back home. And he was right. The storm wound up being the deadliest in Buffalo history, killing nearly 40 people.

The airport remained closed the following day, but we were able to fly into Rochester, New York, and bus back to Orchard Park. We were all looking forward to seeing our families and sleeping in our own beds. And we were all looking forward to the next game, a primetime Monday night matchup against the defending AFC champion Bengals in Cincinnati. This had all the makings of one of the most memorable games in Bills history. And it was. For reasons we never could have imagined.

# CHAPTER 18
## BELIEVING IN MIRACLES

The Monday night game between the Buffalo Bills and Cincinnati Bengals on January 2, 2023 would be another measuring stick. A win would keep the Bills in the driver's seat for the top seed in the conference and home-field advantage throughout the playoffs. This was clearly the most anticipated regular-season game in more than a quarter-century, and I was fired up, just like the players, coaches, and fans. And the more I studied the game, the more I liked Buffalo's chances.

The blizzard had forced me and many other Buffalonians to delay our Christmas plans a week, so, Mary and I decided to have our big family holiday bash on New Year's Eve, two days before the Cincinnati game. We had a full house, and after the party commenced, I was feeling kind of strange. Yes, I'd imbibed a few beers, but I hadn't overdone it by any means. I started slurring my words a bit, which wasn't like me at all, but I thought nothing of it. I also was having difficulty holding onto a napkin. Oddly, it kept falling out of my hand.

As the night went on, I continued having occasional problems articulating and holding onto things, and my face started feeling funny on my right side. Mary and others were concerned. They wanted me to go to the hospital, but I stubbornly kept telling them I was fine.

The next day, I was supposed to head to the airport for the Bills' charter flight to Cincinnati. But I was feeling worse than I had the night before. I called our producer and told him I was under the weather, and it was probably best that I didn't take the flight to prevent others from catching what I had. I told him I'd likely feel better the next day and would hop in my car and be in Ohio well before the broadcast kicked off.

But as that Sunday wore on, I wasn't getting any better; I was getting worse. And around 4:00 PM, I finally stopped being pig-headed and agreed to have Mary drive me to the Gates Vascular Institute at Buffalo General Medical Center. The instant I showed up, the nurses picked up on the warning signs. They could see I had suffered a stroke and sprang into action. The first thing they did was get my blood pressure under control because there was concern it could ignite another stroke. A lot of what happened to me after that remains hazy, kind of a blur. I was having trouble speaking and had suffered some paralysis on my right side.

I was in intensive care for about 36 hours. I do remember watching the Monday night game from my hospital room with my sons. I was very tired and obviously depressed about not being in Cincinnati to call the game. I wasn't sure I even wanted to watch it, but my boys urged me to; they thought it would be good for me.

Well, we all know what happened with about six minutes remaining in the first quarter that night. That's when Bills safety Damar Hamlin suffered cardiac arrest after making a tackle and collapsed to the turf. It was very emotional watching that unfold and it was probably even tougher for me than others because it struck close to home given what I was going through. As I watched the first responders attend to him, I couldn't help but cry. It was too much for me to handle. I eventually decided I couldn't watch it anymore. Like everyone else, I went to sleep that night wondering if Hamlin was going to make it.

Miraculously, he did, and it's been wonderful to see him recover the way he has and to see so many people from around the world rally around him. Although his situation is different from mine, I have taken inspiration from it. Miracles happen. He's living proof.

Once people heard I wouldn't be broadcasting the Cincinnati game and that my friend, Chris Brown, would be pinch hitting for me, my phone blew up with texts and voicemails from people who were concerned. About an hour before the Bengals game kicked off, Sean McDermott called and left me a message, but we didn't see it because he phoned while the doctors were talking to me, Mary, and the boys. McDermott didn't know the extent of what I was going through at the time—nobody outside our immediate family did—but he obviously was aware I hadn't made the trip, and he wanted to check in on me. I really appreciated that. The Bills' biggest game of the season was just an hour

Following Damar Hamlin's frightening injury in the game before, Josh Allen leads his team onto the field while holding a flag in support of the defensive back.

away, and yet he took a moment away from his coaching preparations to tell me he was thinking of me. That says so much about him as a human being.

And that humanity would be on full display for the world to see in the aftermath of Hamlin's cardiac arrest. McDermott and his players were distraught, watching in horror as the training staff administered CPR to Hamlin. McDermott decided there was no way either team could or should play football that night, and he and his Bengals counterpart, Zac Taylor, took steps to ensure the game would *not* go on. The way McDermott handled a shocking, unprecedented situation with such compassion was a shining example of what a caring leader he is.

When it became apparent I wasn't going to be able to broadcast any games for the remainder of the season, we decided to release a family statement through the Bills that I had suffered a stroke. We wanted people to know the truth. Over the ensuing days and weeks, the outpouring of love and concern was truly heartwarming. I received hundreds of cards, letters, emails, texts, and voicemails from friends and loved ones—as well as from acquaintances I hadn't heard from in years—and from total strangers. Sadly, my phone wound up dying, and we lost many of the texts and messages, so I wasn't able to respond. But I want everyone to know how much their well wishes meant to me.

Marv Levy was among those who left a message that we were able to retrieve. He said he and his wife, Fran, were thinking of me and praying for me and my family and he ended the call by thanking me "for contributing so much to the city of Buffalo, to the game of football, and to our friendship." That was so Levy. He's such a wonderful, compassionate human being.

Another voicemail came from Bruce Smith. The Hall of Fame defensive end is on a regular text thread with his old Super Bowl teammates and he told me that he, Jim Kelly, Thurman Thomas, Darryl Talley, and Steve Tasker were all praying for me and thinking of me. I had never been that close to Smith, but for him to take the time to do that meant a great deal.

I heard from numerous fellow NFL play-by-play guys, including Bob Socci (New England Patriots), Dan Hoard (Bengals), Jeff Joniak (Chicago Bears), and Ian Eagle (CBS). And it was very kind of Jim Nantz to give me a shoutout on CBS' nationally-televised broadcast of the Bills' regular-season finale against the Patriots. I also appreciated how my friends Brown and Eric Wood took up the slack in my absence and began and ended each Bills radio broadcast by saying that they were thinking of me and my family and praying for me to make a speedy recovery and return to the booth. They're good friends and class acts. And I'm so proud of my son, Mark, for getting back in the booth and helping out Brown and Eric as a spotter, just as he has filled that role for me for years. It could not have been easy for Mark, given what happened to me, but I was happy to see him back in action, doing the great job he always does.

I've always had a good relationship with NFL commissioner Roger Goodell, a fellow Western New Yorker, and it was uplifting to receive a card from him, in which he wrote:

> Murph,
> It's just not the same without you behind the mic!
> Hope that you are resting and recovering quickly.
> Make sure you are following your medical advice.
> We are all thinking about you. If there is anything we can do, please have Mary reach out to us.
> Go Bills!
> Roger

Andy Cappuccino, the doctor who played a role in helping paralyzed Bills tight end Kevin Everett walk again, wrote a lovely note signed by him and his wife, Helen. It read in part:

> So many people love you, care for you, and look up to you. I think of your beautiful and loving family—you are the patriarch; and in our community, so many people count on you to do all you and Mary do and report on the Bills. Please know that we are cheering you on.

As Mary and I read the cards, letters, texts, and emails, and listened to the voicemails, I couldn't help but cry. One that really tugged at my heartstrings came from my youngest sister, Di. In a card that contained the quotation, "THERE IS SOMETHING INSIDE YOU THAT IS GREATER THAN ANY OBSTACLE," she wrote:

I know I could tell you this face to face when I see you every few days, but sometimes you have to read something for it to really sink in and really believe it. You have a wonderful life and an amazing career and an incredible family. Every day you wake up, start your day thinking of your blessings, then hit the ground running—don't get discouraged if it seems that the progress is slow. Just keep doing the work, and it will bring rewards. Take pride in all you've accomplished already.

Never give up. Remember Dad clawed his way back...and [older sibling] Paulie did, too. Not only do you have all of us but the entire city of Buffalo rooting for you.

There are scores of others I could excerpt, but you get the picture. Each one struck a chord, made me feel like people cared. I can't thank everyone enough. We all hope that our lives have had true meaning, that we've done something that has had a positive impact on others. As I've discovered in the aftermath of this ordeal, perhaps in some small way our broadcasts have enhanced the fans' enjoyment of the games. Their responses boosted my spirits, especially during my darkest moments.

My doctors were encouraged by my progress and released me after a few days. After I got out of the hospital, I began a rigorous daily regimen of occupational therapy, speech therapy, and physical therapy. The therapists put me through the wringer and they gave me a ton of homework. They were tough on me at times, but that's what I needed.

Other people stepped up as well. My brother-in-law, David, has a really good friend named Tim Farrell, who's a physical therapist with experience in stroke rehabilitation, and he has worked with and pushed me. My niece, Kerry Murphy, is a speech pathologist in Philadelphia and she Zoomed with me five, six days a week for half-hour and hour sessions. All told, Mary figured that between my regular therapists and my additional work with Kerry and Tim, there were times I was doing roughly 16 sessions a week.

Another person who really helped was my friend and former Bills athletic trainer Bud Carpenter. He lives near me in Orchard Park, and I occasionally would run into him at the grocery store or gas station. Unbeknownst to me, he suffered a stroke, too, not long after he had retired from the Bills in 2018. After hearing my news, Carpenter reached out and visited me. During his 33 years working with NFL players, he developed a deep understanding of the psychological challenges one faces during rehabilitations from injury or illness. Those challenges can be as daunting as the physical and mental hurdles. And having experienced a stroke himself, he could relate to me on a level others couldn't.

While working with injured players, Carpenter developed a 24-hour rule. For the first day after the injury, he allowed the player to vent his anger and feel sorry for himself to the fullest. But once that day was over, he firmly told the player he needed to move on in order to move forward with his recovery. And that's the same approach he took with me. "Any time you spend feeling sorry for yourself," he harped, "is time you're taking away from truly trying to get better."

It made perfect sense intellectually, but emotionally it's not easy. One of the most frustrating and depressing things about stroke rehab is that progress often can be incredibly slow. There are days when you feel like you are running in place or going backward. Things you took for granted no longer come naturally or easily to you. And in my case it often was even more difficult to deal with since I've made my living talking. Having to re-learn to do mental and physical things you've done your entire life can be disheartening and exhausting. But whenever I started down the self-pity road, Carpenter worked at snapping me out of it.

And so did Mary. She has been my rock, my glue, throughout this. Of course, that's nothing new. She's fulfilled those roles in my life for as long as I've known her. As I said in my dedication at the beginning of the book, I would not have accomplished what I have in my life without her support and encouragement. And my sons, grandkids, siblings, nieces, and nephews all have played roles, too. The Murphys are a tight-knit family. Always have been.

My season and the Bills' 2022 season ended prematurely. I shed some tears while watching them get clobbered by the Bengals in their divisional round playoff game at Highmark Stadium. I know some fans don't want to hear this, but the Bills were emotionally spent by the time they kicked off that game. They had nothing left in the tank. And that was so understandable, given what they had been through—on and off the field. We like to think of these guys as warriors and gladiators while often forgetting they are human beings, too, with feelings and emotions that at times leave them as vulnerable as the rest of us.

So, a season of great expectations ended as so many other Bills seasons had—with disappointment. Like others, I worry that the window of opportunity is closing, but Josh Allen is just entering his prime and still has upside, so that gives us hope. It's a quarterback's league, and we have a great one, and his best years, hopefully, are ahead of him. In the introduction to this book, I wrote that my dream is to one day exclaim over the airwaves: "The Buffalo Bills are Super Bowl champions!"

As I write this in April 2023, it's still a dream; still a carrot I dangle in front of me. Maybe I'll be fortunate enough to return to the booth and say those words; maybe I won't be. Maybe the Bills will finally hoist the Lombardi Trophy; maybe they won't. But this much is certain: we're both going to keep trying because that's what Buffalonians do. Especially after we've been knocked down.

# CHAPTER 19
## BILLS FANS: FAME AND GRACIOUSNESS

There have been few bigger Buffalo Bills boosters than the late Tim Russert, who would go on to become the moderator of the iconic political talk show, *Meet the Press*, and one of the toughest, most respected journalists in our nation's capital. During football season Russert always would end his show with the words, "Go Bills!" It didn't matter if he had just finished interviewing the president of the United States or the head of a foreign country. It was kind of hokey, but people in his hometown loved it.

Russert was Buffalo through and through. The son of a garbage man he fondly referred to as "Big Russ," Tim went to Canisius High School before heading off to John Carroll University. He's one of those people who left Buffalo, but Buffalo never left him, no matter where he worked, whether it was Albany or Washington, D.C.

I first met him back in 1976 when he was an aide to U.S. senator Daniel Patrick Moynihan. My dad was a state legislator at the time, and I headed out to a public market in North Tonawanda with him to attend a campaign appearance by Moynihan. As my dad and Moynihan pressed the flesh, I followed along in back of them and introduced myself to Russert. We kind of hit it off. Not saying we became buddies, but we stayed in touch. He wound up working for Moynihan for several years before making the transition to journalism as a political correspondent for NBC.

Russert and I would stay in touch via email, and I was always amazed at how plugged in he was to what was going on with the team. The Bills definitely were his pride and joy, and I think they provided a much-needed respite from the high-stakes pressures of his job.

Jeff Glor is another network news guy from the Buffalo area (Kenmore) who I text back and forth with about the Bills. He briefly sat in the anchor chair once manned by Walter Cronkite and Dan Rather on the *CBS Evening News* and he occasionally would give Buffalo and the Bills a shoutout. Glor's been back for some games, and we've invited him up to the booth, but it just hasn't worked out yet. Wolf Blitzer from CNN is another network news guy with Buffalo roots and a strong affinity for the Bills. I've seen him post photos of himself in Bills gear on the Internet, but I've never talked to him or been able to get him to come on the air.

Nick Bakay, the famed actor, comedian, and television series producer, also is a Buffalonian. I've spoken to him a few times on the phone, and he's another one who follows the Bills very closely. He'll bring up the tiniest details about the team that indicates how passionately he is into it.

ESPN legend Chris Berman isn't a Buffalonian, but he might as well be. He grew up a New York Jets fan back in the early 1960s, so he's quite familiar with those great Bills AFL teams and names like Cookie Gilchrist and Elbert Dubenion. I've been with Berman on numerous occasions, and he's a fun guy to have a few beers with and shoot the breeze. He's genuine—not one of these blowhard guys who tries to act like a big shot in your presence.

I consider Berman more of a cheerleader than a chronicler of the team, and that's okay; that's the role he's morphed into and made as part of his persona. Berman jumped on the Buffalo fanwagon before most others in the national media did, adopting the Bills just as they were ascending to Super Bowl prominence in the late 1980s. He wound up becoming good friends with Ralph Wilson and Jim Kelly in particular. Mr. Wilson even asked Berman to be his presenter at his Pro Football Hall of Fame induction in 2009. That kind of caught many of us by surprise. We thought he might ask Marv Levy to do the honors. Berman also makes it back to Kelly's charity golf tournament every year. Bills fans always have appreciated the way Berman has adopted them and has rooted for them even during the thin times. He's the guy who coined the "Nobody circles the wagon like the Buffalo Bills" phrase when people were tiring of the team reaching the Super Bowl. On his desk at ESPN headquarters in Bristol, Connecticut, Berman proudly displays a piece of one of the goal posts Bills fans tore down after Buffalo clinched the AFC East crown in 1988.

Although he spent so much time in our nation's capital, where his father, Charles Goodell, worked as a congressman, Roger Goodell has never forgotten his Western New York roots. He grew up in Chautauqua County in the Southern Tier and still has a summer home there. And I really believe that connection to our region gives him a deeper understanding and appreciation of what the Bills mean to us. In his role as NFL commissioner, he works for all 32 owners, so he can't show any bias, but I believe he's been an advocate for keeping the Bills here. He still has friends in the area and he comes home every summer to play golf, drink beers, and eat chicken wings with them. I really believe he gets us. And he has used his clout to remind the owners that it's important for the NFL to have teams in places like Buffalo, that we underdog markets add to the league's national and international appeal.

I first met Goodell at the wedding of former Bills media relations director Dave Senko. He was an outgoing, down-to-Earth guy, and we hit it off. Our paths have wound up crossing several times through the years, and he's always been friendly and helpful. Back in 1999, when the Bills were mandated by the league to sell a specific number of luxury suites, Goodell called me out of the blue at Channel 7 in Buffalo to tip me off about the requirement being met. Goodell was working as an assistant to then-commissioner Paul Tagliabue at the time. I really appreciated him giving me the scoop.

After Mr. Wilson's Pro Football Hall of Fame induction, there was a huge party in a corporate tent in Canton, Ohio, and the instant I walked in, Goodell came over and said, "Murph, let's go grab some beers." We got our brews and headed off to a dark corner of the tent and we sat there for a good hour, shooting the breeze like we were longtime buds. You'd never thought you were sitting with someone who was calling the shots for the most successful sports league in the world. He was just a regular guy, letting his hair down.

Another time his niece was graduating from Maple Grove High School down in the Southern Tier and she asked Uncle Roger if he would deliver the commencement address at her graduation. He was more than happy to do that, and the day before, Goodell called me up and invited me and Mark Gaughan, the longtime football writer for the *Buffalo News*, down there for exclusive interviews with him.

On another occasion Goodell was invited to speak at the Chautauqua Institution as part of a sports symposium. He didn't want to deliver a speech and instead asked me to moderate a question-and-answer session with him. I figured his handlers would tell me in advance that there were certain topics I should steer clear of, but they told me anything was fair game. This was around 2010, and the status of the Bills future was a hot topic, so I peppered him with questions about that subject, and he was candid and forthcoming. That morning I was in the lobby of the Athenaeum Hotel, and I was looking at an exhibit of old voting booths, when I noticed the name of Goodell's father on one of the ballots. When I looked up, I saw Goodell making his way to breakfast and called him over. I figured he would get a kick out of seeing his dad's name—and he did.

I truly believe that he cares about his home region and realizes what the Bills mean to Western New York because he's from there. That's not to say that he hasn't pushed for things such as the construction of a new stadium. But I think he was thrilled to have the Pegulas purchase the team, and I think he's used his influence when possible to remind his bosses—the owners—that small-market teams like Buffalo contribute to the immense popularity the NFL enjoys.

* * *

People look at me strangely when I tell them my choice for the greatest moment in Buffalo Bills sports history. I think many expect me to say it was the 51–3 evisceration of the Las Angeles Raiders that propelled the Bills into their first Super Bowl. Or the Comeback Game. Or the first AFL Championship. Or the head-of-state welcoming for Jim Kelly. Or O.J. Simpson becoming the first player in history to break the 2,000-yard barrier. Or the end to the Miami Dolphins' 20-game win streak. Or the payback demolition of smug Bill Belichick and his New England Patriots during the 2021 playoffs.

Those certainly are worthy candidates and joyous, unforgettable moments. But to me the greatest moment in our city's rich sports history occurred when 25,000 people showed up in Niagara Square in downtown Buffalo on January 28, 1991. That, of course, was the day after the most painful moment in our sports history—when Scott Norwood's kick

Supporters of the Buffalo Bills are the most rabid—but also generous—fans around.

sailed Wide Right, denying the Bills a Super Bowl victory against the New York Giants in Tampa. That gathering said everything you need to know about Bills fans and Buffalo and the love affair between this town and team.

Even during a moment of such agony, Buffalonians felt compelled to show up, say thanks for the incredible ride, and offer encouragement to the team, especially Norwood. Tell me another place on the planet where less than 24 hours after such despair that 25,000 fans show up. Not only do they show up in huge numbers, but they chant for the kicker, who missed the game-winning field goal, to step to the podium so they can cheer him and tell him they love him. Where does this kind of stuff happen? Only in Buffalo.

We don't have the market cornered on sports misery, though our track record is long and painful. Certainly, those Chicago Cubs fans knew a thing or two about curses, having had to wait 108 years between World Series titles. The Boston Red Sox, too, were familiar with such pain, going 86 seasons between championships, though the Curse of Bambino has become but a distant memory after four titles in this century alone. Even the old Brooklyn Dodgers, who had the annual "Wait Until Next Year" lamentation, finally reached the top of the hill back in 1955.

As I learned from my first Bills game at old War Memorial Stadium 56 years ago, you better learn how to deal with heartbreak and somehow maintain hope. And despite having a PhD in agony, Bills fans keep hoping. The thing I've come to really love in recent years is the philanthropy of Bills fans. They're not only extremely loyal, but also extremely generous. And extremely creative. This was driven home after Andy Dalton delivered the miracle play that cleared the way for the Bills to make the playoffs in 2017, ending the Drought that had dragged on for a generation. More than 17,000 donors contributed roughly $442,000 to the Cincinnati foundation created by Dalton and his wife to benefit seriously ill and physically challenged children and their families.

In January 2021, a day after Lamar Jackson had been knocked out of the game during Buffalo's 17–3 playoff victory, Bills Mafia went to work again and wound up donating close to half-a-million dollars to the Baltimore quarterback's "Blessings in a Backpack" program, which provides meals for kids struggling with hunger. Later that same year, they donated $1.1 million to build the Patricia Allen Pediatrics Recovery Wing at Oishei Children's Hospital in Buffalo in memory of Josh Allen's grandmother. They raised another $100,000 for a Western New York visual impairment organization after a close loss to the Tampa Bay Buccaneers, in which NFL officials blew several obvious pass interference calls. And after Buffalo tight end Dawson Knox's younger brother died unexpectedly in the summer of 2022, they raised more than $100,000 in his memory for a pediatric cancer program.

I think these gestures speak to the goodness that is Buffalo. In other places fans waste their money taking out billboards calling for a coach's firing or an owner to sell their team. Like that ever works. The only thing that does is make the company renting out the billboard space more profitable. In the case of Bills fans, the money goes to addressing real-life problems to make a positive difference. That's pretty darn cool. You won't find a bigger fan of Bills fans than I. Nobody supports their team to the extent Bills fans do. And I absolutely love their charitable side. Millions of dollars have been raised for a multitude of worthy causes. That speaks to the soul of Buffalo.

# CHAPTER 20
## RICH STADIUM, RIVALS, AND ROUGHNESS

Perhaps as early as the 2026 season, the Buffalo Bills will have a new home across the street from the place they've called home since 1973. And that's sure to be an exciting occasion for Western New Yorkers because the new place will have all the bells and whistles you'd expect from a new stadium. It has the potential to be spectacular. But it will take a while—a long while—for the new place to measure up to the old one when it comes to history, tradition, and memories. The stadium originally known as Rich has been home to so many special players and moments. From the highs of 51–3 and the Comeback Game to the lows of all those losses to the hated New England Patriots and Miami Dolphins, it became a place to shout and pout. I'm going to truly miss the joint because for me and the millions of fans who watched games there the past half-century it has become hallowed grounds, a place where generations of fans shared in joy and misery. And having broadcast well over 300 games there, the place long ago became my second office and second home.

I was at the first game ever played there. For that exhibition game against the Washington Redskins, more than 80,000 people showed up, and I think about half of them decided to arrive at the exact same time. This was all new to everyone. The access roads wound up becoming parking lots as cars, campers, and trucks came to a standstill. It was a traffic jam to end all traffic jams. My brothers and I rushed to our seats on the scoreboard (west) side of the stadium and saw Washington's speedy return man Herb Mul-Key sprinting toward us. He christened the stadium with a 102-yard touchdown return on its very first play. It was stunning and it took a moment to register. What a bummer. Although it set the tone for a 37–21 Washington victory, I didn't care. I was too enamored with the new digs. The place was state of the art, and after attending all those games in War Memorial and sitting on that cold, uncomfortable concrete, I had to pinch myself that this was indeed real and not some mirage. Our Buffalo Bills were now playing in a palace the equal of any in the NFL. We felt like we were in the big time and we were.

The opening of Rich Stadium marked the end of a long and at times acrimonious battle over whether and where to build a new stadium. There was talk of constructing a domed stadium in Lancaster, a suburb east of Buffalo, with easy access off the New York State Thruway or perhaps some place downtown, though the trend at that time was to build stadiums in the suburbs. There was a lot of rancorous debating, and the rhetoric was similar to the occasionally heated discussions that preceded the state and county's 2022 approval of the new Bills stadium. There were many who said if multi-millionaire Ralph Wilson wants a new playpen, then muti-millionaire Ralph Wilson should build it himself. Mr. Wilson argued that he didn't have the wherewithal to do that and argued that if Buffalo wanted to keep its NFL team it would have to build a new stadium to replace antiquated War Memorial, which had been deteriorating and was in a neighborhood beset by poverty and crime.

Mr. Wilson drove a tough bargain. He even threatened to move the team to some place that would build him a stadium that he and his fellow NFL owners demanded. I, like many, was very concerned the Bills were going to leave town, but fortunately they were able to work things out, settling on Orchard Park, an affluent suburb south of Buffalo. Some of the costs to taxpayers wound up being defrayed by Bob Rich Sr., a longtime Buffalo entrepreneur who agreed to purchase the stadium naming rights. His family owned Rich Products, the world's largest frozen dairy manufacturer, and he and Mr. Wilson worked out a deal where Rich would pay roughly $60,000 a year for 25 years in order for the venue to be called Rich Stadium. It was one of the first corporate stadium naming rights agreements, and the Riches wound up getting plenty of bang for their buck.

One of the things the fans and I have always loved about the place are the sightlines. There really isn't a bad seat in the house. Even in the last row of the upper deck, you have a great view, though you would be subjected to the winds whipping off nearby Lake Erie, and that can be brutal in November and December. We've enjoyed a perfect view from the announcers' booth, which is situated on the mezzanine level near midfield. I've always been grateful for that because many NFL teams have moved announcers' booths and press boxes to out-of-the-way places in their new stadiums, so they can use the space to sell luxury suites and seating. There are some stadiums where you have an awful vantage point, and as a result, it's a lot more difficult calling games. Fortunately, our booth has stayed put at Highmark Stadium. I hope that continues to be the case in the new stadium.

Although the Bills opened Rich Stadium with a loss, that wouldn't be a sign of things to come during that inaugural season thanks to O.J. Simpson and the Electric Company line that turned loose the Juice. That fall Simpson would go where no back in pro football history had gone before. In 1973 he took fans on a 2,003-yard football odyssey and captivated not only Buffalo, but also the sports world.

Like Jim Kelly, Simpson wanted nothing to do with Buffalo initially. In fact, he warned the Bills not to draft him after his Heisman Trophy-winning season at the University of Southern California in 1968. He threatened to stay in Los Angeles and pursue a movie career if Buffalo chose him. Mr. Wilson, as he did with Kelly years later, held fast and wound up paying Simpson big bucks. Juice floundered his first few years. It wasn't until Lou Saban, the coach of the AFL championship teams, returned in 1972 that Simpson's career began gaining traction. And after moving from the uneven grass and dirt of War Memorial to Rich Stadium's fast track AstroTurf the following fall, Juice took his game to another level, becoming the first running back to break the 2,000-yard barrier in a single season.

Simpson would enjoy some spectacular seasons in Buffalo, and like Kelly, he would come to embrace the city. And the love affair would be mutual and continue strong right up until that fateful June day in 1994 when the Juice was charged with double murder. Before that sad and surreal moment, he may have been Buffalo's all-time favorite person. During the height of his popularity in the 1970s and 1980s, when a national survey ranked him as the most admired man in America, Simpson became Buffalo's biggest cheerleader. We had no greater ambassador. When he would come back to broadcast games for one of the networks, the fans would go wild. As he made his way up through the stands to the press box, he'd be stopped every step of the way by people who wanted his autograph, a handshake, or a picture snapped with him.

I have never encountered a more accommodating big-name athlete. It didn't matter if you worked for some Podunk newspaper or radio station, the Juice was accessible and treated everyone as if they were important. And he was the same way with the fans. He loved the adulation. He loved conversing with them. It was never an imposition, never a bother. And that's why the news of him being charged with the murders of his ex-wife and her friend was so jarring to those of us who had interacted with him. I was working at Channel 7 when the story broke and I admit I was in denial for the longest time. *Not O.J. No way!* I was crushed. And so were many others.

In the trial of century, he would be acquitted of criminal charges but later found legally responsible for the deaths of ex-wife Nicole Brown Simpson and Ron Goldman in a civil suit. I don't know of too many celebrities who have suffered a bigger fall than Simpson. And there might not have been any place in America that took his fall harder than Buffalo. He had been our champion, our ambassador, and he had used his celebrity as a Hall of Fame football player, actor, broadcaster, and preeminent product endorser to sing our community's praises to the world. Then, boom, just like that, our biggest cheerleader became a pariah. All these years later, it still doesn't seem real. It's a painful reminder that we think we may know these athletes, but we usually don't. We often only know their public persona. We don't know what goes on behind closed doors. It was only later that we found out more about Simpson's incidents of domestic violence. Sadly, they were stories that either weren't reported or underreported because of Simpson's good-guy public persona.

After he was arrested, I couldn't help but think back to my many interactions with him. In retrospect one incident eerily stands out above the rest. I remember walking around the field with Van Miller at Cleveland's old Municipal Stadium several hours before the Bills–Browns wild-card playoff game kicked off in 1989. Simpson walked over and greeted us. He was doing the game for NBC and he began picking our brains about the Bills' tumultuous season. After finishing our shop talk, the conversation turned personal. Van had been tight with him and innocuously asked Simpson how his family was doing. Simpson shook his head. "The kids are good," he said with exasperation, "but my wife is driving me crazy."

I thought nothing of it at the time, but five years later after he was arrested, those words came rushing back and took on new meaning. Not long after Simpson's epic fall, there was strong sentiment among Bills fans and some media members to remove the running back's name from the stadium's Wall of Fame. I was at the selection committee's meeting in 1995. As delicately as possible, I mentioned the topic and wondered if we should give the removal some consideration. Mr. Wilson, who oversaw the meetings, exploded and quickly ended the discussion before it began. "I don't give a shit what people think about O.J.," he shouted. "He's up there for his football accomplishments."

My fellow committee members, which included the likes of longtime football scribes Vic Carucci and Milt Northrop of the *Buffalo News* and Chuck Pollock of the *Olean Times Herald*, had never seen Mr. Wilson so angry. I thought it was at least worth a discussion, but Mr. Wilson wouldn't even countenance a discussion. All these years later, the topic still comes up, but Simpson's name remains. The committee hasn't met for more than five years, so I have no idea if his name will be removed or if anybody's name will be added. It will be interesting to see if the Wall of Fame continues to occupy a prominent space in the new stadium. I sure hope it does.

\* \* \*

Intense rivalries add spice and misery to a sports fan's experience. And when you look back at Buffalo Bills history, there are two teams that make Western New Yorkers' blood boil—the Miami Dolphins and New England Patriots.

For long-in-the-tooth Bills followers—people over 50—the hatred for the Dolphins remains real, even though Josh Allen and Co. have had their way squishing the Fish in recent years, reeling off seven consecutive victories between 2018 and 2021. But time hasn't completely healed this wound, which was inflicted during the 1970s, when Miami swept the decade. It's still hard to fathom the Bills went 0-for-20 against them, but they did. The series felt like the Harlem Globetrotters against the Washington Generals. The difference, of course, was the Generals were paid to be foils and lose to the clown princes of basketball. The Bills were paid to win and couldn't.

A couple of things made the hurt even worse. Bills fans developed a detestation for Don Shula, the jut-jawed coach who guided Miami to two Super Bowl victories, including the one in January 1973 that capped the NFL's only perfect season. Shula was not only a Hall of Fame coach, but also one of the league's most influential voices, and that power led some Bills fans to subscribe to conspiracy theories. There was a belief that since Shula was on the NFL's rules and competition committee that referees were prone to make calls on behalf of the Dolphins—especially in games against the Bills. Even Ralph Wilson grumbled publicly after some close calls went against the Bills. I hate to sound like a homer, but his grousing might have been justified. Maybe there was some truth to those theories.

Buffalo's loathing for the Dolphins was further stoked by Miami newspaper columnists and radio shock jocks who loved to stir the pot with incendiary comments about our crummy weather and economy. It struck a nerve with many Bills fans, fed into our collective inferiority complex. If we could just squish the Fish, we figured we could exact some revenge. At least that was the hope.

I was at Rich Stadium in 1979 with my friend, longtime college basketball coach John Beilein, when we thought we had witnessed the end to the streak. It was a rainy, miserable day, and the Dolphins had splishsplashed their way to a 9–7 lead, but Joe Ferguson moved the Bills into position to win in the waning seconds. On the final play of the game, kicker Tom Dempsey came on to attempt a 34-yard field goal. While with the New Orleans Saints, Dempsey had set an NFL record with a three-pointer 29 yards farther than that, so we were feeling pretty good about our chances. Beilein and I were sitting even with the goal line. So we didn't have the greatest view. From our vantage point, the kick looked good, and we started jumping up and down. Then, we noticed nobody around us joining in our delirium, and it quickly became apparent the kick was no good. In a matter of seconds, we plummeted from exaltation to deflation.

The hideous losing skid mercifully ended in the 1980 season opener at Rich Stadium and touched off a raucous celebration that saw the fans rush the field and tear down the goal posts. The postgame festivities also saw several Bills players form a victory dance chorus line. I wasn't at the game. I was back in the radio studio producing a postgame show, but I was there in spirit.

Sadly, the Dolphins continued their dominance after the streak was snapped, winning 11 of the next 13 matchups between the teams. Thankfully, it all started to turn after Marv Levy and Jim Kelly arrived.

In 1987 Kelly led the Bills to a 34–31 overtime victory in Miami as Scott Norwood drilled the game-winner. Bill Polian called it a turning point win because Kelly had outdueled Dan Marino on his home turf. Buffalo won the rematch later that year 27–0, giving the Bills a series sweep of the Dolphins for the first time since 1966—Miami's inaugural season. Interestingly, the pendulum swung at that point, and it would be the Bills going on to dominate, winning 19 of 28 meetings in the 1980s and '90s. After the retirements of Levy and Shula and Marino and Kelly, the rivalry lost much of its luster. Some of that had to do with the fact that both franchises experienced long stretches of mediocrity. Allen has the Bills ruling their South Beach foes again, and that's fine with me because I'm one of those old guys who hasn't forgotten the hurt of the 1970s.

The other team Bills fans love to hate are the Patriots, and it's easy to understand why. With Bill Belichick, the Hoodie, as coach and Pretty Boy Tom Brady as their quarterback, the Patriots dominated the Bills for nearly two decades. Brady actually set an NFL record for most wins against a single opponent, going 32–3 against Buffalo. (It's 33–3 if you tack on his one win against them while quarterbacking the Tampa Bay Buccaneers.)

But all things must come to an end, and since the start of the 2020s, Buffalo is 6–1 vs. the Brady-less Patriots. The one loss came on a fluky night at Highmark Stadium in 2021 when gale-force winds made passing treacherous, and Belichick's boys eked out a four-point win despite throwing the ball just three times. Allen atoned for that loss, winning twice against the Pats within the next six weeks. The capper came in the playoffs when the Bills destroyed them 47–17. It was the most lopsided playoff loss in Belichick's illustrious career and it marked the first time in league history that a team went through an entire game without punting, kicking a field goal, or turning the ball over. After so many years of misery, the Bills were finally writing some history worth remembering.

Allen completed 84 percent of his passes for 308 yards and five touchdowns in that blowout. He finished with more touchdown passes than incompletions (four). That's how spectacular he was. And he did it against a defense that had entered the game ranked fifth in the NFL. Belichick, the defensive mastermind with the knack for shutting down Hall of Fame quarterbacks, had no answer for Allen. For good measure Allen added 66 rushing yards on just six carries, a scintillating 11-yards-per-carry average. Few victories in Buffalo history have been more satisfying. The Bills' all-time tormentor was finally tormented. Payback can indeed be a bitch.

\* \* \*

Buffalo takes a lot of crap for its weather, but truth be told, I've broadcast many more good weather games than bad ones in Orchard Park. In fact, many of our games in September, October, and even November, are played in ideal conditions. When you get into December and January, it can be a different story.

People think we're nuts, but we always keep the window to our booth open. It goes back to Van Miller, who said it's important to get a feel for the crowd and the elements, and he's right. As I was reminded during those spectator-less games during the pandemic, a great deal is lost when there isn't crowd noise to feed off. There are places on the road—like Kansas City's Arrowhead Stadium—where you can't open the windows, and I hate that. The audio bounces off the glass. You feel like you're calling the game from a phone booth. It's just not the same.

We have some heat in the booth at Highmark Stadium, but there are times when you freeze your ass off. And while you're shivering you think, *Maybe, we should close that window.* There was one late December game during the Super Bowl run when the wind chill was something like minus-37. My comrades in the press box said the windows were freezing up and they had to keep scraping the frost off with credit cards in order to see the action. We didn't have to do any scraping, but we were worrying about dealing with frostbite. Regardless of the conditions, we try to gut it out. Hey, it could be worse. We could be out in the elements like the fans with no heat except what our body is generating.

Van Miller was known for wearing this flamboyant fur coat on game days once the weather turned cold. He claimed it kept him warm, which I'm sure it did, but I also think he liked to wear it because it was a conversation starter, especially with the fans. Unlike Van, I'm no fashion plate. I'm just trying to find the right socks, boots, gloves, long johns, and parkas to stay warm.

There have been numerous occasions when inclement weather has impacted games I've broadcast in Orchard Park. Perhaps the most famous (or infamous) of these was the Snow Bowl game on December 10, 2017, which also cleverly became known as the "Snowvertime Game." Eight or nine inches of the white stuff fell on New Era Field during the game—prodigious even by Buffalo standards. And the huge amount of snow—coupled with high winds—limited our visibility, making the broadcast extremely difficult. Fortunately, the Bills had opted to wear their all-red uniforms that day, so that made identification a little easier. It was a lot tougher IDing the Indianapolis Colts, who wore all white. It also was tough assessing yardage because no matter how hard the Bills maintenance crew tried, it just couldn't keep up with the rapid accumulation.

Not surprisingly, kicking and passing became treacherous, and the teams were tied at 8–8 apiece at the end of regulation. It looked like the game might end that way, but fortunately Bills running back LeSean McCoy had grown up in Pittsburgh and had some experience playing in the snow. He gained 156 yards rushing and wound up breaking free for the winning touchdown with just two minutes remaining in overtime. The thing I also remember about that game were the fans. Many were on their feet the entire game, but many also remained seated. As I looked out at a bunch of them sitting there and saw the snow accumulating on their ski caps, I wondered if they were suffering from hypothermia because they weren't moving.

Wind games can also wreak havoc—not on our ability to broadcast but on a quarterback's ability to throw the ball. The worst I ever covered was the New England Patriots game at Highmark Stadium on December 6, 2021. Gale-force gusts up to 40 mph made passing next to impossible that Monday night even for Bills quarterback Josh Allen, who I believe has the strongest arm in the NFL. Allen connected on just 15-of-30 tosses for 145 yards. Meanwhile, his New England counterpart, Mac Jones, threw just three times, completing two for 19 yards, but I guess you could say Jones had a pretty good night handing the ball off, as the Patriots ground their way to 222 yards on 46 carries and upset the Bills 14–10. The wind chills were brutal. That was one night I wished we could have closed that window.

A few months earlier in Kansas City, we dealt with a weather situation that I hadn't encountered before—a lightning delay. It lasted at least an hour during that nationally televised Sunday night game that the Bills dominated. The delay harkened me back to my days calling Buffalo Bisons baseball games with Pete Weber. Working with him was a ton of fun. Weber, of course, has gone on to make quite a name for himself in NHL circles as the play-by-play man for the Nashville Predators. It was a little strange broadcasting Bisons games on a diamond laid out in a rectangular football stadium, but it worked. Of course, the most famous baseball games ever played there occurred during the filming of *The Natural*, starring Robert Redford as fictitious slugger Roy Hobbs. They needed to find an old ballpark that had the feel of something from the 1930s, and War Memorial fit the bill perfectly.

I'd later have an opportunity to broadcast games from Pilot Field in downtown Buffalo after the Bisons moved into their new digs. That was exciting, and the Bisons wound up leading the minors in attendance several seasons in a row. Bob Rich Jr. owned the ballclub and looked seriously into bringing a Major League Baseball expansion team to Buffalo two decades after we had been a finalist for a big league club in the late 1960s. That never happened, but we did spend a chunk of the summer of 2021 being home to the Toronto Blue Jays during the pandemic, and the "Buffalo Jays" drew impressive crowds, especially when the New York Yankees came to town. I don't know if we would have been able to support an MLB franchise, but it was fun to be able to say we were in the big leagues that summer.

Anyhow, I know from baseball how you often have to fill in during rain delays, so that's what Eric Wood and I tried to do for awhile during that Sunday night game in Kansas City. Eventually, we sent it back to the studio. It was fun and it was different, but it made for a long, long night. I think we were there until something like 1:30 AM as Sunday Night Football turned into Monday Morning Football.

\* \* \*

There's no sugar-coating it. Football can be a violent game. It's a collision sport. And sometimes those crashes can result in harrowing moments. I'll never forget that game in the Houston Astrodome when Buffalo Bills cornerback Derrick Burroughs crumpled to the turf after lowering his head to make a tackle. He was down for quite some time before they were able to get him onto a stretcher and put him in an ambulance. Fortunately, Burroughs was able to walk again. But he was never able to play again because the doctors discovered he had cervical stenosis in his neck and would be at risk for paralysis.

I witnessed and described a number of the hellacious hits Jim Kelly took through the years. There were a few games he had to be carted off, including the final game of his career in a playoff loss to the Jacksonville Jaguars at Rich Stadium on December 28, 1996. No one was tougher than Kelly. How he got up from many of those blind-side hits, I'll never know. It was sad to see him knocked woozy in his final play as a Bills player.

Speedy wide receiver Don Beebe also endured some brutal hits. In that wild playoff game against the Cleveland Browns in 1989, there was a play when Beebe went up for a pass, had his legs cut out from under him, spun upside down, and landed on his head like a pogo stick. And there was another time against the New York Jets in the Meadowlands when he lay motionless on the turf after being rammed into by a defensive back. The thing I remember about that was his arm quivering reflexively in an upright position while the rest of his body remained limp. That was very unnerving. So, too, was Dane Jackson's neck injury during the Bills home opener in 2022. He was inadvertently hit by teammate Tremaine Edmunds and he wound up twisting his neck in a way it wasn't meant to be twisted. He was on the turf for several minutes before the ambulance took him to the hospital. Fortunately, he didn't suffer any spinal cord or vertebrae damage.

The most harrowing moment I've broadcast occurred in the Bills home opener against the Denver Broncos on September 9, 2007. During the second-half kickoff, Bills tight end Kevin Everett was paralyzed tackling the returner. He was down for the longest time before the trainers and medical staff were able to slide him onto a stretcher and lift him into the ambulance.

I don't mean to sound callous or heartless, but when you're doing play-by-play, you don't have time to dwell on injuries once the game resumes. I stay alert for updates on a player's condition, but my focus has to return to describing the action on the field—as difficult as that might be. When we signed off that day, we didn't have any update other than that Everett had been taken to a local hospital. It wasn't until several hours after the game that night that I learned the severity of the injury. One of the team doctors I called told me that Everett had almost died on the field, and he was paralyzed.

The following Friday, Everett was still lying paralyzed in a Buffalo hospital, and I headed over to practice to tape my pregame radio segment with coach Dick Jauron. Before I met with Jauron, he called the team together near the tunnel end zone at Ralph Wilson Stadium and said there was a woman there who wanted to speak. It was Everett's mom. She wound up delivering this heartfelt talk, thanking everyone in the Bills organization for all their help and she wanted them to know how proud she was of them and of her son. The players and coaches were in tears, and I was, too. Fortunately, there was a happy ending to this story. Everett would walk again. And five years later, he would return to the stadium and walk slowly but surely to midfield, where a podium had been set up so he could address the fans. He thanked them for their support and the support he had received from the Bills training staff, his doctors, his therapists, and his family. Two of his doctors, Andy Cappuccino and Kevin Gibbons, were praised by some in the medical community for employing what's known as cold or hypothermia therapy to aid in Everett's recovery. An unsung hero that day was Bills head trainer Bud Carpenter. The week before the injury, Carpenter and his staff spent about 20 minutes practicing some new protocols regarding handling serious head and neck injuries. Little did they know they would be putting them into action so soon. Thank God they did because everything done that day played a role in helping Everett walk again. Sixteen years later, the Bills medical and athletic training staffs would perform similar heroics when they saved Damar Hamlin's life following his cardiac arrest on the field during that game in Cincinnati.

# AFTERWORD

Igot to know John Murphy professionally and personally after I took over as the head coach of the Buffalo Bills midway through the 1986 season. John interviewed me on numerous occasions, and we wound up collaborating on a radio call-in show on Tuesdays following games. Some coaches hated doing these kinds of shows—treating them as if they were undergoing root canals—but I enjoyed interacting with John and our passionate fan base.

John was one of those people who was always a delight to work with and be around. Even after losses, I found that time with him to be relaxing. He always was well-prepared. He did his homework, knew his stuff about the players and the issues we were facing as a team. John would ask tough but fair questions. Working with him on those shows and in other settings helped make sports a heck of a lot more enjoyable for me—and for the fans. He conveyed the excitement of the game of football so well. He was not hypercritical like some in the media. He had a marvelous sense of humor and kept it fun. And that's what's sports are supposed to be. Fun.

As you learned from reading this book, John is an entertaining and insightful storyteller, and he and another journalist whom I hold in high regard, Scott Pitoniak, have done a wonderful job weaving together many tales about the people, games, and moments that have made the Bills such an integral part of Buffalo for decades.

Bills fans, players, and coaches have been truly blessed when it comes to broadcasters. We were so fortunate to have Van Miller doing play-by-play with John providing the color for all those years, and then when Van retired from the radio booth, the transition was seamless as John took over the play-by-play. Going from Van to John was the broadcast equivalent of going from Jim Kelly to Josh Allen—two different styles, two different personalities, two different perspectives but similar, sterling results. In their inimitable ways, Van and John displayed a knack for entertaining and enlightening us.

Broadcasters helped nurture and develop my passion for sports growing up in Chicago in the 1930s. I have fond recollections of listening to the great Bill Stern describe the exploits of football legends Bronko Nagurski and George "Papa Bear" Halas. Stern's stories added greatly to my enjoyment of the games. Football, especially at the professional level, has never been more popular than it is today, and I've long argued there are three elements that have contributed to that popularity. The first component involves the participants—the players and coaches. The second involves the fans. And the third relies on the media, which connects the first two.

One thing that sets John apart is that he brings the perspective of a native Buffalonian to his broadcasts. He understands what the Bills mean to his hometown and region because he was born and raised there. He understands this special bond because he was once a fan himself, dating all the way back to his boyhood days attending American Football League games with his dad at old War Memorial Stadium. I think that adds historical context and perspective to his broadcasts and to this wonderful book. He gets Buffalo because he is Buffalo through and through.

It's been my pleasure through the years to not only work with John, but also to get to know him. It's an honor to call him and Scott my friends. I hope you enjoyed the book, and go Bills!

—*Marv Levy, winningest coach in Bills history and a 2001 Pro Football Hall of Fame inductee*

# APPENDIX

## ALL-MURPH TEAMS
## AND GAMES

This list is based solely on the players and games I've covered as a color man, play-by-play guy, and as a television sports reporter. So you won't find O.J. Simpson in this all-time Bills lineup nor any of the great players from Buffalo's back-to-back AFL title teams of my youth. This is a list based through the 2022 season. Let the debating begin.

## My All-Time Bills Team
### OFFENSE
### *Quarterback: Jim Kelly*

I love Josh Allen and gave him serious consideration—and I might change my mind down the road—but as I write this, it's hard to argue against Kelly, who went to four Super Bowls. Kelly is in the Pro Football Hall of Fame, and if Allen's career was to end today, I don't think they'd be sculpting a bust for him in Canton, Ohio. Again, that all could change, but for now at least, I have to go with Kelly based on everything he achieved and how he saved the franchise.

### *Running back: Thurman Thomas*

This one isn't even subject for debate. The Thurmanator was a dominating force, leading the NFL in yards from scrimmage four consecutive years. He earned league MVP honors and a bust in the Hall of Fame. He was a great all-around player who beat you with his legs and his hands. In addition to being a fabulous ball carrier and receiver, he also developed into a fantastic blocker, picking up blitzes that gave Kelly that extra second to make a play. I'd put the underrated Fred Jackson as a strong second behind Thomas at this position.

### *Fullback: Jamie Mueller*

He was a hard-nosed player who did a lot of underappreciated things for those Bills Super Bowl teams. The consummate fullback.

### Offensive tackles: Will Wolford and House Ballard

Wolford was a first-round pick who lived up to expectations. House was a late-round pick who far exceeded expectations.

### Guards: Jim Ritcher and Ruben Brown

Ritcher was undersized but was so strong that he played much bigger than he was, and Brown earned nine Pro Bowl invites, eight of them while with Buffalo.

### Center: Kent Hull

Hull's my guy, and my buddy and broadcast mate, Eric Wood, is a close second. Hull was the heart-and-soul and quarterback of those Super Bowl lines.

### Tight end: Pete Metzelaars

Metzelaars was an excellent blocker and dependable receiver for the early 1990s teams. Look out, though, for current tight end Dawson Knox, who's much more athletic and much more of a receiving threat. He could be my No. 1 guy here with a few more productive seasons.

### Wide receiver: Andre Reed and Eric Moulds

Reed is a no-brainer. He made himself into a Hall of Famer through his hard work. He got better every year. Moulds took a while to develop, but when he did, he really took over. He's second all time to Reed in the major receiving categories. Stevie Johnson had a really nice run, and Lee Evans really shone while playing with some weak quarterbacks. If current wideout Stefon Diggs compiles a few more seasons like his first three with the team, he'll merit consideration on future lists.

### Kicker: Steve Christie

He was Mr. Dependable and Mr. Clutch. He made a lot of big kicks, including the one that capped the greatest comeback in NFL postseason history. Scott Norwood is my No. 2. Everyone fixates on Wide Right, but Norwood won a lot of games for the Bills with pressure kicks as time expired.

### Punter: Brian Moorman

He was the best by far and also was an exceptional athlete who executed fake punts better than anybody.

## DEFENSE

### Defensive ends: Bruce Smith and Aaron Schobel

Smith is the NFL's all-time sack leader and enshrined in Canton. So this was another no-brainer selection. The other spot wasn't as easy, but I went with Schobel, who turned out to be one of the better second-round draft picks in team history. He finished with 78 sacks and made the Pro Bowl twice in his 10 seasons with the team. Jerry Hughes also merits consideration for the spot opposite Smith, but he didn't play as long as Schobel.

### Defensive tackles: Fred Smerlas and Ted Washington

Good luck running against these two immovable objects. Smerlas made the Pro Bowl five times, and "Mount Washington," who was listed at 365 pounds but may have played at closer to 400 pounds, earned three Pro Bowl invites in his six seasons in Buffalo.

### Linebackers: Cornelius Bennett, Shane Conlan, and Darryl Talley

Bennett was a superb pass rusher and the perfect complement to Bruce Smith. Conlan was a great run stuffer in the middle. I did give some consideration to Jim Haslett here, as well as Ray Bentley. Talley may have

270

been the most respected and emotional voice on those Bills Super Bowl teams. As was the case with Hull on offense, when Talley spoke, guys listened.

### Cornerbacks: Nate Odomes and Tre'Davious White

Odomes is another of the Bills' great second-round picks. He was selected in the 1987 draft and became an immediate starter. He finished with 26 interceptions in his seven seasons and was an unsung hero on Buffalo's Super Bowl teams. White definitely has justified his first-round selection. He's been a shutdown corner and game-changer for the current Bills. Hopefully, he can bounce back to his pre-injury form.

### Safety: Jordan Poyer and Mark Kelso

Poyer had 22 interceptions in his first six seasons since coming to the Bills and earned All-Pro honors in 2021. I considered teaming him here with fellow safety Micah Hyde but went instead with Kelso. Perhaps, I'm showing some bias because I worked so many years with him in the booth, but Kelso did have 30 interceptions while playing for the Bills Super Bowl teams.

## COACHES

### Head coach: Marv Levy

Sean McDermott has done a stellar job in rebuilding the Bills, leading them to five playoff appearances in his first six seasons while ending Buffalo's 17-season postseason drought. But Levy's the man. He's the all-time leader in victories and took the team to four Super Bowls.

### Offensive coordinator: Ted Marchibroda

He convinced Levy that Kelly could flourish running the no-huddle offense, and that offense befuddled and exhausted opponents, enabling Buffalo to become perennial championship contenders. Brian Daboll did a superb job helping Allen develop and tailoring an offense that utilized the quarterback's skills to the fullest. Had Daboll stayed in Buffalo a few more years, he might have supplanted Marchibroda on my list.

### Defensive coordinator: Walt Corey

I gave serious consideration to Teddy Cottrell and Leslie Frazier, but Corey was the guy during the Bills glory run.

## GENERAL MANAGER

### Bill Polian

He inherited a franchise that had floundered with back-to-back 2–14 seasons and built it into a juggernaut. In addition to signing Kelly back from the USFL, he oversaw a number of exceptional drafts, including ones that yielded Hall of Famers Reed and Smith. He also hired Levy as the head coach and assembled a front office that included future NFL general managers John Butler, A.J. Smith, and Bob Ferguson. Butler—whom I believe was an even better talent assessor than Polian— also merits consideration. As does current GM Brandon Beane, who, like Polian, has raised a franchise from the ashes in short time. Beane deserves immense credit for the massive makeover of the Bills roster and, of course, drafting Allen, who was by no means regarded as a slam dunk to become a franchise quarterback and league MVP contender.

# My Most Memorable Games

### 14. November 24, 2014—Buffalo Bills 38, New York Jets 3 @ Detroit

This was a game moved to Monday night and to Detroit after a massive November snowstorm forced the Bills out of Orchard Park for several days. Doug Marrone went into the game complaining about the NFL schedule and playing a "home" game away from home. But his team was up to the challenge. Two unforgettable moments: One, when the gates opened to spectators, Bills fans raced down the aisles of Ford Field to sit close to the action since there was no assigned seating. Two, Scott Chandler mimicked snow shoveling after his 19-yard touchdown catch as an homage to the snowed-in Bills fans back home.

### 13. November 18, 1984—Bills 14, Dallas Cowboys 3 @ Orchard Park

In my first year on the broadcast, it was pretty apparent the Bills were awful, starting the season with 11 straight losses. But this game started with a bang: an 85-yard touchdown run by rookie Greg Bell on the first play from scrimmage. It led to Buffalo's first win of the year.

### 12. November 20, 1988—Bills 9, Jets 6 (OT) @ Orchard Park

The Bills clinched their first AFC East title since 1980 (in Week 12!) and they did it in a hard-fought overtime battle. Fred Smerlas made the play of the game, blocking Pat Leahy's field-goal attempt in the fourth quarter. Smerlas said, "It feels like we're a team of destiny."

### 11. September 10, 1989—Bills 27, Miami Dolphins 24 @ Miami

This was the season opener, following the Bills' loss in the AFC title game the year before. The Bills got off to a slow start, trailing 24–13 with four minutes to play. But Jim Kelly cemented his stature as a superstar quarterback and led the Bills to two touchdowns. He ran two yards into

273

the end zone as time expired to win it and was immediately mobbed by his teammates.

### 10. January 17, 1993—Bills 29, Dolphins 10 @ Miami (AFC Championship Game)

Two weeks after the comeback game, the Bills locked up their third consecutive Super Bowl appearance with a convincing win on the road. A lasting image of the game was the Bills players walking around the field at the Dolphins' stadium waving the Bills flag in celebration.

### 9. December 31, 2017—Bills 22, Dolphins 16 @ Miami

This unforgettable day in Miami was the regular-season finale. The Bills were playoff longshots but played well and got a touchdown run from defensive tackle Kyle Williams that established the game as a milestone. Then, minutes after leaving the field with a win, they watched the Cincinnati Bengals' last-second touchdown miracle that put Buffalo in the postseason, ending the Bills' 17-year playoff drought. The best New Year's Eve of my lifetime was spent on a bus and a charter flight home.

### 8. January 15, 2022—Bills 47, New England Patriots 17 @ Orchard Park (wild-card game)

The Bills buried their New England Patriots curse emphatically with a 30-point playoff win over Bill Belichick and New England. Josh Allen threw five touchdown passes, and the Bills looked unstoppable moving on through the playoffs. Oh yeah, it was 7 degrees on this Saturday night. Former quarterback Ryan Fitzpatrick enjoyed watching the game in the stands without a shirt. Incredible.

### 7. January 16, 2021—Bills 17, Baltimore Ravens 3 @ Orchard Park (AFC Divisional Playoff Game)

This game was in doubt for almost three quarters. Taron Johnson's 101-yard interception return for a touchdown was in the final minute of the third quarter, when the Baltimore Ravens looked like they were going to make it a game. Johnson's return ranks among the great single plays in Bills history. And it remains my favorite play-by-play call ever.

### 6. January 8, 2000—Tennessee Titans 22, Bills 16 @ Nashville (wild-card game)

Wade Phllips' Bills rolled into the playoffs on a hot streak, winning seven of their final nine regular-season games. But the "Music City Miracle" ruined their dreams. Was the "lateral" that led to the Titans' game-winning touchdown an illegal forward pass? I think so. The game marked the final Bills game for three Hall of Famers—Bruce Smith, Thurman Thomas, and Andre Reed. It was clear that an era was over; the Bills wouldn't see the playoffs again for 17 years.

### 5. January 6, 1990—Cleveland Browns 34, Bills 30 @ Cleveland (AFC Divisional Playoff Game)

Another season ended with a loss, but this one signaled a new era for the Bills. Buffalo went with a no-huddle, fast paced offensive attack after falling behind. It worked so well it became their primary offensive mode for the next several years. Ronnie Harmon's dropped pass at the end cost the Bills a longer playoff run. On the flight home, general manager Bill Polian told me and Van Miller, "he'll never drop another one for us." He never did.

## 4. January 20, 1991—Bills 51, Los Angeles Raiders 3 @ Orchard Park (AFC Championship Game)

The Bills punched the ticket to their first Super Bowl appearance in convincing fashion with this one-sided victory. The Los Angeles Raiders went into the game confident. There's a story that the day before the game and just after the L.A. walk-through practice at Rich Stadium, Raiders defensive lineman Howie Long was heard by Bills personnel arguing on a pay phone in the tunnel of the stadium about how many Super Bowl tickets he could get and the seat locations, fully expecting he and the Raiders would win the next day and represent the AFC in the big game. This incident was relayed to Bills players before kickoff the next day.

## 3. January 27, 1991—New York Giants 20, Bills 19 @ Tampa (Super Bowl XXV)

Did I expect Scott Norwood's 47-yard field goal to go through? I did. Not because it was a gimme but because everything seemed to go Buffalo's way that year. In the postgame rush of emotion and analysis, the overwhelming memory for me was Norwood's grace and patience, as he handled every interview situation (there were dozens) with remarkable poise. Amazing.

## 2. January 3, 1993—Bills 41, Houston Oilers 38 (OT) @ Orchard Park (wild-card game)

"The Comeback" was the most spectacular swing in fortune I've ever seen in any sport. The Bills were as good as dead at halftime. And the game got worse—the Oilers scored in the third quarter to go up 35–3. And then it happened—an avalanche of big plays from Buffalo. Frank Reich's four touchdown passes in the second half gave the Bills the lead. Houston tied it up and sent it to overtime, but the comeback was so stunning that Steve Christie's game-winning kick in overtime was almost anti-climactic.

## 1. January 23, 2022—Kansas City Chiefs 42, Bills 36 (OT) @ Kansas City (AFC Divisional Playoffs)

It's not recency bias that puts this one at the top. This was the greatest game I've ever seen—let alone broadcast. It was a good game through three quarters, a showcase for Allen and Patrick Mahomes, the two best quarterbacks in the NFL. And then it exploded in the final two minutes of regulation and overtime. Allen threw two touchdown passes—both to Gabriel Davis. Mahomes threw two also. The Chiefs forced overtime after Buffalo's special teams and defense collapsed in the final 13 seconds of the fourth quarter. It was a damaging but amazing game for the Bills and one that will be discussed forever.

# ACKNOWLEDGMENTS

The authors would like to thank all the people who made this book a reality, including:

Triumph publisher Noah Amstadter, acquisitions editor Bill Ames, and senior editor Jeff Fedotin for believing in this project and seeing it to fruition; former Buffalo Bills center and current radio color man Eric Wood for generously contributing the foreword; Hall of Fame coach and friend, Marv Levy, for contributing the afterword and for his kindness through the years; the Bills public relations staff past and present—Scott Berchtold, Denny Lynch, Dave Senko, Budd Thalman, and Derek Boyko; our wives, Mary Travers Murphy and Beth Pitoniak, for their understanding, patience, encouragement, and love; Bills players, coaches, administrators, owners, and support staff—past and present; Todd Broady, Chris Brown, Joe Buscaglia, Sal Capaccio, Vic Carucci, Rich "The Bull" Gaenzler, Jay Harris, Greg Harvey, Mark Kelso, Van Miller, Mike Mullane, Jack Murphy, Mark Murphy, Paul Peck, Steve Tasker, and Alex Van Pelt; and Bills fans—before and now, near and far.

# ABOUT THE AUTHORS

**John Murphy** is a native of the Buffalo suburb of Lockport and a 1978 Syracuse University graduate. Murphy has been the "Voice of the Bills" since succeeding legendary broadcaster Van Miller following the 2003 season. Prior to that he spent 16 seasons as the team's color analyst. During his illustrious journalism career, Murphy also worked as a sports anchor and director at Buffalo television stations WKBW and WIVB and hosted a popular radio talk show on WBEN and WGR. In addition to the Bills, he also served as commentator for the Buffalo Bisons minor league baseball team and did basketball play-by-play for Canisius College, the University at Buffalo, and Niagara University. From 2012 through 2020, he hosted the *John Murphy Show* (later renamed *One Bills Live*). He has received numerous honors along the way, including induction into the Buffalo Broadcasters Association Hall of Fame in 2019. He and his wife Mary Travers—a former television journalist and Orchard Park Town Supervisor—have two children (Mark and Jack).

**Scott Pitoniak** is a native of Rome, New York, and a 1977 Syracuse University graduate. Pitoniak is a best-selling author of more than 35 books and a nationally honored journalist now in his fifth decade of covering sports. This is his sixth book about the Buffalo Bills, a team he has been writing about regularly since 1985. Pitoniak spent the lion's share of his career as a reporter and columnist for the [Rochester, New York] *Democrat* and *Chronicle*, Gannett News Service, and *USA TODAY*. He also cohosted an ESPN-affiliated sports radio talk show and provided Bills commentary for television stations in Rochester and Buffalo. He is the recipient of more than 100 journalism awards, including a dozen from the Professional Football Writers of America, and has been inducted into six Halls of Fame. He is married to Beth Adams Pitoniak, a longtime radio journalist. He is the father of two adult children (Amy and Christopher) and has two granddaughters (Camryn and Peyton.)